W9-BUG-514

First Come, First Served...
IN SAVANNAH

A TASTE OF SOUTHERN HISTORY AND HOSPITALITY

St. Andrew's School Parent Teacher Organization
Savannah, Georgia

St. Andrew's School exists to develop active learners by inspiring a passion for knowledge, a deepened social consciousness, and a commitment to personal integrity.

The purpose of the Parent Teacher Organization is to support the Mission Statement of the school, encourage unity among the parents, staff and students through communication and good will, enhance education, and provide emotional, spiritual and financial support.

St. Andrew's School
601 Penn Waller Road
Savannah, Georgia 31410
www.saintschool.com

First Printing	November 2001	5,000 copies
Second Printing	October 2002	7,000 copies
Third Printing	January 2004	5,000 copies
Fourth Printing	February 2006	5,000 copies

©2001 St. Andrew's School
ISBN: 0-9713159-0-6

Cover Art by Sharon Saseen
Interior Art by Ken Wheeler

All rights reserved. No part of this book may be reproduced or utilized in any form or by any means, including photocopying and recording, or by any information storage and retrieval system, without permission in writing from the publisher.

WIMMER
COOKBOOKS
ConsolidatedGraphics
800.548.2537
www.wimmerco.com

Artist Acknowledgments

We are both proud of and immensely grateful to our fine contributing artists. The *St. Andrew's School PTO* extends to both *Sharon Saseen* and *Ken Wheeler* our heartfelt thanks for their time, talent, and treasured support of *First Come, First Served*... IN SAVANNAH.

Sharon Saseen

Sharon Saseen, our award-winning cover artist, is, herself, as beautifully representative of our fair Savannah as are her works of art. An unusually versatile artist, Ms. Saseen is quite proficient in an impressive variety of media, including oil, acrylic, watercolor, and mixed media, as well as pen and ink. Her delightful works are available in Savannah at *The Signature Gallery,* 303 West Julian Street, Savannah, Georgia 31401, phone (912) 233-3082 and also at *Gallery 209,* 209 East River Street, Savannah, Georgia 31401, phone (912) 236-4583; web address, www.saseen.com.

Ken Wheeler

Ken Wheeler, whose photo-technic art brilliantly sets off the interior text of *First Come, First Served*... is an award-winning designer. With two decades of worldwide experience in his field, Mr. Wheeler's works include designing and illustrating books, print media, and multimedia. His multimedia/animation has been well received from Cannes to Tokyo, and his clients include Intel and Microsoft.

Ken Wheeler's wonderfully imaginative works are available at his chic new establishment, *The Angel House Cafe and Art Gallery,* 325 West Broughton Street, Savannah, Georgia 31401, phone (912) 790-5050; web address www.angelhousegallery.com

Table of Contents

From the *first* chapter to the last, *First Come, First Served...* highlights Savannah's many historical *firsts*. Original photo art sets the tone for an accompanying spirited story, whimsical food anecdote or local legend. In this cookbook, the "Hostess City of the South" shares her finest and her favorite recipes, historical tidbits and suggestions for entertaining Southern style.

Savannah Resources

Bland Farms
P.O. Box 506
Glennville, GA 30427
1-800-843-2542
www.Blandfarms.com

Davis Produce
7755 East Highway 80
Savannah, GA 31410

Joe & Nellie's Key Lime Juice
P.O. Box 2368
Key West, FL 33045

Roger Wood Foods, Inc.
7 Alfred Street
Savannah, GA 31408

Russo Seafood
201 E. 40th Street
Savannah, GA 31401

Savannah Candy Kitchen
225 E. River Street
Savannah, GA 31401

Savannah Cinnamon and Cookie Company
2604 Gregory Street
Savannah, GA 31404
1-800-288-0854
www.Savannahcinnamoninc.com

Introduction

Our Amazing Grace

First and foremost, Savannah is a Great Lady. Such a lady meets what life brings with amazing grace, courage and style. Since Savannah *first* carved her home from pine forests and salt marshes, she has weathered wars, fires, epidemics and floods. Savannah has entertained presidents and patriots, as well as her fair share of pirates. She has experienced boom and endured bust, with both bringing her strength and renewal. Perhaps her most special gift is Savannah's ability to preserve the historic and to evolve, still classic, into modern times. Savannah lets her legacy of the past serve as a catalyst for her future. She prevails in a *first* class present of comfortable elegance, greatness and grace.

"America's Thirteenth Colony...The Most Beautiful City in North America"
(LeMonde newspaper, Paris)

First Come, First Served... IN SAVANNAH was created to present Savannah's hospitality and cooking, as well as history and stories, from this fine, fair city. *First Come, First Served...* represents the culmination of efforts put forth by dedicated contributors who gave their advice, time, materials, hard labor, and talents. This book was a long held dream at St. Andrew's School. It came to pass because of families, friends, and the school community, as well as the expanded Savannah community. Our hope was, and is, to showcase the heritage and style which we hold dear in Savannah; proudly reflected at St. Andrew's School.

The importance of interwoven school family and community emphasized by St. Andrew's was proven by the many doors which opened to help us implement our vision. This, we feel, was an amazing grace, for which we are grateful. Further gratitude goes to those who preserve Savannah for the world, and for all of our families.

We often felt very close to our family traditions and cooking, as we reviewed, retested, and re-experienced treasured recipes. As we tested the newest trends in cooking, we found that they blended wonderfully with those that were tried and true. We came to feel that the cooks in our family lines would have been pleased to see their legacies of Southern cooking evolve so well. Here in Savannah, hospitality and cooking have evolved into a most special and delicious style of its own. We have learned to honor the amazing abilities of those who came before us. They could stretch a chicken to feed a crowd in lean times, or serve up a sumptuous banquet in times of abundance. They did this with the same grace and comfortable elegance we willingly live up to today.

First Come, First Served... IN SAVANNAH was organized into 13 recipe chapters representing the 13 original colonies. It was designed to provide information and inspiration, as well as a "gracious plenty" of our finest, most favorite recipes. Each chapter title highlights one of Savannah's many historical *firsts* and focuses on that specific theme throughout the chapter sidebars. We have included a selection of stories and historical tidbits which reveal the personality of this Great Lady, the city of Savannah. Our *Foremost Menus and Perfect Parties* chapter shares our tried and true suggestions for theme based luncheons and dinner parties for large and small groups. Remember, Savannah is both uptown and down home. She abides. Whether with elegant galas, holiday festivities, or simple family fare, Savannah keeps up the standards of excellence. In *First Come, First Served...* we have endeavored to present and emulate Savannah's amazing qualities, and to share them most hospitably with you.

"Make yourself at home!"

St. Andrew's School
Parent Teacher Organization

ST. ANDREW'S
S·C·H·O·O·L

Foremost Menus and Perfect Parties

The *First* Planned City

Savannah is the *first* planned city to be based on a system of squares. The well-ordered arrangements of lots may still be seen, along with the squares and beautiful broad avenues. James Oglethorpe's vision still gives Savannah a sense of orderly grace, unmatched by more than a few cities. "Paris and London are her sisters..." Anita Raskin, from *Sojourn in Savannah*. Quite practically, the squares were set up for defensive purposes. This was due to the Spanish presence to the south and the possibility of hostile Native Americans. Should danger threaten, the residents were expected to gather in their respective squares. Each square was made up of four "Trust" lots for public uses. Each square had four "Tything" lots divided into ten 60 x 90 feet lots. This created 40 sites for houses on each square. Equally, each house measured around 16 x 22 feet to 20 x 30 feet (historians differ on the exact measurements). Each house was a wooden structure, most cheerfully painted red or blue.

Spirited Savannah

Bonaventure was once a beautiful plantation, famed for hospitality and fabulous parties. Indeed, one of those parties has left a lasting impression to this day. It was late autumn around 1800, when in the midst of a party, the owner, Josiah Tatnall, Jr., was told that Bonaventure was ablaze. Fire would soon take the massive wooden structure, and nothing could stop it. Tatnall asked his guests to take their dinner things outside, while the servants moved tables and chairs onto the grounds. There dinner continued far into the night, with guests recalling notable events enjoyed at Bonaventure in the past. Soon toasts were being made, some to "endless joy" for Bonaventure, with the glasses shattered, as was the old custom. By morning, Bonaventure was ash and burnt timbers. In the 1860's, Bonaventure became a cemetery, one of the most beautiful anywhere. On cool autumn nights, the sounds of a party, with laughter and music, are often heard. Most clearly heard are the sounds of glasses shattering against the great oak trees.

"Hostess City of the South"

Savannah knows how to throw a party. She has truly been the "Hostess City of the South" since Colonial times. Savannah's most famous fêtes began with George Washington's visit on May 12-16, 1791. A formal dinner led the activities, with 15 toasts made. At a late lunch the next day, 15 more toasts were made. This was followed by a ball in his honor. Ceremonies, parties, tributes, and more parties continued for the duration of his visit.

President James Monroe, accompanied by John C. Calhoun, visited Savannah in 1819. He was the guest of William and Julia Scarbrough and arrived on the very day that their house was completed. Julia's parties, which she called "blowouts," were famous – and sometimes infamous. In March of 1825, the Marquis de Lafayette arrived in Savannah, to be met with what was called "Lafayette Mania." It was said that Lafayette was "persecuted" with parties and events in Savannah.

Savannah is justifiably proud of its hospitality, style, and grace. In keeping with Savannah's sterling reputation as "Hostess City of the South," the St. Andrew's community has come to be well known for its own parties. Indeed, our parties have been enjoyed by our faculty and parents and are amongst the most sought after items at our annual fund-raising auction. Bidding on these events is both friendly and fierce. Buyers, in the midst of enjoying a party they purchased, have been known to offer "cash on the spot" for whatever party we will create and offer for the next year. *Foremost Menus and Perfect Parties* represents our *first* order favorites. We hope these will be an inspiration to create your own signature parties...with a little help from us, to y'all.

Life's a Game... But Bridge is Serious

There are two things Southern ladies take very seriously - bridge and cooking! This luncheon menu suggests the best of both. Since all recipes may be prepared well in advance, it affords the hostess an opportunity to participate in this competitive game and serve her guests in a most gracious manner. Fashionable tablecloths for card tables can be made from 54 inch cotton duckcloth squares bordered with 1-inch grosgrain ribbon. As the cards are being dealt, serve your guests tall, cool glasses of Peach Iced Tea - just in case the game gets a little "heated." Of course, no card game would be complete without small dishes of Toasted Pecans and Candied Mints for guests to nibble on. After lunch, present your guests with a sweet "finale" to this traditional ladies' pastime. Clear plastic bags tied with festive ribbon make a delightful "goodie-bag" when filled with samplings of Frosted Pecans or Praline Cookies.

Midday in the Garden of Good and Even Better

This luncheon menu was inspired by the book, *Midnight in the Garden of Good and Evil,* that took Savannah and the rest of the country by storm. If you don't have an ivy-covered brick courtyard, create the ambiance of one anywhere. Potted plants and flowers, old moss-covered statuaries and architectural elements set the tone for this very Southern, very Savannah menu. With the availability of small indoor fountains you may even want to consider using one on your buffet table. Ivy topiaries make beautiful centerpieces, as guests are seated at round tables draped with crisp white linens. For our Teacher Appreciation Week luncheon we used indoor-outdoor carpet from a local funeral home to give the effect of a grassy garden. Silk fica trees and park benches created a warm entry as we converted our gym into a Savannah garden. Whether serving a small or large group, this menu is easily adapted to chafing dishes and will still taste "good or even better."

MENU

Peach Iced Tea

❦

Classic Tomato Aspic with
Shrimp Mayonnaise

❦

Squash Boats Florentine

❦

Crêpes Bellisimo
or
Chicken with Linguine &
Artichoke Hearts

❦

Savannah Sour Cream Muffins

❦

Chess Pie
Lace Cookies

MENU

Lime Tea Coolers

❦

Cucumber & Red Onion Salad

❦

Deep South Tomato Pie
Green Bean Bundles
Garlic Cheddar Grits

❦

Honey Pecan Fried Chicken
Martha Nesbitt's Crab Cakes
with Lemon Dill Sauce

❦

Golden Pecan Pie
Best of the Bunch Baked
Banana Pudding

Nothin' but Azaleas, Azaleas, Azaleas

MENU

Orange Blossom
Champagne Punch

❦

Molded Raspberry-Peach Salad

❦

Tomato Basil Dip with
Asparagus

❦

Cheesy Squash and
Tomato Casserole

Grits Soufflé with
Caramelized Onions &
Roasted Red Peppers

❦

Baked Ham
with Spicy Apricot Glaze

Hot Chicken Crunch

❦

Lemon Charlotte

MENU

Pain Killer Rum Punch

❦

Spicy Black Bean Cakes with
Red & Yellow Tomato Salsa

❦

Hearts of Palm Salad with
Spicy Cedar Key Peanut
Dressing

❦

Fresh Summer Vegetables
on the Grill

Black Rice

❦

Salmon Bake with Pecan
Crunch Coating

❦

Key Lime Cake

Though the winters are often short and mild in Savannah, warming temperatures and a profusion of azaleas in bloom, announce the arrival of Spring. Easter Sunday brunch is a special occasion in the Hostess City. Little girls are dressed in their smocked finery - little boys are in white buck shoes. Mothers and grandmothers are adorned with lovely hats and corsages, and gentlemen sport seersucker suits. After sunrise or late morning worship services, families and friends gather for photographs in front of the largest azalea plant in the garden and then the traditional Easter meal. A fresh floral centerpiece of dogwood blooms and azaleas creates the feeling of Savannah in the spring. These dishes are easily prepared the night before allowing the hostess time to be part of the traditional children's Easter egg hunt.

Wild Women Don't Get The Blues

Wild women love to play. They view friendship as a form of art and laughter as a form of medicine. They believe that life should be shared with friends. Most importantly, they know that time spent together is time well spent. Call your best girlfriends for an overnight retreat that will nurture friendships and lift your spirits. Turn on the stereo with your favorite Jimmy Buffet or Reggae tunes and greet your guests with glasses of Pain Killer Rum Punch. Begin your evening with hors d'oeuvres such as Gray's Creek Crab Fritters with Jalapeño Dipping Sauce, Black Bean Salsa with Lime Tortilla Chips and Coconut Chicken Salad with Glazed Pita Chips. To really catch the free-spirit of a "Wild Woman," have brightly colored T-shirts and sarongs (made from a large square of fabric) available for your friends to put on upon arrival. Flip-flops embellished with raffia bows and sea shells are a festive way to accessorize their "outfit." Play games, have a scavenger hunt, act silly and take plenty of pictures! This island-inspired get-a-way will nourish both the body and the soul.

Gone with the Wind

We may not "Know nothin' 'bout birthin' no babies"...but we surely can give birth to a spectacular party! Pull out all the stops for this one - white damask linens, fine china, crystal and the "old family" silver. Floating magnolia or gardenia blossoms will complete a beautiful table setting. Watch the movie several times, make replicas of Scarlett's hats, and practice your best Southern accent. Customize your invitation and invite guests to join you, in costume, on the verandah for the most appropriate of Southern libations, the Mint Julep. Create an arch of magnolia leaves and blossoms at your doorway and have "Dixie" playing as your guests arrive. If your event is just for the girls, consider having lace fans or crocheted gloves as party favors. This meal will delight friends and family from any locale.

Jambalaya and Blues

While Savannah has its own unique style...she isn't afraid to celebrate the traditions and heritage of other Southern states. One of those cultures is that of a "Southern Sister," Louisiana. This great outdoor party is even more fun during the Mardi Gras season. A cool evening, a full moon and lots of great jazz (with a little Cajun and Zydeco thrown in) prepares you to let the good times roll. In-A-Hurry Hurricane Punch or cold, Louisiana brewed beer leaves no one thirsty. As an hors d'oeuvre Jalapeño Cheese Hot Broccoli Dip adds spice to the gathering and kicks off this celebration with a bang. Mardi Gras colors of purple, green and gold make decorating simple and colorful. Beads and doubloons can be tossed on tables around centerpieces crafted from Mardi Gras masks placed on dowl rods inserted into styrofoam in clay pots. Cover the foam with colorful metallic shred and purple, green and gold Christmas ornament balls. Cast iron and enameled serving platters and bowls are both practical and decorative. Send your guests home with a little "lagniappe" - small gift bags filled with beads, doubloons, hot sauce, Savannah Pralines and maybe even a little voodoo doll!

MENU

Mint Juleps or Whiskey Slush

Cucumber Sandwiches
Shrimp Spread

Cucumber Aspic

Savannah Red Rice
Big Mama's Minced Greens

Pork Tenderloin in Tomato
Creole Cream Sauce

Sweet Potato Biscuits

Traditional Southern
Pound Cake

MENU

In-A-Hurry Hurricane Punch

Pennies from Heaven
Summer Corn & Zucchini Salad

Chicken & Crawfish Gumbo
Sausage & Ham Jambalaya
Bourbon Bar-B-Q Chicken

French Bread with Garlic
Cheese Spread

Bread Pudding
with Bourbon Sauce

Savannah Pralines

MENU

Flirtinis

❧

Crab & Pecan Stuffed
Mushrooms
Sun-Dried Tomato Cheese Torte

❧

Gorgonzola & Pecan
Crunch Salad
with Hazelnut Vinaigrette

❧

Vidalia Onion Soup

❧

Broccoli Stuffed Tomato Cups
Accordion Garlic Potatoes

❧

Medallions of Veal
with Shrimp & Chanterelles

❧

Crème Brûlée with
Raspberries & Mint

MENU

Assorted Wines

❧

Smoked Salmon Canapés
Spinach Artichoke Dip
Scallops & Mushrooms in
Pastry Shells

❧

Red Pear Salad with
Raspberry Vinaigrette

❧

Sautéed Asparagus

❧

Creamy Shrimp & Mushrooms

❧

Flaky Dinner Biscuits

❧

Oreo Mousse with
Super Fudge Sauce

Setting the Course

Introduce the idea of this "shared" dinner party to several couples who enjoy fine foods, conversation and good wine. Begin early and schedule plenty of time for this very elegant, course-by-course dinner party. It is surprisingly easy to do, even for the novice. As hostess, you will invite guests to your home and you will take charge of the entrée and side dishes. Assign or have couples choose from the remaining courses. Each couple will prepare their course (at their home) and will serve their course (out of your kitchen). They may also wish to serve a special wine to compliment the dish (so have plenty of wine glasses available). After each course the guest couples will clear the table in preparation for the next course. This type of dinner party allows everyone a chance to enjoy both the cooking and the eating. For those who enjoy cooking (and even for those who don't) and for everyone who enjoys fine dining, this dinner party has all of the elements to set the course.

Boys Night in...
the Kitchen

Ladies, this is your night to get out of the kitchen and the boys night to get in! Dream if you may, for a moment, of being welcomed home from a day of shopping by gentlemen wearing white tuxedo shirts, bow ties and cumberbunds. You are greeted at the door with sparkling glasses of champagne, sumptuous hors d'oeuvres and your favorite tunes playing softly on the stereo. With a little pre-planning, your husband and his closest friends can set the stage for a sophisticated dinner in a relaxed atmosphere. Easy recipes and responsibilities are divided amongst friends and most of the selections can be prepared well ahead of time. Ladies, you may have to drop a few hints for this one, but after a ladies' day out, you are most deserving of a "boys night in...the kitchen."

Who "Dunnit" Dinner

Take a shot in the dark... and set the stage for an evening of mystery and mayhem! For a unique invitation, create and mail a video tape to each guest. Whatever mystery you stage, guests will become immediately intrigued as you assign them a character and introduce clues for the evening. Everything on this menu can be prepared well in advance, so that the host and hostess can participate in the evening's activities. Never hosted a Who "Dunnit" Dinner? Don't worry, there are many boxed games available at party stores for an evening of mystery-solving. For a dramatic presentation, keep things simple by using black and white or silver which is clean and contemporary. If you prefer, recreate a Sherlock Holmes atmosphere for an intriguing English manor style evening. Lay out your clues, become detectives, enjoy your meal and decide...who "dunnit"!

It's a Hard Day's Night

We all know that "manly endeavors" work up "manly appetites." Whatever your manly men do for recreation is certain to bring them home hungry! So, when the guys arrive at your house after a hard day of fun and games, give them each a cold brew, let them kick back and wait for the "war stories" to begin. For fun table decor - lay out a plaid table cloth or table runner. For the men who have been out on the links, consider using clay saucers filled with grass and golf balls or small pin flags. If your guys enjoy "dropping a line," fill a (clean) fishing creel with Bay Street Brown Bread and scatter miniature rods and reels and spools of fishing line on the table. Bring out Hot Rye sandwiches and Hot Beef Dip to stave off hunger until dinner is served. Ladies, choose between Marinated Beef Tenderloin or Roquefort-Stuffed Fillet Mignon and prepare to share in their woes of "the one that got away" or "the putt that no one could have made!"

MENU

Marinated Shrimp
Spinach Cheddar Chutney Loaf
Crab Corners

❧

Spinach & Strawberry Salad

❧

Tomato & Artichoke Bake
Delmonico Potatoes

❧

Stove-Top Pork Tenderloin

❧

Sour Dough Rolls

❧

Brown Sugar Pecan Squares

MENU

Cold Beer

❧

Hot Beef Dip
Hot Ryes

❧

Zucchini Milano
Creamy Garlic Mashed
Potatoes

❧

Marinated Beef Tenderloin
or
Roquefort Stuffed Fillet
Mignon

❧

Bay Street Brown Bread

❧

Banana Nut Pound Cake
with Caramel Glaze

MENU

Mango Margaritas

❧

Taco Cheesecake
Peach Salsa

❧

Yellow Tomato Gazpacho with
Crab Relish

❧

Chili Rellenos
Red Rice

❧

Margarita Salmon
or
Chicken Artichoke Burrito

❧

Margarita Mousse Cookies
or
Key Lime Bars

MENU

Boiled Peanuts

❧

Crab Fritters
Southern Caviar
Tybee Pickled Oysters
with Tangy Seafood Sauce

❧

Saint's Cole Slaw

❧

Low Country Boil
Boiled Blue Crabs

❧

Sliced Watermelon

❧

Peach Ice Cream

Margarita Madness

Explore the Latin culture with your family or gather friends for a lively fiesta. You may want to include other "south of the border" hors d'oeuvres such as Chicken Brie Quesadillas and Picante Rollups. Set the table with bright serapes and fiesta-ware china (look-a-like dishes can be found for just a dollar or two). Miniature cacti and succulents in clay pots, colorful paper flowers and sombreros really add to the festive atmosphere. Don't forget the music! Latin and Salsa rhythms add to the festive mood. Serve plenty of Margaritas - traditional, Mango, or "virgin" for the younger set. Make your tart, refreshing beverage even more special by dipping the glass rims into colored sugar or salt. Tomato Gazpacho is sassy with the addition of Crab Relish. With two great entrées to choose from, you'll be able to satisfy everyone's need for something spicy. Olé and Buenos Nochés!

Oceans of Fun

This party is what summer is all about in Savannah! Whether you're spending the day at the beach, on the dock, or in your own backyard, take advantage of the abundance of seafood and summer fruits, and serve up what has become a local tradition. Low Country Boil has only four ingredients - shrimp, potatoes, corn and sausage. The secret is in the spices used and cooking methods, both of which may vary slightly according to the chef! Make sure you have plenty of boiled peanuts, sliced watermelon and coolers full of icy, cold beverages for everyone. Take advantage of a full crab trap by serving Crab Fritters. Simple red and white checked napkins and tableclothes lend to the casual atmosphere and small galvanized buckets filled with sunflowers or zinnias present a summertime burst of color. If you live on the coast, your guests will greatly appreciate lots of citronella candles and your favorite bug spray.

St. Patrick's Day Picnic in the Square

The St. Patrick's Day Parade is cause for major celebration in Savannah and is truly an all-day affair. Delegation and preparation are key to making this menu work; ensuring that a good time will be had by all. Family and friends bring several folding tables to set up in the square. Cover these with green tablecloths or decorative fabric and to really get in the spirit, add pots of shamrock plants tied with green and white helium filled balloons. Since you must arrive early to ensure a prime spot in your favorite Savannah Square, you'll need to serve breakfast. Begin with Bloody Marys and favorite juices. Bring your chafing dish to keep Garlic Cheddar Grits warm and yes, you may add green food coloring if you must. During the parade, have plenty of fresh vegetables, as well as chips and dip available for snacking. After the parade put out your spread for lunch. Be sure to have enough food for "drop-by" guests as they make their way to their car, City Market, or River Street. *Erin go braugh!*

The Night the Lights Went Out in Georgia

Throw the main breakers on a cool, crisp autumn evening to turn off the lights. Leave only the stove, refrigerator and stereo working. Illuminate your home with candles, light the fire, pour the wine and get ready for a cozy, romantic dinner. Instead of the formal dining room, set your coffee table for dinner in the den. Place large, comfortable cushions on the floor, and turn on romantic music or easy-listening jazz (Georgia-born Gladys Knight singing her popular "Midnight Train to Georgia" would be appropriate.) Leave the dishes until morning, and enjoy "the night the lights went out in Georgia."

MENU

Breakfast
Garlic Cheddar Grits
Melted Swiss and Ham Rolls
Country Breakfast Pie
Mini Cinnamon Rolls

❧

Lunch
Broccoli Bacon Toss
Marinated Cucumbers
Corned Beef Sandwiches
Fried Chicken
Mint-Cream Brownies

MENU

Assorted Wines
❧
Chafing Dish Crab
❧
Portobello Cream Soup
❧
Baked Chèvre Salad with
Red Grape Clusters
❧
Steamed Broccoli in
Olive Nut Sauce
Curried Rice Pilaf
Lamb Shanks with
Red Zinfandel Mushroom
Sauce
❧
Temptation Turtle Cheesecake

Christmas in the South

Make time in your hustle and bustle to enjoy this Christmas season with friends and family. Whether you invite the ladies over after a long day of shopping, entertain couples for cocktails, or gather with family on Christmas Eve, this easy menu will prove to be a true Christmas gift to both you and your guests. Light the trees and the candles, put on your favorite Christmas music and your favorite Christmas sweater and entertain Southern style. "Pick-up" foods on large crystal or silver platters require little attention during the party. For "one of a kind" invitations, attach a Christmas ornament or jingle bells, or nestle the invitation in a Christmas stocking filled with "sugar plums." Use Clement Moore's "T'was The Night Before Christmas…" to word your own "T'was Two Weeks Before Christmas…" invitation. Add your own personal touches to create a new family tradition for Christmas.

MENU

Pop's Nog
Ye Olde Wassail

❧

Buffet Salmon Platter
Asparagus with Garlic Cream
Plains Cheese Ring
Heavenly Ham and
Cheese Bake
Creamy Shrimp Mold
Cucumber Chicken Salad
Incredible Fruit Dip
Assorted Fresh Fruits

❧

Butter Pecan Dreams
Fruitcake Cookies
Savannah Candy Kitchen
Divinity

Southern Suits Us To A Tea

Afternoon tea is a gentle way to relax and is often enjoyed by ladies in the South. This is a very pleasant and inexpensive way to repay small social obligations even though husbands are rarely included. Invitations to informal teas are usually extended in person or by phone. Formal teas, however, call for an engraved invitation. Polish the silver and stack tea plates with a folded napkin between each one. Place the plates on the end of the table, opposite your mother's sterling silver tea service. Guests go to the "pourer" telling her "how they take their tea" and then help themselves to tea sandwiches and confections. Often punch is served, especially during the summer when this event may be called an "ice-water" tea. For a variety of tea sandwiches, use different breads without crusts and choose at least three of your favorite "tea-time" spreads. Open Faced Tomato, Rolled Pimento-Cheese, and Melted Swiss and Ham are a few of our favorites. In the South, no tea would be "proper" without Cheese Straws, Homemade Mints and Classy Tassies. White gloves are "optional" but linen and lace are *de rigeuer.*

MENU

Saints' Graduation Punch
Hot Tea

❧

Cheese Straws

❧

Tomato Sandwiches
Green Chile-Pimento Cheese
Sandwiches
Classic Chicken Salad
Sandwiches

❧

Melted Swiss and Ham
Sandwiches

❧

Classy Tassies
Orange Blossom Bars
Mints

Beverages

The *First* Chatham Artillery

First organized in 1786, the Chatham Artillery has been in service as a field artillery longer than any other unit in the South. The Chatham Artillery was presented with two bronze cannons, one British and one French. These cannons were a gift from George Washington, after his visit to Savannah in 1791. Formally called the Washington Guns, they are nicknamed "George" and "Martha." The British cannon, cast in either 1756 or 1758, bears the monogram of King George II, as well as the royal insignia of The Order of the Garter. Appropriately, it is also inscribed, "Surrendered by the capitulation of Yorktown, October 19, 1781." The French cannon, *first* nicknamed "La Populaire," was cast in 1756. Among its inscriptions is the royal insignia of Louis XIV, The Sun King. Brought to America by Henri Compte d'Estang, the French gun was presented to the Continental Congress by Lafayette. In 1986, at the bicentennial of the Chatham Artillery, a memorial monument was dedicated, bearing the inscription "Soldiers in War, Patriots in Peace."

Spirited Savannah

Savannah holds on to its history and heritage, both naturally and supernaturally. Spirits abound within the old townhouses, plantations and forts. Mostly, these spirits are content coming and going about their business (and sometimes the owner's business, as well.) There are other places wherein the spirits are disturbed and disturbing. Foremost among these is the Hampton-Lillibridge House, a private residence over 200 years old. It was renovated by Jim Williams (of *Midnight in the Garden....*) Inexplicable activities and terrors caused Jim Williams to have an exorcism performed. This did the trick, somewhat. However, many unseen residents remained. In 1964, famed para-psychologist Dr. Roll declared Hampton - Lillibridge to be the "most psychically possessed" house in the USA. It is also the only house in Savannah known to have had an exorcism. Well, publicly known, perhaps.

"Punch and Julep"

On May 1, 1783, "The Georgia Gazette" reported that the Treaty of Paris had been signed, thus ending the War for American Independence. In gleeful response to this news, the "Chatham Regiment of Militia" (Chatham Artillery) joined in the many toasts being made that day. Accounts of the celebrations present the *first* association between the Chatham Artillery and its infamous punch. It was probably concocted of rum and just about whatever else was available.

Another instance with claims to the origin of Chatham Artillery punch happened before the War Between the States. It seems that the Chatham Artillery prepared a punch for their "rivals," The Republication Blues, ostensibly to honor them (or see how well they could hold their liquor). Since this punch is still called Chatham Artillery Punch, and not Republication Blues Punch, one can assume which group was most successful in managing the effects of this punch. In any case, it is a most spirited and fierce punch, traditionally associated with Savannah.

Mint Juleps are also a subject for debate, not only in Savannah but also throughout the South. Here the contentions are not about the origin of a Julep, but its proper preparation. Some favor preparing a simple sugar syrup ahead of time and others like the spur of the moment method. Whichever method is used, Juleps are a welcome addition at traditional Southern gatherings. One point of absolute agreement is that mint Juleps are never to be rushed, either in their creation or their enjoyment.

Chatham Artillery Punch

1	pound green tea	1	gallon rum
2	gallons cold water	1	gallon brandy
	Juice of 3 dozen lemons	1	gallon rye whiskey
	Juice of 3 dozen oranges	1	gallon gin
5	pounds brown sugar, firmly packed	2	quarts maraschino cherries, undrained
3	gallons Catawba wine	15	(750-ml) bottles champagne

Combine tea and cold water and allow to stand overnight. Strain and mix tea with lemon and orange juices. Add sugar, wine, rum, brandy, whiskey and gin. Let stock stand for 2 to 6 weeks, stirring occasionally. When ready to serve, strain stock of pulp. Add cherries with juice and champagne. Stir well before serving.

Makes 12 gallons

Southern Comfort Punch

1	(6-ounce) can frozen orange juice concentrate, thawed	3	quarts lemon-lime soda, chilled
1	(6-ounce) can frozen lemonade concentrate, thawed	1	(750-ml) bottle Southern Comfort blended whiskey
¾	cup lemon juice		Sugar to taste (optional)

Combine concentrates and lemon juice. Add soda, then whiskey. Add sugar to taste. To serve, chill with an ice ring or ice cubes made from juices or lemon-lime soda.

Serves 32 to 36

The original Chatham Artillery Punch recipe used equal parts of rum, brandy, and whiskey, mixed with sugar and lemons. This mixture was allowed to "mature" over several days in tubs or horse buckets! When the mixture was deemed to be ready, ice was added, then champagne was poured over the ice; thus completing the preparation of this most spirited of Savannah's concoctions, the infamous Chatham Artillery Punch.

One version of an old Savannah saying goes like this:

In Charleston, they want to know who your people are;

In Augusta, what your church is;

And in Savannah, what you want to drink.

Savannah is known as a city that loves its spirits. Nothing confirms this better than the powerful brew known as Chatham Artillery Punch.

In A Hurry Hurricane Punch

½ (64-ounce) bottle red fruit punch

1 (6-ounce) can frozen limeade concentrate, thawed

1 (6-ounce) can frozen orange juice concentrate, thawed

1⅔ cups light rum

1⅔ cups dark rum

Stir together all ingredients. Serve over ice in tall glasses.

Makes about 8 cups

Whiskey Slush

2	family-size tea bags	1	(6-ounce) can frozen
2	cups boiling water		lemonade concentrate
1	(12-ounce) can frozen	2	cups whiskey
	orange juice	1	cup sugar
	concentrate	6	cups water

Combine tea bags and 2 cups boiling water in a large container. Let steep 5 to 10 minutes. Remove tea bags. Add concentrates, whiskey, sugar and 6 cups water. Place mixture in freezer, stirring occasionally, for 24 hours or until slushy.

Witch's Ginger Brew

1	(25.4-ounce) bottle sparkling cider, chilled	1	cup dark rum
1	(1-quart) bottle cranberry juice cocktail, chilled	1	recipe spice syrup, strained
1	(1-liter) bottle club soda or seltzer, chilled		Ice blocks in any shape

Spice Syrup

3	cinnamon sticks	⅓	cup water
6	whole cloves	⅓	cup sugar
3	tablespoons minced fresh ginger		

Pour all drink ingredients except ice into a punch bowl. Stir to mix. Add ice blocks.

To make spice syrup, combine all ingredients in a small saucepan. Bring to a boil, stirring until sugar dissolves. Reduce heat and simmer, covered, for 5 minutes. Cool syrup. Cover and store in refrigerator up to 1 week. Strain before using.

Makes 13 cups

Ye Olde Wassail

1	gallon apple cider	1	(6-ounce) can frozen orange juice concentrate
3-4	cinnamon sticks		
1-2	teaspoons allspice		
1	tablespoon whole cloves	1	(6-ounce) can frozen lemonade concentrate, or juice of 2 lemons
1	(46-ounce) can pineapple juice		

Combine apple cider, cinnamon sticks, allspice and cloves in a saucepan. Bring to a boil. Reduce heat and simmer 15 minutes.

Add pineapple juice and concentrates. Bring to a simmer over medium-low heat. Cook 15 to 30 minutes.

Serves 20 to 25

To make in a crockpot, heat cider and spices on high for 30 minutes. Reduce heat to low and stir in juices.

A bottle of dark or spiced rum is often placed beside the wassail so guests may choose if or how much alcohol they prefer in their drink.

Pop's Nog

1	(750-ml) bottle blended whiskey or bourbon	12	eggs, separated
2	cups sugar	2	quarts whipping cream

Combine whiskey and sugar and stir until sugar dissolves. Whip egg yolks. Slowly add whiskey mixture to yolks. Set aside.

Whip cream until soft peaks form. Slowly fold in whiskey mixture. Whip egg whites until stiff peaks form. Gently fold whites into whiskey mixture. Refrigerate 5 hours before serving. To serve, use a ladle to reblend ingredients.

Makes 6 quarts

Savannah Cinnamon Holiday Punch

Delicious, aromatic, hot mulled cider

½ gallon apple juice, or cider

½ cup Savannah Cinnamon Mix

Heat and serve to welcome friends and family.

In 1881, at the Centennial celebration of Cornwallis' surrender, the Washington Guns traveled to Yorktown. Escorted by the Chatham Artillery, the Washington Guns led the parade that day. They were then returned home where they remain as proud reminders of Revolutionary valor.

The Washington Guns were used in the capture of Fort Pulaski, for the Confederate Cause! This event counts among the first of the "Rebel" actions. This also predates the firing on Ft. Sumter by several months, with Pulaski in January of 1861 and Ft. Sumter in April of that same year.

Savannah has the 2nd largest St. Patrick's Day parade in America (with New York 1st). There is quip regarding this "competition" with New York. It says that Savannah has the "2nd largest parade, but New York has the 2nd best." Slainte!

Syllabub

2	pints whipping cream	1	cup sugar
1	cup half-and-half	1	cup blended whiskey

Combine all ingredients and stir until sugar dissolves. Beat on medium or high with an electric mixer or whisk rapidly by hand until frothy. Serve froth in cups or small glasses. Continue to beat as needed to keep frothy while serving.

Serves 12 to 16

Martha Nesbitt's Irish Coffee

Lemon wedge and sugar to prepare glass	½-1	ounce Irish whiskey
½-¾ cup hot strong coffee	2	tablespoons lightly whipped cream
1-2 teaspoons sugar		

Rub lemon wedge around the rim of a glass or mug. Dip rim in sugar. Pour coffee into glass. Stir in 1 to 2 teaspoons sugar. Add whiskey. Float whipped cream on top. Sip coffee slowly through the cream.

Serves 1

Homemade Irish Cream

1	cup Irish whiskey	1	tablespoon chocolate syrup, or 2 tablespoons instant hot chocolate
1	(14-ounce) can sweetened condensed milk		
4	eggs, lightly beaten	1	tablespoon instant coffee
2	tablespoons vanilla		

Combine all ingredients in a blender. Mix well on low speed. Refrigerate at least 12 hours. Serve over ice.

Serves 4 to 6

Bloody Marys

1	quart V-8 juice	
1	cup Vodka	
1	tablespoon	
	Worcestershire sauce	
6-8	dashes Tabasco sauce	
	Juice of 1 lemon	

Salt and pepper to taste
Fresh shucked oyster
   (optional)
Prepared horseradish
   (optional)

Combine all ingredients; pour into tall ice filled glasses. Garnish with celery sticks and lime wedges. Top with oyster (optional).

Serves 6

Lime Tea Cooler

Juice of 6 limes
¾ cup sugar
1½ cups strong tea

2½ cups cold water
1 (2-liter) bottle ginger ale
Lime wedges for garnish

Combine lime juice, sugar, tea and water. Add ginger ale and chill. Serve over ice. Garnish with lime wedges.

Serves 18 to 20

Flirtini

1½ ounces vodka
2 ounces champagne

2 ounces pineapple juice

Mix all ingredients well. Serve over ice in a highball glass.

Serves 1

Increase recipe and make in a pitcher to serve more people. It's a "sippin'" kind of drink.

Bloody Marys

Bloody Marys were named after a queen of England. She was the daughter of Henry VIII and his 1st wife, Catherine of Aragon. Mary was a Catholic and did not care for the new Church of England created by her father (in part so that he could divorce her mother.) During her reign, she reinstated Catholicism as the official religion of England and bloody revolt followed. Thus the name - Bloody Mary.

Most Savannahians begin St. Patrick's Day with the traditional Bloody Mary.

"Sweet Tea" ... House Wine of the South

There are several important points to remember when making tea. One: your water should be clear and not hard. Two: never let boiling water touch the tea; rather it should be just coming up to a boil. Three: do not brew your tea too long or it will be bitter. Four: store in a cool, not cold place; tea stored in the refrigerator will become cloudy.

Infallible Fours: Method for Tea in the Microwave:

4 - regular-size tea bags (or one family-size)

4 - cups of cool water

4 - minutes in microwave on high

4 - minutes to steep

4 - teaspoons or tablespoons of sugar

Poor over ice and enjoy!

Most Southerners agree with the band Cravin Melon that " on the 8th day God made sweet tea!"

Peached Iced Tea

3	orange pekoe tea bags	¼	cup or to taste simple syrup, chilled
4	cups boiling water		
5	(5-ounce) cans peach nectar (about 3⅓ cups), chilled		Fresh peach slices and mint sprigs for garnish

Simple Syrup

1⅓	cups sugar	1¼	cups water

Place tea bags in a 1-quart glass measuring cup or heatproof bowl. Pour boiling water over tea bags. Steep 5 minutes. Strain through a sieve into a heatproof pitcher. Cover and refrigerate 1 hour or until cold.

To make simple syrup, combine sugar and water in a saucepan. Bring to a boil and stir until sugar dissolves. Cover and chill. Store in refrigerator up to 2 weeks.

Stir in peach nectar and simple syrup. Serve tea over ice in tall glasses, garnished with peach slices and mint or serve as a cool summer punch.

Makes about 8 cups tea; about 2 cups simple syrup

Church Social Sherbet Punch

1	gallon pineapple or lime sherbet	3	(1-liter) bottles ginger ale, chilled
		1	quart apple juice, chilled

Place sherbet in a punch bowl. Pour ginger ale and apple juice over sherbet. Stir gently to mix.

Serves 40

Do not use rainbow sherbet...it makes brown punch.

Cool Coffee Punch

1	pint whipping cream	1	gallon vanilla ice cream
5	tablespoons sugar	1	gallon strong coffee,
5	teaspoons vanilla		chilled

Whip cream with sugar and vanilla. Scoop whipped cream and ice cream into a punch bowl. Pour coffee over top. Mix gently and serve.

Serves 34 to 36

Can substitute non-dairy whipped topping instead of whipped cream.

Mango Margaritas

1	(26-ounce) jar sliced mangoes, undrained	1	cup gold tequila
	Colored decorator sugar	½	cup Triple Sec or Cointreau
1	(6-ounce) can frozen limeade concentrate, thawed	¼	cup Grand Marnier
			Crushed ice

Spoon 3 tablespoons of juice from mangoes onto a saucer. Pour mangoes and remaining juice into a blender. Spoon some decorator sugar onto a separate saucer. Dip rims of serving glasses into mango juice, then sugar. Set aside.

Add limeade concentrate and liquors to blender. Process until smooth, stopping once to scrape down sides. Pour half of mixture into a small pitcher. Add crushed ice to remaining mixture in blender to bring volume to 5-cup level. Process until slushy, stopping once to scrape down sides. Pour into sugar-rimmed glasses. Repeat with remaining mango mixture and ice. Serve immediately.

Serves 6 to 8

Hazelnut Cooler

Whisk together 2 cups cooled strong coffee, ¼ cup chocolate syrup, 2 cups milk, and 1 cup Savannah Cinnamon Southern Hazelnut mix. To serve, pour over a scoop of ice cream in a tall glass.

This mixture can be refrigerated for several days. Also good served over ice or warmed in the microwave.

When Union troops began closing in on Savannah, the Washington Guns were buried under the Chatham Artillery Armory where they remained safe until 1872, when they were returned to their position of prominence in our fair city.

Orange Blossom Champagne Punch

3	cups sugar	4	bananas
6	cups water	8	(750-ml) bottles champagne, or 4 to 5 (2-liter) bottles ginger ale, chilled
1	(12-ounce) can frozen orange juice concentrate		
1	(6-ounce) can frozen lemonade concentrate		Orange blossoms for garnish
1	(46-ounce) can unsweetened pineapple juice		

Combine sugar and water in a large saucepan and heat until dissolved. Add concentrates and pineapple juice. Puree bananas in a blender or food processor with enough of juice mixture to liquefy. Add puree to juice mixture and stir until well blended. Pour into a large ring mold, or several smaller ones, and freeze.

Remove ring mold from freezer about 1 hour before ready to serve and place in a large punch bowl. Pour half the chilled champagne over the ring. Float orange blossoms on top. Refill punch bowl with remaining champagne as needed.

Serves 48

Peach Fuzzie

6	peaches, unpeeled and quartered	1	(6-ounce) can frozen lemonade concentrate
		¾	cup vodka or gin

Combine all ingredients in a blender. Add ice cubes and blend. Garnish with fresh mint and serve immediately.

Serves 4

Quick Chill

For a quick chill of wine and champagne, fill the sink with cold water and ice and submerge the bottles. This will cool the liquid faster than the freezer or ice bucket.

Serving Wine

How many wine servings in a bottle? A fifth (25 ounces) of table wine such as Rosé, Chablis, or Burgundy serves four persons. With champagne, a fifth serves five to six. For dessert wines like sherry or port, a fifth serves eight.

Pain Killer Rum Punch

1	part cream of coconut	4	parts pineapple juice
1	part orange juice		Dark rum to taste

Combine cream of coconut and juices. Add rum and mix. Refrigerate until ready to serve. Serve over ice.

Perfect for the beach or boat. Serve garnished with fruit kabobs made of cherries and chunks of pineapple and oranges.

Saints' Graduation Punch

1	(46-ounce) can pineapple juice	1	(2-liter) bottle lemon-lime soda, chilled
1	(46-ounce) can apple juice		

Combine juices in a container and freeze until solid.

Remove mixture from freezer 1 hour before serving. When ready to serve, transfer juice mixture to a punch bowl. Add soda and serve.

Serves about 30

Freeze the juice in a container that can be easily opened. A clean, 1-gallon ice cream bucket works well. Also, you may wish to cut the frozen juice mixture into chunks before placing in punch bowl or serving pitcher.

For a garnish and to help keep punch cool, cut 3 oranges and 4 limes into thick slices and freeze. Float frozen slices in punch bowl.

For an alcoholic "Saints' Preserve Us" Spiked Punch, add 1 to 1½ cups orange liqueur and 1 to 1½ cups light rum or blended bourbon.

River "Raft-Ups"

A favorite summer activity for area boaters is our regular "Raft-Up" River Party. Ten to twelve boats hook together around an anchored fishing trawler in any of our nearby rivers. The trawler serves as the entertainment hub, and stage, while the locally infamous "Crabettes" delight us with their own style of river music and folklore. We hop from boat to boat, enjoying a variety of beverages and freshly prepared hors d'oeuvres, such as Richardson Creek Crab Dip, boiled peanuts, and fresh-out-of-the-creek boiled shrimp with a variety of dipping sauces. These impromptu parties are easy - no planned agenda, just good friends, a high tide, and great food!

Mint Juleps

Mint Syrup

3	cups water	2	cups sugar
2-3	cups fresh spearmint	1	cup bourbon
	leaves, lightly packed		Sprigs of fresh mint

To make syrup, combine water, spearmint and sugar in a heavy saucepan. Bring to a boil over medium heat, stirring constantly until sugar dissolves. Boil gently for 3 minutes. Remove from heat, cover and chill at least 3 hours. When ready to serve, strain syrup into a bowl or wide-mouth pitcher, pressing mint leaves to extract flavors. Discard mint.

For individual drinks, fill tall, frosted glasses or julep cups with finely crushed ice. Add 1 to 1½ jiggers of syrup and 1 to 1½ jiggers of bourbon to each glass. Stir gently and garnish with fresh mint.

Serves 8 to 10

To make Mint Julep Sorbet, add ¼ cup crème de menthe to the strained mint syrup. Freeze in an ice cream maker according to manufacturer's instructions. Spoon into parfait or rounded wine glasses, cover and freeze 2 hours longer. Garnish with mint and serve.

Mint Juleps served on the verandah, shaded by the branches of ancient live oak trees, have long been a cherished Southern tradition. Mint Juleps, in frosted sterling cups with silver spoon straws, are a luxurious experience to be certain. However, tall frosted glasses and decorative stirrers will serve just as well for the enjoyment of this most classic Southern drink. Your best bet is to always have plenty of extra mint (preferably fresh, from under the dripping spigot in the garden) sugar, ice and sour mash bourbon.

Appetizers

The *First* Capital of Georgia

Savannah was the *first* capital of the 13th colony and later of Georgia.
A charter signed in 1732 by King George II established Georgia as what turned out to be the
last British colony in America. This new colony was founded on the vision of James Edward
Oglethorpe, an active member of the British Parliament. Oglethorpe's political and military
service made him acutely aware of social problems in England. In particular was the
problem of indebtedness, which landed many an otherwise worthy person in prison.
British Parliament was expecting Georgia to provide new sources of wealth, as well
as help relieve unemployment. There was also the Spanish threat to the Carolinas, which
could be buffered by the Colony of Georgia. Thus, the Charter was granted to 21 "Trustees
for Establishing the Colony of Georgia for America." Georgia's original boundaries were
defined by the Savannah River to the North, the Altamaha to the South, the
Atlantic Ocean to the East and the Pacific Ocean to the West.

Spirited Savannah

Among the most fervent supporters of the Cause for American Independence was James Habersham, Jr., owner of the Pink House. He helped finance the war and also served in the Continental Army. As with many other of Savannah's Sons of Liberty, Habersham, Jr., did this in opposition to his father's loyalty to the Crown. During the War of 1812, the Pink House held captured British gold in its vaults, after it had been paraded victoriously through the streets. When Savannah surrendered to Sherman, one of his generals, Brigadier Lewis York, seized the house for his headquarters.

Having endured three wars, the Pink House could certainly have a cadre of spirits in residence. That seems to not be the case. The primary spirit is said to be James Habersham, Jr., whose ghostly appearance "matches" his portrait quite clearly. So real are these appearances that guests have commented on the "gentleman in Colonial dress." They assume "he" was hired to create more atmosphere in this revolutionary period restaurant, now called The Olde Pink House.

"Keeping up the Standards, To a Tea"

Once in a while, usually in the summertime, it will come upon a fine Southern lady that it has been far too long since she had a formal tea. Often called "ice-water" teas, the standards for these were set long ago by our foremothers. Although this kind of event is rather inelegantly called "putting on the dog," it is the time to bring out your most elegant things, both old and new. Savannahians attractively mix their fine old linens and period piece table settings with new – or at least newer – items.

Regardless of whatever else you serve, it is not a tea without at least two kinds of cutout sandwiches. These bread cutouts can be done weeks ahead of time and frozen. Your foremothers had more help but they didn't have refrigeration or plastic zipper bags. Thawing frozen bread cutouts will also help to dry them out a little. This will keep the sandwiches from getting soggy on their platters. Once the sandwiches have been spread completely, they must then be covered with a damp cloth and stored in a covered container until time to put them on the platter. This keeps them from drying out too much. This may seem to be working at cross-purposes, but it is not. If a tea sandwich is properly prepared, it can survive a hot summer afternoon. (It can also withstand any lingering guests who have had too much punch.)

Toasted Pecans

6   **cups pecan halves**
1   **cup butter or margarine,**
      melted

Salt to taste

Preheat oven to 275 to 325 degrees. Place pecans in a large mixing bowl. Pour butter over pecans and stir until evenly coated. Arrange in a single layer on baking sheets. Sprinkle lightly with salt. Bake 30 to 45 minutes or until lightly browned, stirring every 10 minutes. Sprinkle with more salt, as needed.

If nuts seem to be getting brown enough but are not crisp, they need to dry out a little longer. Turn off oven and crack door slightly. Leave nuts in oven until cool, checking every 5 minutes.

Makes about 2 pounds

Frosted Pecans

1   **cup sour cream**
3   **cups sugar**

1   **tablespoon vanilla**
6   **cups pecan halves**

Combine sour cream, sugar and vanilla in a heavy 4- to 6-quart saucepan or cast-iron skillet. Cook over medium to medium-high heat until mixture reaches soft-ball stage (234 degrees on a candy thermometer.) Stir frequently while cooking to prevent scorching. Add pecans and stir until evenly coated. Turn onto lightly greased baking sheets, separating nuts with 2 forks. When completely cooled, store nuts in an airtight container.

Makes about 3 pounds

These are especially good if pecans have been lightly toasted before adding to candy coating. Makes great Christmas gifts.

Pecans

Since toasting pecans, like frying chicken, is a matter of style, use the rule: Cook low and slow, to come and go. Cook high, on the fly, then stand close by!

Whether you say "pee-cans" or "pah-khans" is regional, and also depends to whom you are speaking. Pecans are used in a multitude of Southern dishes, and are delicious just by themselves. Wild pecans were one of the staples for the Native Americans and have been under cultivation since the early 1700s. Pecan trees were planted by many of the colonists who used them for pies and confections. Pecan Pie and the classic Pecan Praline are most familiar and delightful.

Peanut Boilings

"In South Georgia, where former President Carter was raised, peanut farmers used to celebrate the harvest with peanut boilings. These were large outdoor parties where the peanuts were boiled in iron wash pots. A good boiling drew several hundred people. I can't give you quantities for a serving. If you love boiled peanuts, you won't be able to stop eating them; if you hate them, you won't eat more than it takes to find out. There isn't anybody in the country who is in between."
Damon Fowler from Classical Southern Cooking, 1995.

Boiled Peanuts

2	pounds raw peanuts in the shell	1	gallon water
		1¼	cups salt

Wash and rinse peanuts until water runs clear. Place peanuts in a large pot. Combine water and salt to make a brine. Pour brine over peanuts until covered. Bring to a boil and cover pot. Boil 45 minutes or until shells are tender. Remove from heat and let stand about 15 minutes; drain. Crack open shells and eat or store peanuts in refrigerator for up to 1 week.

"How we boil 'dem Davis Produce 'nuts'"

Take about 5 lbs fresh green Georgia peanuts, "right out of the ground."

Boil in a large cooking pot with water almost to the top.

Add salt, "about a large shaker full."

Boil on medium high for 1 hour.

Make sure to check your water, keep the pot full.

Taste after 1-hour. If peanuts are soft, turn off heat.

Then eat 'em!

For something different, boil nuts with some jalapeños or place a ham hock in panty hose with a knot and boil with peanuts! Both are "mmm good"! When on your way to Tybee, stop by Davis Produce for free samples!

Cheese Straws

1	pound New York sharp Cheddar cheese, grated
½	cup butter, softened
1½	cups all-purpose flour
1	teaspoon baking powder
¼	teaspoon salt
¼	teaspoon cayenne pepper or to taste

Preheat oven to 300 degrees. Cream together cheese and butter. Sift together flour, baking powder, salt and cayenne pepper. Add dry ingredients to creamed mixture. Knead well. Transfer to a pastry press with a star disc. Squeeze straws onto a greased or parchment-lined baking sheet. Bake 30 minutes or until light brown. Store in an airtight container.

For a biscuit-type treat, shape dough into logs, cover and chill 8 hours. Cut into ¼-inch slices and place on ungreased baking sheets. Bake at 350 degrees for 15 minutes. Cool on wire racks. Store in an airtight container.

Makes 8 dozen

Savannah Cheese Squares

2	eggs
2	tablespoons flour
½	teaspoon salt
⅓	cup milk
1	(4-ounce) can chopped green chiles
8	ounces sharp Cheddar cheese, grated
8	ounces sharp Monterey Jack cheese, grated

Preheat oven to 350 degrees. Beat eggs. Add flour, salt and milk and beat well. Add chiles and cheeses and mix well. Pour into a flat, well-greased 8x12-inch glass baking dish. Bake about 35 minutes. Cut into tiny squares and serve hot.

Makes 8 dozen

Cheese Straws

The most favorite of Southern standby snacks or "pick-ups" are cheese straws. It is wonderful to make a batch of these to keep on hand for guests (the problem is staying out of them). Cheese straws are a delicacy, crafted from flour, butter, cheese and red pepper. Therefore, they are to be enjoyed slowly and sparingly. A cookie press or pastry bag is used to make the most formal cheese straws. Dough rolled out and cut in strips is less difficult. For the quickest cheese straws, roll the dough into a log and slice to desired width.

Benne Seeds

Benne seeds have a legendary mystical power in the Orient. They were a charm that could "secure entrance and exit through any portal," thus "Open Sesame," as Ali Baba said. Africans, who planted them for luck, first brought benne seeds to the colonial coast. Black plantation cooks brought benne seeds into the Southern kitchens and toasted them into seed cakes and candies for good fortune. Even in the early days of the 20th century, Afro-Americans would sprinkle benne seeds on their doorsteps for luck and to scare off the "haints." The most well loved use of benne seeds is still the delicious toasted bits.

Benne Bits

A staple for Savannah cocktail parties.

½	cup benne (sesame) seeds	4	tablespoons butter, chilled and cut into pieces
1	cup all-purpose flour		
¼	teaspoon salt		
	Cayenne pepper to taste	1	tablespoon milk
		1	tablespoon water

Preheat oven to 350 degrees. Scatter seeds evenly on a baking sheet. Toast 10 minutes, stirring often or until golden brown; cool.

In a mixing bowl, combine flour, salt and cayenne pepper. Work in butter with your fingertips until mixture resembles coarse meal. Add benne seeds, milk and water and mix with your hands until dough is smooth. Roll out dough onto a floured surface to about ¼-inch thick. Cut into 1-inch rounds and place on an ungreased baking sheet. Bake 12 minutes or until golden. Let cool, then serve with cocktails.

Makes about 40 bits

Two cups of grated sharp Cheddar cheese can be added to the dough for Benne Cheese Bits.

Cucumber Sandwiches

1   cup mayonnaise
1   (8-ounce) package cream
      cheese, softened
1   loaf white sandwich bread

2   cucumbers, peeled and
      sliced ⅛-inch thick
    Chopped fresh dill

Mix mayonnaise and cream cheese until smooth. Cut a round piece out of each slice of bread using a 2-inch biscuit or cookie cutter. Spread each round with mayonnaise mixture. Place a cucumber slice on each round and top with fresh dill.

Thinly sliced baguette bread or baked refrigerator French bread can be used in place of sandwich bread rounds.

For the cucumber, run the tines of a fork down the length of an unpeeled cucumber. Slice paper thin and cut a slit to the middle in each slice. Twist slices and place 2 on each slice of bread, forming an "X". Sprinkle with dill.

The sandwiches can be topped with cooked cocktail shrimp.

Cucumber Sandwich

Another fine summertime sandwich is a slice of cheddar "hoop" cheese, with a slice of tomato and cucumber. Thinly sliced cucumber with mayonnaise, open faced on white bread rounds is most classic. Both cucumbers and tomatoes are the tried and true sandwiches for any Southern event. Casual or formal, they are a treat.

Swiss and Bacon Ryes

1   cup finely grated Swiss
      cheese
¼   cup cooked and crumbled
      bacon
1   (4½-ounce) can chopped
      black olives

¼   cup minced green onion
1   teaspoon Worcestershire
      sauce
¼   cup mayonnaise
    Party rye bread

Preheat oven to 375 degrees. Combine all ingredients except bread. Spread on bread slices. Bake 10 minutes or until browned. Serve immediately, or freeze and reheat when ready to serve.

Makes 36

Tomato Sandwiches

1	loaf white bread	½	cup mayonnaise
3	tomatoes, sliced	1	(3-ounce) jar bacon bits
½	cup horseradish sauce		

Cut a round piece out of each slice of bread using a cookie cutter. If preparing ahead, store bread rounds in an airtight container until ready to use. Place tomato slices on paper towels to dry. Mix horseradish sauce and mayonnaise and spread on each bread round. Top with a tomato slice and sprinkle with bacon bits. Serve open-faced.

Chicken Brie Quesadillas

¼	teaspoon garlic powder	4	(10-inch) flour tortillas
⅛	teaspoon salt	¼	cup bottled barbecue sauce
⅛	teaspoon freshly ground black pepper	4	ounces Brie cheese, thinly sliced
⅛	teaspoon ground cumin	1	green onion, minced
4	ounces boneless, skinless chicken breast, cut into strips	¼	cup chopped fresh cilantro
2	tablespoons unsalted butter, divided		

Mix garlic powder, salt, pepper and cumin. Add chicken strips and toss to coat. Sauté chicken in 1 tablespoon butter for 3 minutes.

Place 2 tortillas on a flat surface. Spread a thin layer of barbecue sauce over tortillas. Layer chicken, Brie, green onion and cilantro on top. Spread a thin layer of barbecue sauce on remaining 2 tortillas and place, sauce-side down, on top of first 2 tortillas.

Melt ½ tablespoon butter in a 12-inch skillet over medium-high heat. Place one quesadilla in skillet. Place a small oven-proof plate on top. Cook about 30 seconds or until bottom is golden brown. Remove plate and carefully turn quesadilla and brown on other side. Remove quesadilla and repeat with second quesadilla. Cool quesadillas slightly and cut into wedges. Serve with sour cream or salsa.

Tomato Sandwiches

In the summertime, when garden fresh tomatoes beckon from the produce stand, even the most gourmet of Southern cooks yearns for a simple tomato sandwich. People who have been health conscious all year, eating multi-grained breads, will suddenly buy the softest white, processed bread that they can find...along with a jar of mayonnaise which is not free of anything. For this finest of all summertime sandwiches, remember to slice your tomatoes evenly and thinly, press them lightly, with a paper towel, then salt the tomatoes and you're set.

Tea Sandwiches

Tried, true and traditional tea sandwich spreads.

2   (8-ounce) packages cream cheese, softened

½-¾ cup mayonnaise or softened butter

Blend together cream cheese and mayonnaise. Add any ONE of the following combinations:

1   cup crushed pineapple, drained and patted dry
    Zest of 1 medium orange

2   cups finely chopped pimiento-stuffed green or black olives
1   cup chopped celery
1-1½ cups minced pecans

Turkey-Spinach Rollups

1   (8-ounce) package cream cheese, softened
3   tablespoons chutney
2   tablespoons mayonnaise
8   (8-inch) flour tortillas

1   pound thinly sliced cooked turkey
1   bunch green onions, chopped
1   (6-ounce) package fresh spinach

Combine cream cheese, chutney and mayonnaise. Spread mixture evenly over tortillas. Top with turkey, green onions and spinach. Roll tightly and cut in half.

Serves 8

Can also add caramelized onions and/or cooked and crumbled bacon.

Cut rollups into 1-inch pieces to serve as appetizers or small snacks, or cut in half and serve as a sandwich for a picnic or a day at the beach.

Tea Sandwiches

Small sandwiches became fashionable towards the end of the nineteenth century when tea parties became socially acceptable and are still enjoyed today at Southern socials and receptions. Tea sandwiches also make, "a cooling quick lunch in the dead heat of summer. As an afternoon reception refreshment, they are predictable and maybe even a little hokey, but I've never known anyone who's gotten tired of them." Damon Fowler from Classical Southern Cooking, *1995.*

Damon Lee Fowler, author of Classical Southern Cooking, *our "cookbook bible", is an architect, culinary historian, food writer, and cooking teacher. Damon Lee Fowler embraces the notion that a Southern table is not only a place to gather for good food, but rather a place to share timeless traditions. Damon Lee Fowler lives in Savannah, Georgia.*

Plains Cheese Ring

(A favorite of Jimmy Carter's)

1 pound sharp Cheddar cheese, grated

1 cup pecans, chopped

1 cup mayonnaise

1 small onion, grated

Black pepper

Dash cayenne

Strawberry preserves

Mix cheese, pecans, mayonnaise, onion and peppers in a medium size mixing bowl. Remove and press into a ring mold. Place in refrigerator until chilled. When ready to serve, invert and fill center with strawberry preserves. Serve with crackers.

Green Chile-Pimiento Cheese Sandwiches

2	(8-ounce) packages grated extra sharp Cheddar cheese	1	(4-ounce) jar diced pimiento, drained
1	(8-ounce) block Monterey Jack cheese with peppers, grated	1	medium poblano chile pepper, seeded and minced
1	cup mayonnaise	¼	small onion, minced
1	(4-ounce) can chopped green chiles	2	teaspoons Worcestershire sauce
		12-16	slices whole grain bread

Combine all ingredients except bread in a large bowl. Spread ½ cup of mixture over half of the bread slices. Top with remaining slices. Trim crusts and cut sandwiches lengthwise into thirds. Reserve remaining cheese filling for other uses.

Makes about 6 cups cheese filling or 42 finger-sandwiches

Picante Rollups

1	(8-ounce) package cream cheese, softened	½	cup green onions, chopped
1	(8-ounce) container sour cream		Hot pepper sauce to taste (optional)
1	(8-ounce) package grated Cheddar cheese	1	(12-ounce) package small flour tortillas
1	(4-ounce) can green chiles	1	(16-ounce) jar picante sauce
1	(4-ounce) can black olives, chopped		

Mix cream cheese, sour cream, cheese, chiles, olives, onion and hot pepper sauce. Spread mixture over tortillas. Roll tightly and wrap in foil. Refrigerate rolls 1 hour or up to 1 day in advance. Slice rolls when ready to serve. Serve with picante sauce.

For a change of flavor, add 2 teaspoons spicy mustard and 2 teaspoons prepared horseradish to filling mixture. Before rolling, top filling with 8 ounces sliced roast beef and 1 chopped medium Vidalia onion.

Melted Swiss and Ham Rolls

1 cup butter or margarine, softened
3 tablespoons dry mustard
3 tablespoons poppy seeds
1 medium onion, finely diced
1 teaspoon Worcestershire sauce
4 packages party rolls (in foil pan)
1 pound ham, thinly sliced
12 ounces Swiss cheese, thinly sliced

Preheat oven to 400 degrees. Combine butter, mustard, poppy seeds, onion and Worcestershire sauce. Set aside. Remove rolls intact from foil pans. Slice whole package of rolls horizontally through the middle. Return bottom layer to pans. Arrange ham and cheese on bottom layer and cover with top layer of rolls. Spread butter mixture over top of rolls. Cover tightly with foil. At this point, rolls can be frozen for later use wrapped in aluminum foil. Bake 10 minutes or 20 to 30 minutes if frozen. Slice and serve.

A must for Christmas morning brunch or to keep on hand, frozen, for impromptu cocktail gatherings.

Southern Caviar

2 (16-ounce) cans black-eyed peas, drained
1 (15-ounce) can white hominy, drained (optional)
1 green bell pepper, diced
1 red bell pepper, diced
2 cloves garlic, minced (optional)
1 jalapeño pepper, diced (optional)
1 medium onion, chopped
1 teaspoon parsley
1 (8-ounce) bottle Italian dressing

Combine all ingredients and refrigerate for at least 2 hours; drain. Serve with large corn chips or tortilla chips.

This is best when prepared 24 hours in advance.

Hot Ryes

1 pound hot bulk sausage, cooked and drained

1 pound Velveeta cheese, melted

2 tablespoons ketchup

2 tablespoons Worcestershire sauce

¼ teaspoon dried oregano

2 loaves party cocktail rye bread

Preheat oven to 400 degrees. Combine all ingredients except bread. Spread on bread slices and place on a baking sheet. Bake 10 minutes.

or

Spread mixture over bread slices and place on baking sheet. Place baking sheet in freezer for 20 minutes. Remove bread and store in ziplock freezer bag until ready to serve. Replace onto baking sheet and bake 12 to 15 minutes or until bubbly. Serve hot.

Chipped beef on toast, once served to WWII soldiers, can be a delicious breakfast idea. Sauté a jar of dried beef in 4 tablespoons butter or margarine until crisp. Drain and crumble. Make a basic white sauce or use a can of cream of mushroom soup, add cooked beef, and serve over toast points. For an easy hors d'oeuvre, wrap sweet gherkin pickles with slices of dried beef and skewer with toothpicks.

Hot Beef Dip

2	(8-ounce) packages cream cheese, softened	3	tablespoons minced onion
1	(8-ounce) container sour cream	1	bell pepper, finely chopped
2	(2½-ounce) jars dried beef, chopped or shredded	3	tablespoons butter, melted
		1	cup finely chopped nuts

Preheat oven to 350 degrees. Combine cream cheese, sour cream, beef, onion and bell pepper and place in a baking dish. Stir together butter and nuts and sprinkle over cream cheese mixture. Bake 30 minutes or until hot. Serve warm with crackers.

Men especially enjoy this dip.

Black Bean Salsa

2	(16-ounce) cans black beans, rinsed and drained	1	large avocado, chopped (optional)
1	(17-ounce) can white shoepeg corn, rinsed and drained	1	purple onion, chopped
		¼	cup chopped fresh cilantro
		¼	cup lime juice
2	large tomatoes, peeled, seeded and chopped	2	tablespoons red wine vinegar
		1	teaspoon salt
		½	teaspoon black pepper

Combine all ingredients in a bowl and mix gently. Cover and chill until serving time. Garnish with avocado slices and sprigs of cilantro. Serve with tortilla chips.

Makes 6 cups

Tomato Basil Dip with Asparagus

4	pounds fresh asparagus	½	cup chopped fresh basil
1	cup mayonnaise	1	tablespoon tomato paste
½	cup sour cream	1	tablespoon lemon zest

Blanch asparagus in boiling water, then plunge into cold water to stop cooking process. Place drained asparagus in a kitchen towel and roll up and refrigerate until ready to use. Combine mayonnaise, sour cream, basil, tomato paste and lemon zest. Mix well and chill. When ready to serve, spoon into a small dip bowl and place on a serving platter. Surround with asparagus for dipping.

Serves 12 to 15

Jalapeño Cheese Hot Broccoli Dip

1½	pounds jalapeño Monterey Jack cheese, grated	1	(8-ounce) container sour cream
1	(10¾-ounce) can condensed cream of chicken soup	1	teaspoon cayenne pepper or to taste
1	large Vidalia or other sweet onion, minced	1	teaspoon lemon pepper
		1	teaspoon garlic powder
½-1	cup mayonnaise		Salt to taste
		1	(16-ounce) package frozen chopped broccoli, thawed and minced

Combine all ingredients except broccoli in a crockpot. Cook on high, stirring frequently, until melted and hot. Add broccoli and blend well. Reduce heat and adjust seasonings as needed. Serve with bread cubes, pita bread or corn chips.

Serves 12 to 15

For a milder version, use plain Monterey Jack cheese and reduce cayenne pepper and garlic powder.

Substituting 1 cup cream cheese for the sour cream will create more of a spread.

The freshness of asparagus is determined by the tightness of the flower bud. Both thick and thin stalks have the same degree of tenderness. Refrigerate asparagus upright in a container with ½ inch of water if asparagus is purchased ahead of time. Wrap the ends with paper towels. Also, use a knife to cut ends off of asparagus, instead of snapping.

"A man taking basil from a woman will love her always."

Sir Thomas Moore

It has been said that there are two Georgias. There is "federally-occupied" Atlanta, and there is the rest of Georgia. In truth, there are three Georgias. There is the Free State of Chatham (Savannah!), the rest of Georgia, and "federally occupied" Atlanta - in that order. Just ask anyone - outside of "federally-occupied" Atlanta, that is.

Asparagus with Garlic Cream

1	(8-ounce) container sour cream	⅛	teaspoon salt
2	tablespoons milk	⅛	teaspoon freshly ground black pepper
1	tablespoon white wine vinegar	2	pounds fresh asparagus
1	tablespoon olive oil		Chopped fresh chives for garnish
1-2	cloves garlic, minced		

Combine sour cream, milk, vinegar, oil, garlic, salt and pepper. Cover and chill at least 2 hours. Trim ends of asparagus and if desired, remove scales from stalks with a knife or vegetable peeler. Cook asparagus in a small amount of boiling water in a covered saucepan for 4 minutes or until crisp-tender. Drain and plunge into ice water to stop cooking process. Drain and chill. Place a small bowl in the center of a large bowl. Stand asparagus tip-end up between bowls. Place garlic cream in small bowl. Garnish with fresh chives.

Serves 16 to 20 appetizers, or 8 side dish servings

Peach Salsa

2	cups peeled and coarsely chopped peaches	¼	cup sliced green onions, white part only
¼	cup chopped red bell pepper	1-2	jalapeño peppers, seeded and minced
¼	cup chopped green bell pepper	2	tablespoons honey
¼	cup chopped yellow bell pepper	2	tablespoons fresh lime juice
¼	cup chopped cucumber	1	tablespoon minced fresh cilantro

Combine all ingredients. May be made up to 1 day ahead. Drain before serving.

Spinach Artichoke Dip

1	(10-ounce) package frozen chopped spinach, thawed and squeezed dry	1	(8-ounce) container sour cream
1	(14-ounce) can artichoke hearts, quartered and drained	½	cup mayonnaise
1	(5½-ounce) container garlic-herb cheese spread	1	(2-ounce) jar chopped pimiento, drained
1	cup shredded Parmesan cheese	¼	cup pine nuts
		1	medium purple onion, chopped
		8-10	slices bacon, cooked and crumbled

Preheat oven to 400 degrees. Combine all ingredients except bacon and place in a lightly greased 11x7-inch baking dish. Bake 20 minutes. Sprinkle with warm bacon. Serve with crackers or tortilla chips.

Serves 8 to 10

Can also be served as a spinach casserole side dish.

Baked Artichoke Party Dip

1	large round loaf dark bread, unsliced	1	(16-ounce) container sour cream
1	bunch green onions, chopped	12	ounces Cheddar cheese, grated
4	tablespoons butter	1	(14-ounce) can artichoke hearts, drained and chopped
6	cloves garlic, minced		
1	(8-ounce) package cream cheese		

Preheat oven to 350 degrees. Cut a 5-inch diameter slice off top of bread. Remove inner bread, leaving crust shell intact and reserving top slice for a cover. Sauté onions in butter. Stir in garlic, cream cheese, sour cream, Cheddar cheese and artichoke hearts. Mix well and spoon into bread shell. Cover with top slice. Wrap in double thickness foil. Bake 1½ to 2 hours. Serve with crackers.

Heavenly Ham and Cheese Bake

1 (8-ounce) package cream cheese, softened

1 (8-ounce) container sour cream

1 (8-ounce) package grated Cheddar cheese

¾ cup shredded cooked ham

½ cup chopped green onion

1 (4-ounce) can chopped green chiles

2 dashes Worcestershire sauce

1 large round loaf sour dough bread

Preheat oven to 350 degrees. Combine cream cheese, sour cream, Cheddar cheese, ham, onion, chiles and Worcestershire sauce. Mix well. Cut a thin slice off top of bread. Remove inner bread, leaving crust shell intact and reserving top slice for a cover. Inner bread can be cubed and reserved. Fill bread with cream cheese mixture. Cover with top slice of bread. Wrap in foil and bake 45 to 60 minutes. Serve with bagel chips or reserved bread cubes.

Spinach Cheddar Chutney Loaf

2	(8-ounce) blocks sharp Cheddar cheese, grated	2	(8-ounce) packages cream cheese, softened, divided
½	cup chopped pecans, toasted, plus extra for garnish	¼	teaspoon salt
		½	teaspoon freshly ground black pepper
½	cup mayonnaise	¼	cup chutney
1	(10-ounce) package frozen chopped spinach, thawed and squeezed dry	1-3	dashes cayenne pepper
		¼	teaspoon nutmeg

Line a 9x5-inch loaf pan with heavy-duty plastic wrap, allowing some to hang over edges. Combine Cheddar cheese, pecans and mayonnaise. Spread half of mixture evenly into pan. Mix together spinach, 1 package cream cheese, salt and pepper and spread evenly over Cheddar cheese layer. Stir together remaining package cream cheese, chutney, cayenne pepper and nutmeg and spread over spinach layer. Cover with remaining Cheddar cheese mixture. Fold plastic wrap over top and refrigerate overnight, or freeze up to 1 month. If frozen, thaw overnight in refrigerator before serving. Unmold and garnish with extra toasted pecans. Serve with assorted crackers.

Serves 25

Frozen cheese loaf travels well in the boat or to the beach in a cooler.

Vidalia Onion Dip

4 cups mayonnaise

4 cups chopped Vidalia onion

4 cups grated Swiss cheese

1 tablespoon Tabasco sauce

Preheat oven to 350 degrees. Combine all ingredients and place in a 3-quart casserole dish. Bake 20 minutes or until bubbly and lightly browned. Serve with crackers.

Sun-Dried Tomato-Cheese Torte

½	cup sun-dried tomatoes in oil, drained and chopped	4	tablespoons butter or margarine, softened
1½	cups freshly grated Parmesan cheese, divided	2-3	cloves garlic, minced
		¼	cup minced fresh parsley
1	(8-ounce) package cream cheese, softened	1	tablespoon minced fresh basil
4	ounces goat cheese, crumbled	½	teaspoon freshly ground black pepper

Line a 3-cup mold or 4-cup measuring cup with plastic wrap, allowing 5 to 6 inches to hang over edges. Coat with cooking spray. Sprinkle tomato into mold.

Beat 1 cup Parmesan cheese, cream cheese, goat cheese, butter and garlic with an electric mixer until smooth. Reserve 1 cup of mixture and spread remainder evenly over tomato. Beat reserved 1 cup of mixture with remaining ½ cup Parmesan cheese, parsley, basil and pepper until smooth. Spread mixture evenly into mold. Fold plastic wrap over the top and chill up to 8 hours. Unmold and serve with crackers.

Serves 20

Saints' Hot Sausage and Cheese Dip

1 pound hot bulk sausage, cooked and drained

1 pound mild bulk sausage, cooked and drained

1 (8-ounce) package cream cheese

1 (16-ounce) jar picante sauce, hot or mild

1 pound Velveeta cheese

1 (10¾-ounce) can condensed cream of mushroom soup

Combine all ingredients in a crockpot. Heat and stir until well mixed and cheese is melted. Serve with tortilla chips.

Taco Cheesecake

1½ cups crushed tortilla chips
1 tablespoon butter or margarine, melted
1 pound ground beef or chuck
1 (1¼-ounce) package taco seasoning mix, divided
2 tablespoons water
2 (8-ounce) packages cream cheese, softened
2 large eggs
1 (8-ounce) package grated Cheddar cheese
1 (8-ounce) container sour cream
2 tablespoons all-purpose flour
Shredded lettuce and chopped tomato, bell pepper and green onion for toppings

Preheat oven to 325 degrees. Mix together chips and butter and press into the bottom of a 9-inch springform pan. Bake 10 minutes. Cool on a wire rack.

Brown beef in a large skillet over medium heat, stirring to crumble. Drain and pat dry with paper towels. Return beef to skillet. Stir in taco seasoning, reserving 1 teaspoon. Add water and cook over medium heat, stirring occasionally, for 5 minutes or until liquid evaporates.

Beat cream cheese with an electric mixer on medium speed until fluffy. Add eggs and reserved 1 teaspoon taco seasoning. Beat until smooth. Beat in Cheddar cheese until blended. Spread cream cheese mixture evenly over tortilla chip crust and 1 inch up sides of pan. Spoon in beef mixture. Spread cream cheese mixture from around sides of pan over beef mixture, forming a 1-inch border. Combine sour cream and flour and spread over cheesecake. Bake 25 minutes. Cool on a wire rack for 10 minutes. Run a knife around edges and release sides. Serve warm with toppings. Store in refrigerator.

Serves 12

It is noteworthy that Savannah's city hall has a gilded dome. If James Oglethorpe had envisioned this golden structure, would he have included his proposed 5th prohibition? This prohibited the use of silver or gold on clothing and furnishings. Then again, he didn't mention buildings.

Cucumber Chicken Salad

5	cups diced cooked	⅔	cup mayonnaise
	chicken	½	cup sour cream
1	small onion, diced	1	teaspoon salt
1	cup peeled and diced	¼	teaspoon black pepper
	cucumber	½	teaspoon poultry
1	cup finely chopped green		seasoning
	bell pepper (optional)	½	teaspoon celery seed
¼	cup light cream	2	teaspoons sugar

Combine chicken, onion, cucumber and bell pepper. In a separate bowl, mix cream, mayonnaise, sour cream, salt, pepper, poultry seasoning, celery seed and sugar. Pour over chicken mixture. Toss lightly, cover and refrigerate until chilled. Serve on lettuce. Garnish with almonds, if desired.

This salad can be spooned into 1-inch hollow cucumber slices or small phyllo pastry shells.

Raspberry Brie en Croûte

1	sheet frozen puff pastry,	¼	cup raspberry preserves
	thawed according to	¼-½	cup sliced almonds,
	package directions		toasted
1	(8-ounce) round Brie		
	cheese		

Preheat oven to 350 degrees. Place pastry on a lightly greased baking sheet. Place cheese in center of pastry. Spread preserves over cheese and sprinkle with almonds. Wrap cheese with pastry, trimming excess. Seal seams by moistening edges with water and pressing together with fingers. Bake 30 to 40 minutes or until pastry is golden brown. Serve warm with crackers.

Serves 6 to 8

For a creative effect, twist the pastry into a knot or braid, or use the trimmed excess to decorate the outside.

Spicy Apricot Sauce over Cream Cheese Balls

1 (12-ounce) jar apricot preserves

1 (12-ounce) jar pineapple preserves

¼ cup prepared horseradish, drained

1 teaspoon black pepper

1 tablespoon dry mustard

1 (8-ounce) package cream cheese

Combine preserves, horseradish, pepper and mustard. Refrigerate until chilled. Using an ice cream scoop, scoop cream cheese into 3 balls and place on a serving plate. Spoon sauce over balls. Serve with assorted crackers.

Sauce makes an excellent glaze for baked ham.

Tomochichi presented King George with an Eagle feather as a tribute, which appears to be the first time the Eagle was associated with America.

Incredible Fruit Sauce

½ cup margarine

1 cup brown sugar, firmly packed

1 (8-ounce) container sour cream

1 tablespoon vanilla

Melt margarine in a small saucepan. Add brown sugar and stir until blended. Add sour cream and vanilla and stir until well blended. Refrigerate 30 minutes. This sauce is delicious poured over fresh fruit or used as a dip for fresh fruit.

Coconut Chicken Salad with Glazed Pita Chips

1	(46-ounce) can pineapple juice	1	teaspoon salt
1	teaspoon minced garlic	¼	teaspoon black pepper
2	tablespoons minced onion	½	teaspoon coconut flavoring
8-10	boneless, skinless chicken breasts	½	teaspoon almond flavoring
1	(14-ounce) can cream of coconut milk	1	(16-ounce) can crushed pineapple, drained
1	cup mayonnaise	1	(7-ounce) package flaked coconut
1	(8-ounce) container sour cream	1	cup sliced almonds

Combine pineapple juice, garlic and onion. Pour mixture over chicken in a saucepan. Add water to cover. Cook until tender. Drain and cool chicken, then chop into small pieces and place in a mixing bowl. In a separate bowl, combine coconut milk, mayonnaise, sour cream, salt, pepper and flavorings. Stir in drained pineapple, coconut and almonds. Pour mixture over chicken, toss lightly, cover and chill. Serve with Glazed Pita Chips.

Salad can be served in a scooped out pineapple half. Garnish with almonds, toasted coconut and red cherries.

Glazed Pita Chips

2	(8-ounce) packages flat pita bread	1	cup brown sugar, firmly packed
		1	cup butter, melted

Cut bread into triangles. Combine sugar and butter and brush over top of triangles. Broil or bake for a few minutes or until lightly browned.

Piña Colada Fruit Dip

½   **cup flaked coconut, toasted, 1 tablespoon reserved**
1   **(16-ounce) container sour cream**
1   **(8-ounce) can crushed pineapple, drained**
2   **tablespoons brown sugar, firmly packed**

1-2   **tablespoons rum or reserved pineapple juice**
    Assorted fresh fruit, such as red or green apple slices, pear slices, strawberries, pineapple wedges or grapes

Combine all ingredients except fresh fruit and reserved coconut in a medium bowl. Cover and refrigerate at least 2 hours. Garnish with reserved coconut and serve with fresh fruit.

Makes 2 cups

Dip can be served in a scooped out pineapple half.

To prevent pears, apples, or bananas from turning brown after slicing, dip in Sprite or any lemon-lime soda.

Pepperoni Pizza Dip

2   **(8-ounce) packages cream cheese, softened**
½   **tablespoon garlic powder or to taste**
½-1   **tablespoon Italian seasoning or to taste**

½   **cup finely chopped pepperoni or to taste**
    Pizza sauce
1   **cup or more grated mozzarella cheese**
    Sliced pepperoni

Preheat oven to 350 degrees. Beat cream cheese with an electric mixer until fluffy. Mix in garlic powder and Italian seasoning. Add pepperoni and mix well. Spread mixture in a pie plate or casserole dish. Cover with pizza sauce. Sprinkle with cheese and top with whole slices of pepperoni. Bake 15 to 20 minutes or microwave 3 to 5 minutes or until heated through and cheese is melted. Serve with bread cubes.

Add your favorite pizza toppings, such as olives, peppers or onions. Also good with shredded chicken or shrimp mixed into cream cheese. For more texture, instead of pizza sauce, try chunky Italian-style tomato sauce.

Just prior to the War for Independence, the Olde Pink House was the secret meeting place for Savannah's Sons of Liberty. These "Liberty Boys" planned and executed a raid on the King's army in 1775, and the "arrest" of the much-respected royal governor of Savannah, Sir James Wright. When Wright "escaped," both sides were relieved.

Spicy Black Bean Cakes

3	cups dried black beans, picked over and rinsed	1	tablespoon seeded and chopped jalapeño pepper
12	cups water		
6	chicken bouillon cubes	2	tablespoons chopped fresh cilantro
1	teaspoon salt		
2	smoked pork neck bones	1	tablespoon ground cumin
2	tablespoons olive oil		Dash of cayenne pepper
½	cup minced yellow onion	2	teaspoons salt
½	cup minced green onion	1	teaspoon freshly ground black pepper
½	cup minced red onion		
2	tablespoons minced garlic	2	cups cornbread crumbs
¼	cup minced red bell pepper	2	cups stone-ground yellow cornmeal
		1	cup olive oil for frying

Combine beans, water, bouillon, salt and neck bones in a large heavy saucepan. Bring to a boil. Reduce heat and simmer 2 to 2½ hours or until beans are very soft and their skins have broken. Add extra water as needed, 1 cup at a time. Remove neck bones. Drain beans.

Heat 2 tablespoons olive oil in a skillet until very hot. Add onions, garlic, bell and jalapeño peppers and cilantro and sauté 2 to 3 minutes or until just tender. Add cumin, cayenne pepper, salt and black pepper and mix well. Place mixture on a plate to cool.

Mash the beans by hand with a potato masher or with an electric mixer with a flat paddle. Add cooled vegetable mixture and mix well. Add cornbread crumbs and mix well. Adjust seasonings as needed.

Lightly press ¼-cup scoops of mixture into ½-inch thick cakes. Dust lightly in cornmeal. Pan-fry cakes in olive oil in batches, each cake needing only about 2 tablespoons of oil to cook in as oil will be absorbed by the cakes. Keep cooked cakes warm in a 250 degree oven while cooking remaining batches. If cakes are made ahead and refrigerated before cooking, it is best to return them to room temperature before frying. Serve with Red and Yellow Tomato Salsa and sour cream or as a side dish.

Makes 20 (2-ounce) cakes

This makes an elegant hors d'oeuvre when individually plated and served to accompany a Caribbean menu.

Red and Yellow Tomato Salsa

5 medium red tomatoes, cored and halved

5 medium yellow tomatoes, cored and halved

1 cup finely diced yellow onion

½ cup thinly sliced green onion

1 tablespoon minced garlic

½ cup chopped fresh basil

⅓ cup red wine vinegar

½ cup plus 2 tablespoons extra virgin olive oil

1 teaspoon salt

½ teaspoon freshly ground black pepper

Lightly squeeze each tomato half, without crushing, to remove seeds; dice. Place tomatoes, onions, garlic and basil in a bowl. Add vinegar, oil, salt and pepper and toss. Serve or store in refrigerator for up to 2 days.

Makes 6 cups

If yellow tomatoes are not available, use all red tomatoes.

Shrimp Spread

1	(8-ounce) package cream cheese, softened	2	tablespoons lemon juice
½	cup unsalted butter, softened		Dash of Worcestershire sauce
1	small onion, finely chopped	⅛	teaspoon hot pepper sauce
2	stalks celery, finely chopped	1	pound shrimp, cooked, peeled and finely chopped
2	tablespoons mayonnaise		Salt and pepper to taste

Cream together cream cheese and butter. Add onion, celery, mayonnaise, lemon juice, Worcestershire sauce, hot pepper sauce and shrimp. Season with salt and pepper. For best flavor, refrigerate overnight.

Mold in a ramekin and cover with chopped fresh chives before refrigerating or serve spread on Belgian endive leaves, mini bagel chips or crackers.

Creamy Shrimp Mold

1	(10¾-ounce) can tomato soup	¾	cup finely chopped celery
1	(8-ounce) package cream cheese	½	cup finely chopped onion
		1	cup mayonnaise
1	pound shrimp, cooked, peeled and chopped	1½	(¼-ounce) envelopes unflavored gelatin
		¼	cup cold water

Heat soup and cream cheese in a medium saucepan over medium heat until melted. Stir in shrimp, celery, onion and mayonnaise. Dissolve gelatin in cold water and add to mixture. Pour mixture into a lightly greased fish, shell or ring shaped mold. Refrigerate several hours or until firm. To unmold, dip mold briefly in warm water. Place a serving plate over mold and flip over. Garnish with lettuce tucked under mold. Serve with buttery crackers.

Serves a large group

Damon Fowler says, "Savannah cooks have their favorite recipes for shrimp paste or spread, but the 'traditional' ones which have withstood the test of time and the canned-soup craze, are simple almost to the point of austerity, having little more in them than butter and shrimp. To me, those are the best, for their apparent simplicity is deceptive; rich, creamy butter is a perfect background for the delicate taste of the tiny inlet shrimp that inhabit our coast. One needs only the barest trace of onion or pepper to point up and enliven the taste; too much of either throws the entire dish out of balance." Damon goes on to say that traditionally, shrimp paste is served on tea tables, supper buffets and even at breakfast. We often enjoy it with cocktails or as an entrée for a summer luncheon.

"The word 'shrimp' comes from the Middle English 'shrimpe' or 'puny.' Small, but oh, so good!"

Georgia Entertains, *1993*

Quantities for appetizers can be estimated:

- plan to serve 4 bites per person if dinner is to follow.

- plan to serve 10 bites per person for a cocktail party.

- plan to serve 10 to 15 bites per person for an event such as a reception with no dinner afterwards.

Shrimp Toast

8	ounces fresh shrimp			Pinch of nutmeg
1	small lemon, halved and seeded, divided	½	teaspoon salt
			Black pepper to taste
2	green onions, halved	1	egg white, room temperature
5	whole water chestnuts		
1	teaspoon prepared horseradish	10	slices toast, crusts trimmed

Preheat oven to 400 degrees. Place shrimp in a saucepan. Add enough water to cover. Squeeze 1 lemon half into water, then drop it in. Bring to a boil. Drain and cool shrimp, then peel and devein. Place shrimp in a blender or food processor. Add juice of remaining lemon half, green onions, water chestnuts, horseradish, nutmeg, salt and pepper. Blend until ingredients are finely ground. Scrape down sides. In a small bowl, beat egg white with an electric mixer until stiff peaks form. Fold egg into shrimp mixture. Cut each slice of toast into 3 strips. Spread shrimp mixture over strips and place on 2 ungreased baking sheets. Bake 5 minutes or until lightly browned. Serve hot or at room temperature.

Serves 6 to 8

An excellent recipe to serve for cocktail parties since these are baked with no frying necessary.

Marinated Shrimp

1	large onion, sliced	2	tablespoons Worcestershire sauce
1	large green bell pepper, thinly sliced		
	Fresh sliced mushrooms	1	teaspoon salt
⅔	cup vegetable oil	½	teaspoon black pepper
2	cups ketchup		Tabasco sauce
1	cup cider vinegar		Garlic powder
2	tablespoons sugar	3	pounds shrimp, cooked and peeled
2	tablespoons Dijon mustard		

Combine all ingredients except shrimp in a large bowl. Mix well. Stir in shrimp and marinate in refrigerator 8 hours or overnight.

Fresh Fruit with Prosciutto

1	red apple, unpeeled and cut into 6 wedges
1	green apple, unpeeled and cut into 6 wedges
3	tablespoons lime juice
1	honey dew, cantaloupe or Persian melon
1	ripe papaya or mango, peeled, cored and seeded
8	ounces prosciutto, sliced paper thin

Generously brush apple wedges with lime juice to prevent browning. Cut away melon rind, halve lengthwise and discard seeds. Cut each melon half in half horizontally and slice into wedges about the same size as apple wedges. Cut papaya into wedges about the same size of other fruit. Wrap a strip of prosciutto around each piece of fruit, allowing ends of fruit to show. Arrange on a platter and sprinkle with remaining lime juice. Cover and chill up to 2 hours before serving time.

Makes 30 wedges

Crab Corners

8	ounces white or claw crabmeat
1	(5-ounce) jar Old English cheese
2	tablespoons mayonnaise
1	teaspoon garlic salt or garlic powder
½	cup butter or margarine, softened
	Dash of Tabasco sauce or cayenne pepper
4	English muffins, split and lightly toasted

Combine all ingredients except muffins. Divide mixture evenly over muffin halves and spread. Score each muffin half into quarters and place on a baking sheet. Freeze. When frozen, break into fourths and store in a plastic zip-top bag in freezer until ready to use.

When ready to serve, preheat oven to 425 degrees. Place frozen pieces on a baking sheet and bake 10 minutes. Serve hot.

Serves 8

Excellent to keep on hand in freezer for drop-in company. Muffin halves could be served whole as plated appetizers.

Buffet Salmon Platter

1 head curly leaf lettuce

1 smoked salmon, preferably Alaskan

Sprigs of fresh dill

2 hard-cooked eggs, diced

1 purple onion, diced

1 (2-ounce) jar capers, drained

2 cucumbers, sliced

Lemon Dill Sauce (page 158)

Line a large oval serving platter with lettuce leaves. Place whole salmon in center. Sprinkle with sprigs of fresh dill. Along bottom of platter, place separate mounds of eggs, onion and capers. Along top of platter, arrange cucumber slices, overlapping slightly. Place a bowl of Lemon Dill Sauce on the side. Serve with plain round crackers or baguette slices.

Serves many, depending on size of salmon

If you prefer, wrap the hearts of palm in prosciutto ham instead of smoked salmon.

Smoked Salmon Canapés

1 baguette bread

1 (8-ounce) package cream cheese, softened

8 ounces thinly sliced smoked salmon, cut into 24 pieces

½ cup sour cream

24 sprigs fresh dill

Preheat oven to 400 degrees. Cut bread into 24 (½-inch thick) slices and place on a baking sheet. Bake 5 minutes or until lightly toasted. Remove to wire racks to cool. Spread each bread slice with cream cheese. Top each with a piece of salmon and a teaspoon of sour cream. Garnish each canapé with a sprig of dill or serve with Lemon Dill Sauce (page 158).

Makes 24

Hearts of Palm Wrapped in Smoked Salmon with Raspberry-Dijon Vinaigrette

1	(14-ounce) can hearts of palm, chilled and drained	½	pound smoked salmon, cut into thin strips
			Lettuce leaves or fresh parsley for garnish

Vinaigrette

2	tablespoons raspberry vinegar	½	teaspoon salt
1	tablespoon lemon juice	¼	teaspoon dried tarragon
1	tablespoon Dijon mustard	½	cup olive oil

Cut hearts of palm lengthwise into halves or thirds to make uniform long sticks. Wrap salmon around each stick. Arrange in a serving dish or on a platter in a spoke wheel fashion. Cover and refrigerate for several hours or overnight. Just before serving, generously spoon vinaigrette over top. Garnish with lettuce leaves or parsley.

To make vinaigrette, combine all ingredients in a jar. Seal tightly and shake well. Refrigerate until needed or up to 3 days.

Serves 8 to 10

Wrapped Pickled Okra

1	(5½-ounce) container garlic-herb cheese spread	1	(12-ounce) jar medium hot pickled okra
12-14	slices deli baked ham or prosciutto		

Spread cheese on ham. Wrap ham around okra and secure with a toothpick.

Scallops and Mushrooms in Pastry Shells

1	pound fresh mushrooms, sliced	½	cup flour
2	medium onions, sliced	2	cups half-and-half
4	tablespoons butter, divided		Salt and pepper to taste
2	pounds bay scallops	8	baked regular size or 30 individual baked puff pastry shells
½	cup sherry		

Sauté mushrooms and onion in 1 tablespoon butter until tender. Add scallops and sherry and bring to a boil. Reduce heat and simmer 10 to 12 minutes, stirring occasionally. In a medium saucepan, melt 3 tablespoons butter. Blend in flour until smooth. Cook 1 minute, stirring constantly while adding half-and-half. Season with salt and pepper and cook over medium heat until thickened and hot. Stir sauce into scallop mixture until thoroughly mixed. When heated, spoon into pastry shells, using regular size for appetizers, or smaller individual size for hors d'oeuvres.

***Makes 8 regular size
or 30 individual appetizers***

Richardson Creek Crab Dip

1¼	cups mayonnaise	1	teaspoon horseradish
1	cup crabmeat	¼	cup French dressing
½	cup grated Cheddar cheese		

Combine all ingredients. Serve with crackers.

To make extra tangy, don't be afraid to add more horseradish or French dressing.

Everyone needs to "go crabbing" at least once in their lifetime. You only need string, chicken, and a net. Simply tie the string around the chicken and drop the line in the water. Many "seasoned crabbers" tie weights to their lines so they will rest on the bottom of the river. When you feel a crab nibbling on your bait, pull the line up slowly and scoop the crab into your net. Keep crabs in buckets or coolers with river water covering them until ready to cook.

Quick Crab Ball

For a quick, delicious appetizer, try this crab ball. Mold an 8-ounce package of softened cream cheese into a ball. Roll in 8 ounces of fresh crabmeat until ball is completely covered. Place on a plate and drizzle cocktail sauce over top. As ball is devoured, add more cocktail sauce. Serve with crackers.

Chafing Dish Crab

1	(8-ounce) package cream cheese, softened	1	teaspoon Worcestershire sauce
1	(6-ounce) can crabmeat	2	tablespoons grated onion
1	tablespoon milk	2	tablespoons horseradish
1	tablespoon mayonnaise		

Preheat oven to 375 degrees. Combine all ingredients and place in a baking dish. Bake 15 minutes. Serve with crackers.

Serves 8 to 10

Crab and Pecan-Stuffed Mushrooms

24	large mushrooms, stems reserved	1	(6-ounce) can crabmeat
	Salt and pepper to taste	½	cup minced pecans
1	clove garlic, minced	2	tablespoons minced green onion
4	tablespoons butter, divided	½	teaspoon horseradish
1	(8-ounce) package cream cheese, softened	1	teaspoon Worcestershire sauce
1	tablespoon milk	½	cup fine bread crumbs

Preheat oven to 350 degrees. Season mushroom caps with salt and place in a shallow baking dish. Chop mushroom stems and sauté with garlic in 2 tablespoons butter. In a mixing bowl, combine sautéed mushroom stems, cream cheese, milk, crabmeat, pecans, green onion, horseradish and Worcestershire sauce. Season with salt and pepper and mix thoroughly. Spoon mixture into mushroom caps. Dot with remaining butter and sprinkle with bread crumbs. Bake 12 to 15 minutes or until mixture is bubbly.

Makes 24

Tybee Pickled Oysters with Tangy Seafood Sauce

Oysters

2	pints oysters		Dash of allspice
¼	cup vinegar	6	whole cloves
	Salt to taste		Cayenne pepper to taste

Tangy Seafood Sauce

1	cup chili sauce		Prepared horseradish to
1	teaspoon lemon juice		taste
½	teaspoon Worcestershire sauce		

Drain and wash oysters, reserving drained liquid. Place reserved liquid in a saucepan with washed oysters. Add vinegar, salt, allspice, cloves and cayenne pepper. Bring to a boil. Reduce heat and simmer until oysters curl. Remove oysters with a slotted spoon and place in a medium bowl. Bring cooking liquid to a boil and immediately remove from heat. Cool slightly, then pour over oysters. Cover and refrigerate overnight. To serve, drain and serve oysters with crackers and Tangy Seafood Sauce.

To make sauce, combine all ingredients. Cover and let stand to allow flavors to blend or refrigerate overnight.

Serves 8

The term "hors d'oeuvre" literally means "outside the work." In America, this translates into food that is served separately from the meal, usually to complement it.

Oysters are in season from September to May (months containing the letter "r"). Shucked oysters should be plump and cream-colored and their liquid should be clear.

Tomochichi, Chief of
the Yamacraw
Indians, gave
Oglethorpe permission
to settle on his land. A
year later, in 1734,
Oglethorpe took
Tomochichi and his
family to England.
During the visit, one
elder in Tomochichi's
family died and
became the first
Native American to be
buried in a foreign
land.

Southern Angels on Horseback

Marinade

2	tablespoons olive oil	½	teaspoon salt
¼	cup lemon juice	⅛	teaspoon black pepper
1	clove garlic, minced		Dash of Tabasco sauce

Oysters

24	fresh oysters, shucked and drained		Lemon wedges and fresh parsley sprigs for garnish
24	basil leaves		
12	slices bacon, halved		

In a medium bowl, whisk together all marinade ingredients. Add oysters and marinate 2 hours; drain. Wrap each oyster with a basil leaf and then a piece of bacon. Secure with a toothpick that has been soaked in hot water for 30 minutes. Arrange oysters on a greased baking sheet. Broil or grill 3 minutes on each side or until bacon is crisp or bake at 450 degrees for 10 minutes. Remove toothpicks before serving. Garnish with lemon wedges and parsley.

Makes 2 dozen

Soups and Stews

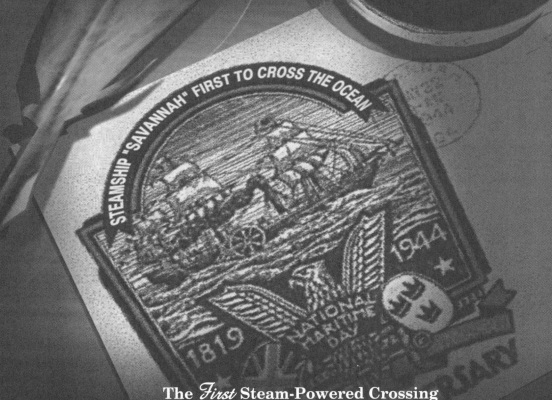

The *First* Steam-Powered Crossing

The S.S. Savannah was the *first* steam-powered ship to cross an ocean. She was the special project of William Scarbrough, one of Savannah's "Merchant Princes," and a score of stockholders. They hoped to quicken delivery time for cotton headed for the mills in England. The S.S. Savannah was actually another ship, which was modified with both conventional sail rigging and a steam powered paddle wheel. On May 22, 1819, the SS Savannah left port. After 29 days and 11 hours, she arrived in Liverpool. She continued her tour to St. Petersburg, Russia, where it was hoped that the Czar (or some other European royalty) would purchase the ship. She did not sell and returned home in November of 1819, beating her own record across the Atlantic by four days. While at sea both times, the S.S. Savannah was chased by several ships who thought initially that the ship was on fire. Perhaps because she was ahead of her time, the S.S. Savannah was not a commercial success. In time, her engine was removed and she was converted to sail. In 1821, she sank in a storm off Long Island Sound.

Spirited Savannah

There is a bronze statue of a young woman on River Street. She stands facing the river, with her dog beside her as she waves a towel in greeting to the ships entering Savannah harbor. This statue was erected in 1971, to honor Florence Martus (1869-1943), known as "The Waving Girl of Savannah." Florence was the sister of the lighthouse keeper on Elba Island, and a familiar sight to sailors as she waved her greeting. At night, Florence would flash a lantern, in welcome. It is said that Florence was waiting in vain for a sailor who had stolen her heart, then left Savannah never to return. Still, Florence waved to each ship hoping against hope. It is also said that Florence waves still, decades after her death. One account from 1950 tells of a Savannah man who had left home for 20 years, unnecessarily on the run. When this man mentioned that he had seen "The Waving Girl" as he came into port, an old friend laughed and said that she had been dead for 7 years.

"The Cooking Pot Cure"

There is something magic in homemade vegetable soup, which gives solace for our worldly woes and fortifies us physically. It may be unsophisticated in a modern gourmet society, which swirls a scallion (or some such) in hot water, then serves it with more unidentifiable garnish than substance. That is not soup!

Even the best of other soups pales in comparison to a hearty pot of vegetables and broth. This is particularly true when that homemade elixir is spoon fed to you when you are not well. At the very least, it is prepared especially for you, because you looked "peaked" (pea-ked), and by all rights ought to be treated as though you were near death. Other reasons for having homemade vegetable soup prepared just for you are because you are "under the weather," tired, worried, in pain, or even in love. You can lay down your troubles at the kitchen door, and be welcomed by this heart-warming sustenance. (Say Amen). The memories of having such a soup "cooked up" for you are irreplaceable. If you have to do it for yourself or others, allow for a " sinking spell" or take a break while you are preparing this most healing of all potions. (One woman we knew called this "prescription soup.")

Whether beef or chicken, the broth must be allowed to absorb all of the vitamins and minerals from the meat to make a truly sustaining soup. The choice of tasteful additions of vegetable depends on the ingenuity of the cook, and the preference of the family. Small children (and some adults) who seem repulsed by most vegetables will chase a favorite one in this soup, thereby taking in a healthy portion of the broth. Who knows, they may grow up to create cooking pot cures of their own - especially if you spoon-feed them once in a while.

Stellar Vegetable Beef Soup

Truly a healing potion

1	(4- to 5-pound) beef chuck roast with bone in, fat trimmed	1-2	cups sliced carrots
10-12	cups water	1-2	(10-ounce) packages frozen chopped okra, thawed
3-4	beef bouillon cubes		
1-2	teaspoons salt or to taste	1-2	(10-ounce) packages frozen mixed vegetables, thawed (optional)
½-1	teaspoon black pepper or to taste		
3	(28-ounce) cans crushed tomatoes	1	teaspoon filé powder or arrowroot powder (optional)
1	bunch celery, chopped		Dash of cayenne pepper
2	large white onions, chopped		Dash of Worcestershire sauce
½	head cabbage, chopped or grated		

Cook beef roast in a large pot in water seasoned with bouillon, salt and pepper for 1½ to 2 hours or until meat falls from bone. Remove meat and bone from pot, reserving broth. Cube beef into bite-size pieces. Allow broth to cool, then skim fat from surface.

Add beef back into broth and slowly increase heat. Add tomatoes, celery, onions, cabbage and carrots. Bring just to a boil. Reduce heat to medium-low and cover. Cook 1 hour, stirring occasionally.

Add okra and mixed vegetables. Cook 1½ to 2 hours on low. Add filé powder if thick soup is desired. Add cayenne and Worcestershire sauce. Taste and season with salt and pepper as needed. Serve with hot cornbread.

Makes about 1½ gallons

Creamy Tomato-Parmesan Soup

2 (14-ounce) cans Italian plum tomatoes, undrained

1 cup whipping cream

¼ cup chopped fresh basil, plus extra for garnish

¼ cup chopped fresh parsley

1 teaspoon freshly ground black pepper

¼ teaspoon salt

½ cup freshly grated Parmesan cheese

Combine all ingredients except cheese in a food processor. Pulse until mixture is smooth. Pour mixture into a saucepan. Cook over medium heat until thoroughly heated. Stir in cheese and heat until melted. If desired, garnish with extra basil.

Serves 4

Choice of soup depends entirely on the occasion. For a formal dinner, a clear soup sets the stage for richer foods to come. In fact, a simple consommé will enhance the appetite. A cream soup, served before an entrée which has a cream sauce, is redundant and takes away from the dish. Substantial and filling soups are a perfect meal, when accompanied with bread and wine.

Yellow Tomato Gazpacho with Crab Relish

3	pounds yellow tomatoes, chopped	½	teaspoon salt
1	cucumber	¼	teaspoon black pepper
1	cup chopped sweet onion	1	teaspoon olive oil
1	yellow bell pepper, chopped, ¼ cup reserved	½	cup finely chopped red bell pepper
1	clove garlic, minced	½	cup lump crabmeat
2	tablespoons sherry vinegar	1	teaspoon lime juice
		2	tablespoons finely chopped fresh basil

Process tomatoes, cucumber, onion, yellow bell pepper and garlic in a food processor, in two batches, until just chunky. Transfer mixture to a large bowl. Add vinegar, salt and pepper to mixture. Chill at least 2 hours or up to 24 hours.

To make relish, heat oil in a small skillet. Finely chop reserved yellow bell pepper and add to skillet along with red bell pepper. Sauté 2 minutes. Add crab and cook until heated, being careful to keep crab lumps intact. Add lime juice and basil.

To serve, divide soup among 4 soup bowls. Top each with a generous mound of the relish. Serve immediately.

Serves 4

Cool as a Cucumber Soup

1	large cucumber, peeled	1	soup can milk
1	large green onion	1	large dollop sour cream
1	(10¾-ounce) can condensed cream of celery soup		Finely chopped fresh parsley

Combine cucumber, onion and soup in a blender. Process until blended. Mix in milk and sour cream. Serve cold with parsley sprinkled over individual servings.

Makes 4 cups

Vidalia Onion Soup

½	cup butter	8	(1-inch thick) slices
2	pounds Vidalia onions,		French bread
	thinly sliced		Garlic butter
3	tablespoons flour		Freshly grated Parmesan
8	cups beef broth		cheese
	Salt and pepper to taste		

Melt butter in a 6-quart Dutch oven. Add onions and sauté 20 to 30 minutes or until golden brown. Sprinkle flour over onions and cook and stir 2 to 3 minutes longer. Remove from heat. Gradually stir in broth. Simmer 30 to 40 minutes. Season with salt and pepper.

Preheat oven to 350 degrees. Toast bread slices on a baking sheet in oven for 15 minutes. Using a pastry brush, lightly coat each side of bread with garlic butter. Bake 15 minutes longer. Just before serving, pour soup into individual ovenproof bowls. Top each with a bread slice. Sprinkle heavily with cheese. Brown under the broiler.

Serves 8

Winter Cheese Soup

½	cup margarine	2	pounds Velveeta cheese,
1	cup minced carrots		cubed
1	cup minced yellow onion	1	tablespoon finely
1	cup minced celery		chopped fresh parsley
½	cup flour		Chopped tomato
3	cups chicken broth		Minced jalapeño pepper
3	cups half-and-half		

Heat margarine in a stockpot until melted. Add carrot, onion and celery and sauté until tender but not brown. Mix in flour. Cook and stir until mixture is light brown. Gradually add broth and mix well. Cook over medium heat, whisking constantly, until thickened. Add half-and-half and mix well. Stir in cheese. Cook until cheese melts and soup is heated. Stir in parsley when ready to serve. Top individual servings with tomato and jalapeño.

Serves 12

Vidalia Onions

Just the mere mention of these gourmet onions brings to mind the savory sweet taste of this beloved vegetable. Bland Farms has become the largest grower, packer, and shipper of these culinary treasures. These are a few of their tips on storing and handling these delicious onions. Wrap onions individually in tissue paper, paper towel, or newspaper and store in refrigerator. Be sure onions are dry before storing in paper. Store in the legs of sheer pantyhose and tie a knot between each Vidalia onion. Hang in a cool, dry, well-ventilated area. Cut below the knot when ready to use.

*Elizabeth Terry
is an award-winning
chef. Her family
enterprise, Elizabeth's
on Thirty-Seventh,
is world renown.
Elizabeth Terry
quite simply elevates
Southern cooking to a
new level of excellence,
"5 Star Dining."*

Elizabeth Terry's
Crab Bisque Thirty-Seventh

6	tablespoons butter	¼	teaspoon white pepper
1	cup minced green onion		Dash of cayenne pepper
½	cup minced celery	1	cup cream
1	tablespoon minced carrot	¼	cup sherry
6	tablespoons flour	1	pound claw crabmeat
2½	cups milk		Fresh parsley or mint
2½	cups chicken broth		leaves for garnish
¼	teaspoon nutmeg		

Melt butter over low heat in a saucepan. Add onion, celery and carrot and cover. Steam 5 minutes or until tender. Whisk in flour and cook 2 minutes. Whisk in milk and broth. Bring to a boil, whisking occasionally. Add nutmeg, white pepper, cayenne pepper, cream, sherry and crab. Garnish and serve immediately.

Serves 12

Waving Girl Oyster Stew

2-3	stalks celery, diced	½	teaspoon salt
1	small onion, minced	⅛	teaspoon black pepper
½	cup butter	⅛	teaspoon mace
1	pint oysters with liquid	1	pint half-and-half

Sauté celery and onion in butter until softened. Add oysters with liquid, salt, pepper and mace. Simmer just until oysters curl; do not overcook. Add half-and-half. Heat until bubbles form around edges; do not boil. Remove from heat and serve immediately.

Serves 4

Savannah Shrimp Bisque

1	tablespoon unsalted butter	1	bay leaf
1	tablespoon vegetable oil	1	teaspoon dried marjoram
½	cup finely chopped yellow onion	⅛	teaspoon nutmeg
½	cup finely chopped celery	1	pound medium shrimp, peeled and deveined, cut into ½-inch pieces
⅓	cup finely chopped carrot		
2	tablespoons all-purpose flour	1	cup whipping cream
		½	teaspoon salt
3	cups chicken broth	2	tablespoons fresh lemon juice
1	(14½-ounce) can whole tomatoes, drained and chopped		Fresh marjoram sprigs for garnish
½	cup dry white wine or fish stock		

Heat butter and oil in a large saucepan over medium-high heat. Stir in onion, celery and carrot and sauté 5 minutes or until tender. Add flour and cook and stir until bubbly. Stir in broth, tomatoes, wine, bay leaf, marjoram and nutmeg. Bring to a boil. Reduce heat and simmer, covered, for 15 minutes. Discard bay leaf and let mixture cool.

Puree soup until smooth in batches in a food processor or blender. Return soup to saucepan. Add shrimp and cook, uncovered, over medium heat for 1 minute. Blend in cream and cook 2 minutes longer or just until soup is heated through and shrimp are firm and pink. Remove from heat and season with salt and lemon juice. Garnish with marjoram sprigs.

Makes 6 (1-cup) servings

A luscious, light and elegant beginning for any dinner.

For a lighter version, use 1 cup low-fat milk and 2 tablespoons whipping cream instead of the 1 cup whipping cream.

The S.S. Savannah made a trial run to Charleston (Savannah's loving rival). This voyage took only an unbelievable 11 hours. Cheers from Charlestonians on the docks made the Savannahians proud. Soon after this, President James Monroe and Secretary of War John C. Calhoun took a more leisurely voyage from Tybee Island to Savannah, where both were guests of William and Julia Scarbrough. The slow pace was probably due to the fact that the brand new Scarbrough House was not quite ready to receive a President.

Chicken and Crawfish Gumbo

3	ounces andouille sausage, diced	⅓	cup flour, baked to dark brown
8	ounces raw chicken breast, diced	2	quarts chicken broth
1	large onion, finely diced	1	quart beef broth
1	green bell pepper, finely diced	2	bay leaves
2	stalks celery, finely diced	1	teaspoon dried oregano
1	jalapeño pepper, seeded and diced	1	teaspoon onion powder
2	cloves garlic, chopped	½	teaspoon dried thyme
¾	cup sliced okra	½	teaspoon dried basil
2	large tomatoes, seeded and diced	1	pound crawfish tail meat or lobster
		1	pound dry rice, cooked
		1	tablespoon filé powder
			Salt to taste
			Cayenne pepper to taste

Sauté sausage and chicken in a large pot until chicken is no longer pink. Add onion, bell pepper, celery, jalapeño pepper, garlic, okra and tomatoes. Sauté until onion is translucent. Stir in flour to make a roux. Add broths, bay leaves, oregano, onion powder, thyme and basil. Bring to a boil. Reduce heat and add crawfish and cooked rice. Simmer 10 minutes. Season with filé powder, salt and pepper.

Makes 1 gallon

To brown all-purpose flour, bake flour in a shallow baking pan at 300 degrees for 3 hours, stirring occasionally. This ensures a rich, nutty flavor for your roux. Can be stored like regular flour.

The word "gumbo" is usually reserved for stews, which are thickened with okra. Okra, which is native to Africa and to India, is actually a member of the hibiscus family. Okra seems to have been introduced into the West Indies by Africans and migrated to the ports of Charleston and New Orleans. The West African name for gumbo is "nkruma." The English thought it sounded like "okra" and the French heard the word as "gombaut." Thus, the source of the word "gumbo."

Pine Bark Seafood Stew

3	quarts chicken broth	1½	cups chopped fish (flounder is an excellent choice)
¾	cup diced celery		
¾	cup diced onion	1	cup peeled and deveined shrimp
¾	cup diced green bell pepper		
		1	cup crabmeat
1½	cups diced potatoes	1	cup scallops
1½	teaspoons thyme	1	cup oysters, shucked and drained
¾	teaspoon white pepper		
¾	teaspoon salt	¾	cup sherry
½	cup margarine		
¼	cup flour		

Combine broth, celery, onion, bell pepper, potato, thyme, white pepper and salt in a large pot. Simmer until vegetables are tender. In a small saucepan, melt margarine. Blend in flour. Add mixture to stew and simmer 5 minutes. Add fish, shrimp, crab, scallops and oysters to stew. Simmer 10 minutes. Remove from heat and stir in sherry.

Serves 8

Christ Church Crab Stew

1	medium onion, chopped	1	dozen crabs, cooked and picked
1	cup finely chopped celery		
	Zest of 1 lemon		Salt and pepper to taste
4	tablespoons butter		Lemon juice to taste
1	tablespoon cornstarch		Sherry to taste
3	cups milk		

In a saucepan, sauté onion, celery and lemon zest in butter until slightly browned. Dissolve cornstarch in milk and add to saucepan. Cook until slightly thickened. Add crabmeat and heat thoroughly. Season with salt and pepper. Cook for 10 minutes. Add lemon juice and sherry to taste just before serving.

Serves 6 to 8

Origin of Pine Bark Stew

There was a young priest who came upon a group of poor folks on the bank of the Savannah River, fishing for whatever they could catch for their cooking pot. The priest was drawn to the delicious aroma. As the priest closed his eyes to take a deep sniff, a large piece of pine bark fell into the cooking pot. This was unseen by the priest until he opened his eyes to see the pine bark being stirred into the cooking pot. He asked if this was a secret ingredient. The cook just kept stirring and let the priest think what he wanted. After three bowls full, the priest declared that it was the finest stew in the world because of the pine bark. (Today's version omits the pine bark but is just as delicious.)

Sausage and Ham Jambalaya

2	tablespoons vegetable oil	¼	cup minced fresh parsley
1	cup chopped onion	2	cloves garlic, minced
1	bell pepper, chopped	1	bay leaf
3	stalks celery, chopped	1	teaspoon thyme
5	green onions, chopped	1	teaspoon basil
1	(10-ounce) can tomatoes, chopped, juice reserved		Salt and pepper to taste
		¼	cup Worcestershire sauce
1	(10-ounce) can chopped tomatoes and green chiles, juice reserved	3	cups water, divided
		12	pork sausages, halved
2	cups diced ham	1	pound smoked sausage, cut into 1-inch slices
¼	cup tomato paste	2	cups dry converted rice

Heat oil in a Dutch oven. Add onion and bell pepper and sauté until tender. Add celery, green onions, drained tomatoes and tomatoes and green chiles. Cook until vegetables are softened. Add ham and tomato paste. Cook until mixture begins to brown. Add parsley, garlic, bay leaf, thyme, basil, salt, pepper, Worcestershire sauce, reserved tomato juices and 2 cups water. Simmer 1 hour.

In a large skillet, cook pork and smoked sausage; discard drippings. Add sausage to vegetable mixture in pot. Rinse skillet with remaining 1 cup water and add to pot along with rice. Cover tightly and bring to a boil. Reduce heat and cook until rice is tender, stirring frequently to prevent sticking. Add extra water while cooking as needed.

Serves 8 to 10

Portobello Cream Soup

4 tablespoons butter

¼ cup flour

2 cups chicken broth

½ teaspoon salt

¼ teaspoon black pepper

1-2 bay leaves

⅔ cup finely chopped celery

¼ cup finely chopped onion

3 tablespoons vegetable oil

4-5 cups sliced portobello mushrooms

⅔ cup half-and-half

Melt butter in a saucepan. Add flour and stir until blended. Gradually stir in broth. Stir in salt, pepper and bay leaves. Simmer 15 minutes, stirring occasionally. In a skillet, sauté celery and onion in oil until tender. Add mushrooms to skillet and sauté until tender. Add sautéed vegetables to saucepan. Bring to a boil. Reduce heat and simmer 15 minutes, stirring occasionally. Slowly add half-and-half and mix well. Cook just until heated. Discard bay leaves before serving.

Serves 4

Southern Belle Pepper Chili

2-3	pounds ground beef chuck		1	teaspoon oregano
4	cups chopped yellow onion		1	teaspoon cumin
2	cups chopped green bell pepper		1	teaspoon salt
1	cup chopped red bell pepper		1-2	teaspoons cayenne pepper or to taste
1	cup chopped yellow bell pepper		1	(28-ounce) can diced tomatoes, undrained
1-2	tablespoons flour		1	(30-ounce) can kidney beans, drained
1	tablespoon minced garlic		1	(28-ounce) can tomato sauce
1	tablespoon black pepper			
1	tablespoon chili powder			

Brown beef with onion and bell peppers in a large saucepan. Drain excess fat. Sift flour over mixture. Stir until flour is no longer visible. Reduce heat to low. Stir in garlic, black pepper, chili powder, oregano, cumin, salt and cayenne pepper. Add tomatoes with juice, beans and tomato sauce. Gradually bring to a boil. Reduce heat to low and simmer 1½ to 3 hours, stirring regularly to prevent sticking. Add more flour if chili is too thin.

Makes 1 gallon

For Rompin', Stompin' chili:

Substitute 2 to 3 (4-ounce) cans chopped green chiles for the bell pepper; or mix 2 cups green bell pepper and 2 cans green chiles, omit the red and yellow bell peppers.

About Chili

The one thing that is known about chili is that it did not originate in Mexico. Instead, chili evolved from dried meat and peppers, called jerky, or pemmican. These dried "bricks" were boiled with spices and chilies until edible and fed to prisoners in Texas. This chili was so good that prisoners often rated the jails by the quality of their "chili."

Saints' Brunswick Stew

Brunswick Stew

*Both Brunswick,
Georgia, and
Brunswick, Virginia,
claim that Brunswick
stew originated in
their own fair cities.
An annual cooking
competition is held,
with a rivalry,
that matches the
controversies
concerning barbeque.
More than likely,
Brunswick stew
evolved, as did many
cooking pot creations,
simply from what was
available. Brunswick
stew can also sit on the
stovetop for hours at a
time, and not lose
any flavor.*

2	fryer or 1 hen chickens (about 6 pounds)	1	(14-ounce) bottle ketchup
1	teaspoon salt	2	teaspoons dried red pepper flakes
1	(5-pound) pork roast	6	medium onions, chopped
1	(4-pound) beef roast	½	cup Worcestershire sauce
4	(16-ounce) cans tomatoes	2	tablespoons sugar
3	(16-ounce) cans corn	¾	cup vinegar

Boil chicken with salt in a large pot in enough water to cover until meat falls from bones. At the same time, roast pork and beef separately, discarding pork drippings and reserving beef drippings. Remove chicken from broth, reserving broth. Bone and skin chicken. Remove and discard fat from cooked roasts. Coarsely chop or grind chicken, pork and beef.

Add tomatoes, corn, ketchup, pepper flakes, onions, Worcestershire sauce and sugar to broth. Simmer. Add chopped meats along with reserved beef drippings. Add vinegar and cook over low heat, stirring frequently to prevent sticking, until mixture thickens; do not boil. Adjust seasonings and serve or freeze for later use.

Makes about 3 gallons

Salads

The *First* Experimental Garden

Trustees' Garden, laid out by James Oglethorpe on a 10-acre plot in Savannah, was the *first* experimental agricultural garden in North America. Trustees' Garden was created to determine the suitability of numerous plants, herbs and trees for Georgia's climate. The cultivation of mulberry trees, to feed and house silkworms, was of primary importance. Production of silk in a British colony was hoped for, in order to compete with the French. One of the *first* big buildings in Savannah, the Filature House, was built for reeling silk. An Italian silk maker was even sent in to help, but to no avail. The silkworms did not thrive in Georgia, and the process required more labor than could be spared in the new colony. While the silk experiment failed, other agricultural projects thrived. Especially successful for Georgia in later years were cotton, peaches, and pecans.

Spirited Savannah

"Fifteen men on a dead man's chest...and the Devil take the rest." So, it is told, said Flint, the most treacherous of all pirates, as he lay dying in an upstairs room of what is now The Pirates' House Restaurant. Built in 1753, it is legendary for strange happenings. There are still rooms today which no-one willingly enters alone.

As a tavern and inn, The Pirates' House welcomed the buccaneer brothers, Jean and Pierre Lafitte. It also saw the likes of "Billy Bones," "Black Dog," and "Blackbeard." (In *Treasure Island,* Robert Louis Stevenson says, "Blackbeard was a child to Flint.") Most believe it is Flint's murderous voice heard on moonless nights, along with the cursing of his crew, and the cries of those they killed. A veil of sadness hangs over parts of the Pirates' House. It may be those who were shanghaied. Drunk or unconscious, they were often dragged through secret tunnels which led to the Savannah River. They awoke to find themselves, enslaved, on an outward going ship. Some may have preferred the quick death that followed any failure to swear to the pirates' oaths.

"Oh So Sweet Southern Salads"

Someone once said that a Southerner's idea of a salad was a half of a banana on a lettuce leaf, topped with mayonnaise. Well, that won't get it as a salad, unless you add peanut butter to the banana *first* (don't knock it if you haven't tried it.) Of course, you can slice the banana *first,* then heat the peanut butter until it will drizzle artfully. It will still be delicious.

Another sweet Southern salad, which everyone's grandmother seems to have made, is simply a canned pear half (or two, if they were small) placed on a lettuce leaf, topped with mayonnaise, then sprinkled with grated cheddar cheese and topped with a maraschino cherry. Perfection. Admittedly, there are some Southern salads that sound like an ice cream sundae. Southerners eat enough vegetables to have no difficulty using the word "salad" to describe a concoction that seems more like a dessert. One all-time favorite has cherries, bananas, mandarin oranges, pineapple, marshmallows (the little ones), and coconut. This is stirred into a cool whipped topping or vanilla pudding, and topped with pecans. A few spoonfuls of this provide a cool respite from spicy foods.

The most famous of the sweet Southern salads are those which are congealed. These have fruit and other ingredients beautifully bound in colored gelatin. Southern cooks rather daringly choose the heat of summer as their favorite time to "set up" some classic congealed salads. The congealed salad has evolved in Savannah, both artfully and formally in variety. Still, it is only right to mention a few of the old standby salads. Briefly, there is "Green Salad," with pineapples, celery, cream cheese, mayonnaise and nuts in green jello. There is "Orange," or "Sunshine Salad," with grated carrots and pineapple in orange jello. Finally, there is something mysteriously called "Spanish Cream," which consists mainly of sugar, whipped topping, and vanilla "set up" in simple gelatin.

Fried Green Tomato Salad with Cayenne Mayonnaise

Cayenne Mayonnaise

4	egg yolks	½	teaspoon dry mustard
¼	cup fresh lemon juice	¼	teaspoon cayenne pepper
½	teaspoon salt	¼	teaspoon paprika
½	teaspoon black pepper	1½	cups olive oil
9	cloves garlic		

Salad

6	large green tomatoes	3	eggs, beaten
1½	cups cornmeal		Vegetable oil for frying
½	cup flour	1½	cups shredded Boston or Bibb lettuce
	Salt and freshly ground black pepper to taste	2½	cups shredded Romaine lettuce or arugula
¼	teaspoon cayenne pepper or to taste		

To make mayonnaise, process egg yolks, lemon juice, salt and black pepper in a food processor until well blended. Add garlic, mustard, cayenne pepper and paprika. Process until smooth. With machine running, add olive oil in a steady stream. Process until mixture thickens. Season to taste with extra salt and pepper.

For the salad, cut tomatoes into a total of 24 (¼-inch thick) slices. Combine cornmeal, flour, salt, black pepper and cayenne pepper in a bowl. Dip tomato slices in eggs, then dredge in cornmeal mixture to coat. Heat vegetable oil in a cast-iron skillet over medium heat to 375 degrees. Add tomatoes, a few at a time. Fry 2 to 3 minutes per side or until golden brown. Drain on paper towels.

Toss lettuces in a bowl. Divide lettuce among 8 salad plates. Top each serving with 3 fried tomato slices. Drizzle mayonnaise on top.

Serve 8

Yes, Virginia, there really is a Santa Claus...and yes, Southerners really eat fried green tomatoes! This recipe was made famous following the movie version of Fannie Flagg's novel, Fried Green Tomatoes at the Whistle Stop Cafe. *For your first attempt at this Southern treat be sure to select very green tomatoes without a hint of pink or they won't have the trademark crisp tartness you desire.*

Homemade mayonnaise may not seem worth the effort until you taste what mayonnaise ought to taste like. You may suddenly want to use it with everything you can think of. As with all recipes with raw eggs, mayonnaise must be kept very cold.

Tomatoes Vinaigrette

12 thick tomato slices

1 cup olive oil

⅓ cup red wine vinegar

2 tablespoons crushed oregano

1 teaspoon salt

½ teaspoon black pepper

½ teaspoon dry mustard

2 cloves garlic, crushed

Lettuce leaves

Minced green onions

Minced fresh parsley

Arrange tomato slices in an 8x8-inch dish. In a mixing bowl, whisk together oil, vinegar, oregano, salt, pepper, mustard and garlic. Spoon mixture over tomatoes. Cover and chill at least 2 hours, occasionally spooning marinade over tomatoes.

To serve, arrange tomatoes on lettuce leaves. Sprinkle with a small amount of marinade. Garnish with mounds of green onion and parsley.

Serves 4 to 6

Saints' Coleslaw

⅓	cup sugar	1	teaspoon black pepper
1	tablespoon white vinegar	1	tablespoon dry mustard
1⅔	cups mayonnaise		Dash of paprika
	Pinch of celery seed	1	head cabbage, coarsely
	Salt to taste		shredded

Mix sugar and vinegar and let stand until dissolved. Add mayonnaise, celery seed, salt, pepper, mustard and paprika. Mix well. Place cabbage in a large bowl. Pour dressing mixture over cabbage and stir until well coated. Refrigerate, stirring several times before serving. Best if made ahead.

Serves 8 to 10

Summer Corn and Zucchini Salad

3	cups fresh or frozen corn kernels	¼	teaspoon salt
		⅛	teaspoon black pepper
1	large onion, chopped	2	teaspoons sugar
1	bunch green onions, sliced	1	teaspoon ground cumin
2	medium zucchinis, unpeeled and cubed	2	teaspoons Dijon mustard
		½	teaspoon hot pepper sauce
1	red bell pepper, chopped	⅔	cup vegetable oil
1	green bell pepper, chopped	⅓	cup white vinegar
¼	cup minced fresh parsley	1	clove garlic, minced (optional)

Cook fresh corn in boiling water for 5 to 8 minutes. If using frozen corn, cook according to package directions. Drain and cool. Combine cooled corn with green onions, zucchini, onions, bell peppers and parsley.

In a separate bowl, mix together salt, black pepper, sugar, cumin, mustard, hot pepper sauce, oil, vinegar and garlic. Stir well. Pour mixture over vegetables and refrigerate 8 hours, stirring occasionally.

Serves 8 to 10

Cucumber and Red Onion Salad

3	cucumbers	⅓	cup sour cream
	Salt to taste	¼	cup sugar
2	red onions, thinly sliced	⅓	cup white vinegar

Peel cucumbers, leaving some skin intact. Thinly slice cucumbers and season with salt. Toss and refrigerate 1 hour. Rinse and drain cucumbers and add onion. Thoroughly mix sour cream, sugar and vinegar to make a dressing. Pour over cucumbers and onions. Refrigerate at least 4 hours, stirring occasionally. Refrigerate until ready to serve.

Serves 6 to 8

Bacon-Broccoli Toss

Sauce

¼	cup vinegar	3	tablespoons flour
¼	cup sugar	½	cup water
1	tablespoon dry mustard	¾	cup mayonnaise

Salad

6-8	cups fresh broccoli florets (about 2 bunches)	12	slices bacon, cooked and crumbled
½	cup raisins	1	small purple onion, finely chopped

For sauce, combine vinegar, sugar, mustard, flour and water in a saucepan. Cook over medium heat until thickened. Let cool. Add mayonnaise.

Combine all salad ingredients in a bowl. Add sauce and mix. Refrigerate. Toss just before serving.

Serves 10 to 12

For Crunchy Marinated Cucumbers, score five large unpeeled cucumbers lengthwise with a fork to create a striped pattern. Cut cucumbers into ¼ inch slices. Pour a mixture of ½ cup vegetable oil, ¼ cup rice wine or red wine vinegar and 2 tablespoons sugar over the cucumbers. Season with Kosher salt and freshly ground pepper. Marinate, covered, in the refrigerator for one hour or longer. Toss gently before serving.

Shrimp Mayonnaise

½ teaspoon dry mustard

½ teaspoon salt

1 egg

1 cup peanut oil

1 tablespoon fresh lemon juice

6 shrimp, cooked and peeled

Combine mustard, salt and egg in a blender. Process about 20 seconds. With machine running, add oil, very slowly at first, blending until all the oil has been added and the mixture is thick and creamy. Scrape down sides with a rubber spatula. Add lemon juice and blend. With machine running, add shrimp, one at a time, blending well after each addition. Cover and store in refrigerator for up to 3 days.

Classic Tomato Aspic

2	cups tomato or V-8 juice, divided	1	tablespoon Worcestershire sauce
1	(3-ounce) package lemon gelatin		Dash of Tabasco sauce
½	(¼-ounce) envelope unflavored gelatin	½	small onion, minced
¼	cup vinegar	¾	cup chopped bell pepper
			Salt and pepper to taste

Heat 1 cup of tomato juice. Add gelatins and stir to dissolve. Add remaining tomato juice, vinegar, Worcestershire sauce, Tabasco sauce, onion and bell pepper. Season with salt and pepper. Pour into individual ramekins or a large greased mold. Refrigerate until firm.

When ready to serve, allow molds to stand at room temperature for 10 minutes before removing. To unmold, gently run a knife around the edges and/or briefly dip bottom of mold into hot water. Serve on a bed of lettuce with Shrimp Mayonnaise.

Serves 8 to 10

Chopped canned asparagus can be added to the aspic.

Pennies from Heaven

2	pounds carrots, sliced	½	cup vinegar
1	medium onion, sliced	½	cup vegetable oil
½	green bell pepper, sliced	¾	cup sugar
1	(10¾-ounce) can condensed tomato soup	1	tablespoon prepared mustard

Cook carrots in a small amount of boiling salted water until tender; drain. Combine carrots, onion and bell pepper. Set aside. Mix together soup, vinegar, oil, sugar and mustard. Stir until well mixed. Pour mixture over vegetables and toss lightly with a fork. Refrigerate overnight.

Serve 12

Oriental Asparagus Salad

1	pound asparagus, cut into 2-inch pieces	1½	teaspoons sugar
2	tablespoons soy sauce	1	teaspoon sesame seeds, toasted
1	tablespoon vegetable oil	¼	teaspoon ground ginger
1	tablespoon vinegar	¼	teaspoon ground cumin

Cook asparagus in a saucepan in a small amount of boiling water for 3 to 4 minutes or until crisp-tender. Drain well and place in a large bowl. In a separate bowl, mix together soy sauce, oil, vinegar, sugar, sesame seeds, ginger and cumin. Pour mixture over asparagus and toss to coat. Cover and chill 1 hour. Drain before serving.

Serves 4

Walnut-Blue Cheese Salad

3	heads Boston or Bibb lettuce, washed and dried	¾	cup coarsely chopped walnuts
		4-6	ounces blue cheese, crumbled

Vinaigrette

¼	cup red wine vinegar	1	tablespoon chopped fresh parsley
¾	cup olive oil	1	teaspoon basil
1	tablespoon finely chopped onion	½	teaspoon oregano
1	teaspoon Dijon mustard	½	teaspoon garlic powder
2	tablespoons water		Salt and pepper to taste

Tear lettuce into bite-size pieces. Toss lettuce and walnuts together in a large bowl. Pour vinaigrette over salad and toss. Sprinkle with cheese.

To make vinaigrette, mix all ingredients in a jar. Cover tightly and shake well. Store covered in refrigerator for up to 2 days.

Serves 8

Basil, Tomato Summer Salad

Surprise your guests with an elegant basil, tomato summer salad. Alternate layers of fresh basil (leaves only), sliced fresh tomatoes and sliced mozzarella cheese on a platter. Drizzle with olive oil, balsamic vinegar and sprinkle with freshly ground pepper and salt. Chill and serve. This can also be served as an individual plated stacked salad. For an interesting twist, add a layer of grilled portobello mushroom.

Another agricultural experiment in Savannah began in the 1890s, when Mrs. Smith planted several bamboo shoots. This expanded into a 46-acre complex, with two acres of Giant Japanese Timber, called the Bamboo Farm. Not only is this a beautiful garden, its cut bamboo is sent to feed pandas in zoos.

Hearts of Palm Salad with Spicy Cedar Key Peanut Dressing

Dressing

½	cup chunky peanut butter	1	teaspoon Thai hot sauce
½	cup unsweetened coconut milk	1	teaspoon minced fresh ginger
2	tablespoons soy sauce	1	teaspoon minced garlic
1	tablespoon fresh lime juice	2	teaspoons minced green onion
1	tablespoon sugar		

Salad

4	cups thinly sliced iceberg or green leaf lettuce	1	tablespoon minced candied ginger
1	cup diced pineapple, fresh preferred	2	cups thinly sliced hearts of palm
½	cup diced pitted dates	1	teaspoon chopped green onion for garnish

To make dressing, combine all ingredients in a blender. Process until well mixed. Refrigerate until ready to use. Add water or chicken broth if dressing is too thick.

For salad, combine all ingredients except green onion. Divide mixture among individual salad plates or place in a large salad bowl. Toss with dressing and garnish with chopped green onion.

Serves 4

Gorgonzola and Pecan Crunch Salad with Hazelnut Vinaigrette

Pecan Crunch

⅔	cup chopped pecans
2	tablespoons butter
1	tablespoon sugar
½	teaspoon salt

Freshly ground black pepper

¼ teaspoon cayenne pepper

Hazelnut Vinaigrette

1	teaspoon Dijon mustard
1	teaspoon orange zest
2	teaspoons honey
2	tablespoons red wine vinegar

¼	cup orange juice
¼	cup hazelnut oil
¼	cup light olive oil

Salad

7 cups mixed lettuces, such as red or green leaf, Bibb or butterhead, torn into bite-size pieces

6 ounces Gorgonzola cheese, crumbled

For pecan crunch, combine all ingredients in a small saucepan. Sauté until sugar caramelizes. Transfer to a small paper bag to cool, shaking occasionally to break into pieces. Store in an air-tight container for up to 1 week, or freeze up to 1 month.

To make vinaigrette, mix all ingredients except oils in a medium mixing bowl. Whisk in oils. Refrigerate up to 2 days.

To assemble salad, combine lettuce and cheese and divide among individual salad plates. Sprinkle with pecan crunch and drizzle vinaigrette over the top.

Serves 6

Red Pear Salad with Raspberry Vinaigrette

¼ cup raspberry vinegar

1 teaspoon Dijon mustard

¼ cup honey

¾ cup extra-virgin olive oil

Salt and pepper to taste

Mixed salad greens, such as red leaf lettuce, arugula and endive

3 red pears, thinly sliced

½-¾ cup crumbled blue cheese

⅓-½ cup walnuts, toasted

Mix vinegar and mustard in a bowl. Stir in honey. Whisk in oil. Season vinaigrette with salt and pepper. Arrange salad greens on individual salad plates. Top with pear slices and sprinkle with cheese and walnuts. Drizzle vinaigrette over salad.

Serves 8

Cucumber Aspic

**1 (3-ounce) package
lime gelatin**

1 cup hot water

1 cup diced cucumber

1 tablespoon lemon juice

¼ teaspoon salt

**1 small green bell pepper,
finely diced**

Boston lettuce leaves

Mayonnaise

Dissolve gelatin in hot water. Add cucumber, lemon juice, salt and bell pepper in order listed. Pour into a large mold or individual ramekins. Refrigerate until firm. Line a serving plate or individual salad plates with lettuce leaves. Unmold salad onto lettuce and top with a dollop of mayonnaise.

Serves 6

Mandarin Orange Company Salad with Pecan Croutons

Candied Pecan Croutons

½   **cup sugar**
2½ **tablespoons water**
½   **teaspoon vanilla**

1   **cup pecan halves or
almonds**

Orange Vinaigrette

⅓   **cup olive oil**
2   **tablespoons red wine
vinegar**
1½ **teaspoons fresh orange
juice**

½   **teaspoon orange zest**
¼   **teaspoon poppy seeds**
¼-½   **teaspoon salt**
⅛   **teaspoon black pepper**

Salad

8   **cups mixed salad greens**
1   **(11-ounce) can Mandarin
oranges, drained**

1   **green onion, sliced**

To prepare croutons, combine sugar, water and vanilla in a saucepan. Mix well and bring to a boil. Reduce heat to low and cook 5 minutes, stirring occasionally. Add pecans and stir to coat. Spread pecans on a baking sheet. Let stand until cool. When cool, break apart.

For vinaigrette, combine all ingredients in a jar. Cover with a tightly fitting lid and shake to mix.

To assemble salad, toss together salad greens, Mandarin oranges and green onion in a salad bowl. Drizzle with vinaigrette and toss gently. Sprinkle with croutons.

Serves 8

Baked Chèvre Salad with Red Grape Clusters

1	head butterhead lettuce, washed and dried	3	tablespoons red wine vinegar
2	(4-ounce) logs chèvre goat cheese		Salt and pepper to taste
1	cup dry bread crumbs	4	green onions, chopped
½	cup olive oil	½	cup coarsely chopped walnuts
¼	cup walnut oil		Red seedless grapes for garnish

Preheat oven to 400 degrees. Tear lettuce into bite-size pieces; set aside. Slice cheese logs into four (½-inch) thick rounds. Coat each round with bread crumbs and place on a lightly greased baking sheet. Bake 3 to 5 minutes or until golden brown.

Make a dressing by whisking together oils, vinegar, salt and pepper. Toss lettuce with green onions and enough dressing to lightly coat leaves. To serve, arrange lettuce on individual salad plates. Place warm goat cheese rounds in center of lettuce. Sprinkle with walnuts and garnish each plate with grapes.

Serves 4

Indian Chutney-Spinach Salad

¼	cup white wine vinegar	1	teaspoon dry mustard
¼	cup vegetable oil	1½	cups diced apples
2	tablespoons chutney	½	cup raisins
2	teaspoons sugar	½	cup unsalted peanuts
½	teaspoon salt	1	(10-ounce) package fresh spinach
1½	teaspoons curry powder		

Whisk together vinegar, oil, chutney, sugar, salt, curry and mustard to make a dressing. Blend until sugar dissolves. Toss together apple, raisins, peanuts and spinach or arrange on individual salad plates. Drizzle dressing on top.

Serves 4

Feast of Flowers

Brighten up your table and palate with a feast of edible flowers used as a garnish both on individual plates and serving plates. Edible flowers include pansies, violets, roses, forget-me-nots, scented geranium leaves, nasturtiums, daisies, lavender, marigolds and honey suckle.

Spinach and Strawberry Salad

Salad

8	ounces fresh tender spinach, washed and dried	1	pint fresh strawberries, sliced
		2	ounces almonds, toasted

Dressing

½	cup sugar	¼	teaspoon Worcestershire sauce
2	tablespoons sesame seeds		
1	tablespoon poppy seeds	¼	teaspoon paprika
1½	teaspoons minced onion	¼	cup cider vinegar
		½	cup oil

This strawberry and spinach salad takes only a quarter of an hour to create and combines sweet and sour flavors into a refreshing crunchy delight. A family favorite.

Arrange spinach and strawberries on individual salad plates or in a large clear glass bowl. Drizzle dressing over salad. Garnish with almonds.

To make dressing, combine all ingredients except oil in a blender. Process to blend. With machine on low speed, add oil in a steady stream, blending until dressing is creamy and thick.

Serves 4

Waldorf Salad

2	Red Delicious apples, chopped	1	cup halved red grapes
		1	cup chopped celery
2	Golden Delicious apples, chopped	½	cup sour cream
		½	cup mayonnaise
	Juice of ½ lemon	2	teaspoons sugar
1	cup raisins (optional)	⅛	teaspoon salt
1	cup broken pecan halves, toasted		

This famous salad was created at the Waldorf-Astoria Hotel in New York. The tart combination of apple and celery makes it an excellent counter balance to rich meats, such as duck and pork.

Toss apples with lemon juice in a bowl. Stir in raisins, pecans, grapes and celery. In a separate bowl, mix sour cream, mayonnaise, sugar and salt. Add to apple mixture and toss gently to mix. Cover and chill until serving time.

Serves 16

Romano Spinach Salad

Salad

2	pounds fresh spinach, washed and trimmed	5	green onions, chopped
10	slices bacon, cooked and crumbled	1	(10-ounce) package frozen green peas, thawed (optional)
2	hard-cooked eggs, chopped		

Creamy Dressing

1	(8-ounce) container sour cream	½	cup grated Romano cheese
1	cup mayonnaise	½	teaspoon lemon pepper
		⅛	teaspoon garlic powder

Layer all salad ingredients in order listed in a large salad bowl.

To prepare dressing, combine all ingredients in a mixing bowl. Spread dressing over top of salad. Cover and chill 8 to 10 hours. Toss just before serving.

Serves 10

Always Ambrosia

10-12	navel oranges, sectioned and membranes removed	1	(14-ounce) can crushed pineapple, undrained
2-3	blood oranges, sectioned and membranes removed	1	cup fresh or canned shredded coconut
		¼	cup sugar (optional)
		2	bananas
		1	cup broken pecan halves

Combine orange sections, undrained pineapple and coconut in a large bowl. Toss to mix. Taste and add sugar if needed. At this point, salad can be covered and refrigerated up to 1 day in advance.

An hour before serving, slice bananas and add with pecans to salad. Chill until served.

Serves 12

Salad can be topped with Grand Marnier or served as a dessert.

Southern Salads

Most Southern ladies could eat a salad for lunch every day of their lives. Seafood, meat and poultry salads are religiously included on restaurant, church and country club menus. Likewise, congealed salads are so wildly popular in the South that they are almost always served at ladies' bridge clubs, church bazaars and charity gatherings.

Congealed Cranberry Salad

Topping

1	(8-ounce) package cream cheese, softened
1	(8-ounce) container sour cream

Salad

1 (20-ounce) can crushed pineapple, drained with juice reserved

¾ cup water

1 (16-ounce) package frozen cranberries

1½ cups sugar

2 (3-ounce) packages raspberry gelatin

1 bunch seedless red grapes, halved

1 cup chopped pecans

To make topping, beat cream cheese and sour cream in a mixing bowl until creamy. Cover and chill in refrigerator.

For salad, combine ¾ cup of reserved pineapple juice, water and cranberries in a saucepan. Cook until cranberries pop open, stirring occasionally. Add sugar and mix well. Simmer, stirring frequently, until sugar dissolves. Stir in gelatin and cook until dissolved. Remove from heat and cool. Stir in pineapple, grapes and pecans. Pour mixture into a greased 2-quart mold. Refrigerate until set.

To serve, dip bottom of mold in hot water for 10 to 20 seconds. Invert onto a serving platter. Top each serving with a dollop of cream mixture.

Serves 8

Gelatin was used in ancient Egypt. Sometimes, it seems that the congealed salad you are striving to set-up just started congealing about that long ago.

Molded Raspberry Peach Salad

2	(¼-ounce) envelopes unflavored gelatin
1½	cups water
1	(6-ounce) can frozen orange juice concentrate, slightly thawed
2	teaspoons sugar
3	tablespoons lemon juice
1	(16-ounce) package frozen peaches, thawed and drained with juice reserved, cut into ½-inch pieces
1	(10-ounce) package frozen raspberries in syrup, thawed and drained with juice reserved
1	medium banana, sliced ¼-inch thick (½ cup) Sweetened whipped cream or Fake Crème Fraîche

Soften gelatin in water in a 1-quart saucepan for 1 minute. Cook over low heat, stirring occasionally, for 3 to 5 minutes or until gelatin dissolves; set aside. In a large bowl, combine orange juice concentrate, sugar, lemon juice, reserved peach and raspberry juices and gelatin mixture. Refrigerate 45 minutes or until slightly thickened. Carefully fold in peaches, raspberries and banana. Pour into a greased 8-cup mold. Refrigerate 6 hours or until firm. Unmold onto a serving plate and serve with cream.

Serves 12

Fake Crème Fraîche

Real crème fraîche is both difficult to find and expensive. Try this "fake" version for a delicious alternative topping.

1 (8-ounce) container sour cream

1 (8-ounce) package cream cheese, softened

1 teaspoon vanilla extract

½ cup sugar

Blend together and chill.

This topping is so delicious that guests have been known to simply eat the topping without the salad.

The first eight pounds of silk were sent to Queen Charlotte to make a dress for her birthday. The (yellow) dress was praised by all, particularly for the silk, which everyone said was far superior to French silk.

Spiced Peach Aspic

1	(29-ounce) can or jar spiced or pickled peaches, pitted, juice reserved	1	cup finely chopped pecans or nut of choice
3	oranges, peeled, seeded and diced	2	(3-ounce) packages lemon gelatin
1	(15-ounce) can pear halves, drained and diced	1	(¼-ounce) envelope unflavored gelatin
		1½	cups boiling water
		2	cups cold water

Combine drained peaches, oranges, pears and pecans in a bowl. Mix gently.

In a separate bowl, dissolve gelatins in boiling water. Add cold water and reserved peach juice. Chill until slightly thickened. Stir in fruit mixture. Pour into a mold and refrigerate 6 hours or until set.

Serves 16 to 20

A small jar of chopped maraschino cherries can be substituted for the canned pears.

Wonderful Creamy Fruit Salad

2	(20-ounce) cans pineapple chunks, undrained	2	Granny Smith apples, peeled and chopped
2	(11-ounce) cans Mandarin oranges, undrained	1	(3-ounce) can pecans, chopped (optional)
3	bananas, sliced	1	(3-ounce) package instant vanilla pudding

Mix undrained pineapple and oranges, bananas, apples and pecans. Sprinkle with pudding. Toss and refrigerate.

Serves 6

Maraschino cherries and marshmallows can be added to the salad, if desired.

Strawberry Pretzel Salad

2	cups coarsely crushed pretzels	1	(6-ounce) package strawberry gelatin
¾	cup margarine, melted	1	cup boiling water
3	tablespoons plus 1 cup sugar, divided	½	cup miniature marshmallows
1	(8-ounce) package cream cheese, softened	2	(10-ounce) packages frozen sliced strawberries, thawed
1	(8-ounce) container frozen non-dairy whipped topping, thawed		

Preheat oven to 400 degrees. Combine pretzels, margarine and 3 tablespoons sugar. Mix well and press into a 9x13-inch baking dish. Bake 8 minutes. Cool completely.

Beat remaining 1 cup sugar and cream cheese in a large mixing bowl with an electric mixer. Blend well. Fold in whipped topping and spread over cooled crust. Refrigerate until chilled.

In a separate bowl, dissolve gelatin in boiling water. Add marshmallows and stir until melted. Add strawberries with their juice. Let stand 10 minutes. Pour mixture over cream layer. Refrigerate until set. Cut into squares and serve as a salad or a dessert.

Serves 12

Blueberry-Pecan Congealed Salad

2 (3-ounce) packages blackberry or black raspberry gelatin

3 cups boiling water

1 (8¼-ounce) can crushed pineapple, drained with juice reserved

1 (15-ounce) can blueberries, drained

1 (8-ounce) container sour cream

1 (8-ounce) package cream cheese, softened

½ cup sugar

Chopped pecans

Dissolve gelatin in boiling water. Stir in reserved pineapple juice. Chill until mixture is the consistency of unbeaten egg whites. Stir in pineapple and blueberries. Pour into a 10x6x1¾-inch pan and refrigerate until set.

Combine sour cream, cream cheese and sugar. Mix until smooth and well blended. Spread cream mixture over firm salad. Top with pecans. Chill until ready to serve.

Serves 6 to 8

So good - can be a salad or dessert.

In 1963, the Garden Clubs of Savannah created a Fragrant Garden for the Blind. Located in Forsyth Park, it is the first such garden in the Southeastern US.

Cold Dillied New Potatoes with Carrots and Scallions

16	small new potatoes	2	tablespoons chopped fresh parsley
6	hard-cooked eggs, quartered	1	tablespoon caraway seeds
1	medium carrot, grated	½	teaspoon salt
2	medium scallions or green onions, thinly sliced	½	teaspoon freshly ground black pepper
3	tablespoons chopped fresh dill, or 1 tablespoon dried	¾	cup sour cream
		¾	cup mayonnaise

Cook potatoes in boiling water in a medium saucepan for 20 to 25 minutes or until just tender. Drain, cool and cut potatoes in half. Combine potatoes, eggs, carrot and scallions in a large bowl. Add dill, parsley, caraway seed, salt and pepper. Toss gently to combine. Fold in sour cream and mayonnaise. Refrigerate several hours or up to 1 day before serving.

Serves 8

Hot German Potato Salad

8	ounces bacon	½	cup vinegar
½	cup chopped onion	1	cup water
2	tablespoons all-purpose flour	6	cups sliced or cubed cooked potatoes
2	tablespoons sugar	2	hard-cooked eggs, sliced or chopped
1½	teaspoons salt		Parsley, pimiento and
1	teaspoon celery seed Dash of black pepper		bacon curls for garnish

In a skillet, cook bacon until crisp. Drain and crumble bacon, reserving ¼ cup fat in skillet. Add onion to fat and sauté until tender. Blend in flour, sugar, salt, celery seed and black pepper. Stir in vinegar and water. Cook and stir until thick and bubbly. Add crumbled bacon, potatoes and eggs. Heat thoroughly, tossing lightly. Garnish and serve.

Serves 8 to 10

Savannah Chicken Salad

3 cups chopped cooked chicken
½-1 cup finely chopped celery
½ cup finely chopped pecans
¾-1 cup mayonnaise
2 tablespoons sweet pickle relish
1 medium white onion, minced

2 hard-cooked eggs, finely chopped, (optional)
1 tablespoon prepared yellow mustard, (optional)
1 cup sliced white seedless grapes, (optional)
Salt and pepper to taste
Lemon pepper to taste
Paprika to taste

Combine all ingredients in a large bowl. Mix gently but thoroughly. Cover and refrigerate until well chilled.

Serves 6 to 8

Hoppin' John Salad

3 cups cooked long-grain rice
2 cups cooked or canned black-eyed peas, drained
½ cup chopped purple onion
¼ cup chopped celery
1 jalapeño pepper, seeded and minced

¼ cup chopped fresh parsley
1 clove garlic, minced
¼ cup olive oil
½ teaspoon salt
3 tablespoons fresh lemon juice
Black pepper to taste
Cayenne pepper to taste

Combine rice, black-eyed peas, onion, celery and jalapeño in a bowl. Mix in parsley and garlic. In a separate bowl, whisk together olive oil, salt, lemon juice and pepper. Pour over rice mixture and toss gently to coat.

Serves 8

For those who are new to chicken salad, the many variations and choices may seem daunting. In Savannah, we are not faced with those choices because we are all making our mother's or our grandmother's chicken salad (none other is quite right). We are polite about it, with appropriate comments such as "How interesting," or "My, my. I would never have thought to add…" The truly brave cook might even say, "I put some…in Mama's chicken salad. What do y'all think?" Then everyone can discuss their differences, and agree that everyone's chicken salad is just lovely, lovely…even if it isn't quite right.

Saffron Rice and Snow Peas Salad

Salad

1 (10-ounce) bag yellow saffron-seasoned long-grain rice

1 large red bell pepper, chopped

1 (3¼-ounce) can pitted black olives

1 carrot, chopped

¾ cup chopped sweet onion

18 raw snow pea pods, ends and strings pinched off

Dressing

⅔ cup vegetable oil

2 tablespoons olive oil

1 teaspoon salt

1 teaspoon black pepper

1 teaspoon oregano

2 teaspoons minced garlic

¼ cup sugar

¾ cup red wine vinegar

Prepare rice according to package directions, being careful to not overcook. Cool. Add bell pepper, olives, carrot, onion and pea pods to cooled rice.

Combine all dressing ingredients and pour over salad. Mix well. Cover and refrigerate overnight or up to 2 days.

Wild Rice and Chicken Salad

Salad

4	cups cooked long-grain and wild rice, cooked in chicken broth is best	½	red bell pepper, sliced
2	chicken breasts, cooked and cubed	1-2	medium avocados, chopped
3	whole green onions, chopped	1	cup pecan halves, toasted Lettuce leaves

Dressing

1	large clove garlic, minced	¼	teaspoon freshly ground black pepper
1	tablespoon Dijon mustard		
½	teaspoon salt	¼	cup rice wine vinegar
¼	teaspoon sugar	⅓	cup vegetable oil

While still warm, toss cooked rice in a medium bowl. Cool. Add chicken, onions and bell pepper. Toss with dressing. Cover and refrigerate 2 to 4 hours. Just before serving, add avocados and pecans. Toss gently and transfer to a salad bowl garnished with lettuce leaves.

To make dressing, combine all ingredients in a food processor or blender and mix, or mix thoroughly in a bowl.

Serves 6

Chinese Noodle Salad

1	cup slivered almonds	1½	teaspoons salt
½	cup sesame seeds	⅓	cup rice vinegar
1	head cabbage, chopped	2	(3-ounce) packages
8	green onions, chopped		Ramen noodles,
1	cup vegetable oil		crushed, seasoning
¼	cup sugar		packets reserved
1	teaspoon black pepper		

Toast almonds and sesame seeds under a broiler. Combine almonds, sesame seeds, cabbage and green onions in a bowl. Mix oil, sugar, pepper, salt, vinegar and season packets from noodles to make a dressing. Refrigerate. When ready to serve, pour dressing over salad. Add crushed noodles and toss.

Serves 8 to 10

Diced cooked chicken or turkey can be added to salad.

Chicken Apple Salad

3	cups chopped cooked chicken	1	tablespoon curry powder or less to taste (optional)
1	large red apple, finely chopped	⅓	cup chopped fresh parsley
½	cup plain yogurt	¼	cup grated onion
⅓	cup mayonnaise		Salt and pepper to taste
2½	tablespoons fresh lemon juice		Boston lettuce leaves
			Crushed peanuts or pecans

Combine chicken and apple in a large bowl. In a small bowl, blend yogurt, mayonnaise, lemon juice and curry powder. Mix well and add to chicken mixture. Toss to coat. Stir in parsley, onion, salt and pepper. Cover and chill until ready to serve. Serve on lettuce leaves with crushed nuts sprinkled on top.

Serves 4 to 6

Greek Marinated Garden Salad

3 medium tomatoes, each cut into 8 wedges

1 green bell pepper, sliced into rings

1 small purple onion, sliced into rings

1 medium cucumber, peeled and sliced

1 cup kalamata olives

¼ cup mild olive oil

2 tablespoons red wine vinegar

½ teaspoon salt

¼ teaspoon black pepper

¼ teaspoon oregano

Lettuce leaves

1-2 (4-ounce) packages crumbled feta cheese or to taste

1 (2-ounce) can anchovies, drained (optional)

Combine tomatoes, bell pepper, onion, cucumber and olives in a bowl. In a separate bowl, whisk together oil, vinegar, salt, black pepper and oregano. Drizzle over vegetables and toss. Serve immediately, or cover and chill 1 hour. Serve on lettuce, sprinkle with cheese and top with anchovies, if desired.

Serves 6 to 8

Spiced Cold Beef Salad

¼	cup red wine vinegar	1	small onion, thinly sliced
¼	cup water	1	head romaine lettuce,
2	tablespoons lemon juice		torn into small pieces
2	tablespoons sugar	1	cup sour cream
¼	teaspoon dill		Artichoke hearts and
½	teaspoon salt		tomato wedges for
	Black pepper to taste		garnish
3	cups cold roast beef, cut		
	into strips		

Simmer vinegar, water, lemon juice, sugar, dill, salt and pepper in a saucepan for 15 minutes; cool. Combine mixture with beef and onion and refrigerate several hours or overnight. Drain, reserving marinade. Place lettuce in a large bowl. Top with beef and onion. Combine sour cream with reserved marinade. Pour over salad and toss. Garnish with artichokes and tomatoes.

Serves 6

Marinated Shrimp Salad

⅓	cup olive oil	1	bunch green onions,
⅓	cup white wine vinegar		chopped
⅓	cup Dijon mustard	2	stalks celery, chopped
2	tablespoons paprika	2	cloves garlic, minced
2	teaspoons sugar	2½	pounds cooked, peeled
½	teaspoon dried basil		and deveined shrimp
½	teaspoon salt	8	cups mixed salad greens
¼	teaspoon freshly ground		Lemon wedges and
	black pepper		paprika for garnish

Combine oil, vinegar, mustard, paprika, sugar, basil, salt and pepper in a large bowl. Whisk until blended. Stir in onions, celery and garlic. Add shrimp, tossing to coat. Cover and refrigerate 3 hours.

To serve, drain shrimp and arrange on a bed of salad greens. Garnish with lemon wedges and paprika.

Serves 8

Deep South Shrimp Salad

¼ (8-ounce) package cream cheese

¾ cup chopped celery

½ cup chopped onion

¼ teaspoon black pepper

Dash of seasoning salt

¾ cup mayonnaise

2 pounds shrimp, cooked, peeled, deveined and chopped

Combine all ingredients except shrimp. Mix well. Fold in shrimp. Cover and refrigerate overnight for best flavor. Serve on croissants or on a bed of lettuce, garnished with parsley.

Serves 6

Breads

The *First* Building Over a Public Street

The Savannah Cotton Exchange was the *first* building in America to be constructed entirely over a public street and to have "air rights." The building was supported with iron columns and piers made of stone. Underneath, the ramp remained open to the river as was required. Thus, a lane was created called Factor's Row or Commerce Row, now called Factor's Walk (a factor was a cotton buyer). Small bridges connected the cotton warehouses, which were usually five stories high, down on River Street and two stories high from their sidewalks up on Bay Street. At that time, there were only two places in the world where cotton prices were set and quoted, Liverpool and Savannah. Cotton was king in the 1880's and Savannah was dubbed the "Wall Street of the South." Today, the Cotton Exchange is occupied by Solomon's Masonic Lodge #1. This is the oldest continuously operating lodge of freemasons in the Western Hemisphere. Established by James Oglethorpe on February 21, 1734, it still houses his personal Bible.

Spirited Savannah

Not far from the area where Eli Whitney invented the cotton gin, there is still one of the oldest plantations in the area, called Coldbrook. In *Savannah Spectres*, Margaret DeBolt relates several intriguing tales concerning two centuries of Coldbrook and its mostly unseen inhabitants. These stories were recounted by the caretakers of Coldbrook, Mr. and Mrs. Jaspar Cooler. Of the many stories, the tale of Eliza is the dearest. Once, when her little granddaughter was spending the night, the bed seemed very crowded. Mrs. Cooler asked her six year old granddaughter to move over, only to be told that another (unseen) little girl, named "Eliza," was sharing the bed. "Eliza" informed the granddaughter that she was nine years old and that she had to leave. Mrs. Cooler's curiosity continued until the *first* frost when it would be safe to explore the completely overgrown parts of the old Coldbrook cemetery. When she had made her way through the winter briars, Mrs. Cooler discovered a little headstone. The headstone read "Eliza Ann Ulmer, age nine, died April 1818."

"Hush Puppy! Hush Puppy!"

There are several versions of how the name "hush puppy" came to be. All, except one (later in this chapter), involve keeping a dog quiet with fried cornmeal balls. The classic version is that hunters and trappers traveling with their hunting dogs would keep them quiet with cornmeal batter fried in their cooking pot. As they threw these to the dogs (after they were cool!) they said "Hush Puppy." Plausible, but do wild men in the woods really use the word "puppy"?

Still another version comes from "federally occupied" Atlanta. There, a cook at one of the hotels used a plateful of fried cornmeal balls to "hush a puppy." The name was cute, so it stayed. Could be, but a plate full for a puppy? The name might have stuck, but the practice wouldn't have.

More than likely, the name and the practice arose in the old days from the need to carry food from the kitchen to the main houses. In those days, kitchens were detached to help prevent fires from spreading to the main houses. Everyone had dogs loose in the yards for protection. Therefore, it was very difficult to carry prepared food without being knocked down. Fried cornmeal balls carried in pockets could be tossed out as far as possible, allowing enough time to get across the yard. As the balls were tossed, the cooks called out "Hush Puppy, Hush Puppy."

Caramel-Pecan and Sour Cream Coffee Cake

Batter

1½	cups sugar	2	cups all-purpose flour
1	cup butter, softened	½	teaspoon baking soda
2	eggs, beaten	1	teaspoon baking powder
1	teaspoon vanilla	1	cup sour cream

Filling

1½	teaspoons cinnamon	1	cup finely chopped
⅓	cup brown sugar, firmly packed		pecans

Caramel Topping

½	cup butter	¾	cup brown sugar, firmly packed
6	tablespoons milk	1	cup finely chopped pecans

Preheat oven to 350 degrees. For batter, cream sugar and butter in a large bowl. Add eggs and vanilla. In a separate bowl, combine flour, baking soda and baking powder. Add dry ingredients and sour cream alternately to creamed mixture. Beat until fluffy.

Combine all filling ingredients in a small bowl. Pour half the batter into a greased and floured 9x13-inch baking dish. Spread evenly and sprinkle with half the filling. Spread remainder of batter over filling and sprinkle remaining filling on top. Bake 35 minutes.

Meanwhile, prepare caramel topping. Melt butter in a medium saucepan over medium heat. Add milk, sugar and pecans. Cook and stir 3 to 4 minutes, then remove from heat. When cake is done, pour caramel over top and spread evenly. Place under broiler for 3 minutes or until topping begins to bubble. Cool cake completely. To serve, cut into squares and place on a large platter.

Serve 24

Cake can be prepared one day ahead. Cover and refrigerate until ready to serve. Cut just before serving.

In 1793, Eli Whitney invented the first cotton gin at Mulberry Grove Plantation. This was the home of Caty Greene, widow of the revolutionary war hero, General Nathaniel Greene. Caty Greene encouraged Eli Whitney's desire to solve the time consuming problem of separating cottonseeds from the fiber. His invention, the cotton gin, was granted a patent by Thomas Jefferson himself. However, the gin was too easily duplicated, and Whitney did not make the money he deserved. Less well known is that Eli Whitney is regarded by many historians as the father of mass production in America.

A mythical guardian, the Griffin, stands in front of the Cotton Exchange protecting the treasures inside. With the head of a lion and the wings of an eagle, the griffin may also symbolize the connection between Britain (Lion) and America (Eagle) when cotton was King.

Apricot Cream Coffee Cake

Coffee Cake

1¾	cups all-purpose flour	½	teaspoon baking powder
½	cup sugar	½	teaspoon baking soda
¾	cup butter or margarine	¼	teaspoon salt
2	eggs	1	teaspoon vanilla

Filling

¼	cup sugar	1	teaspoon lemon zest
1	(8-ounce) package cream cheese, softened	1	(10-ounce) jar apricot preserves
1	egg		

Glaze

⅓	cup powdered sugar	2-3	teaspoons lemon juice

Preheat oven to 350 degrees. Combine all coffee cake ingredients in a large mixing bowl. Beat with an electric mixer on medium speed, scraping bowl often, for 1 to 2 minutes or until well mixed. Spread batter over bottom and 2 inches up sides of a greased and floured 10-inch springform pan.

To make filling, combine sugar, cream cheese, egg and zest in a small bowl. Beat on medium speed, scraping bowl often, for 2 to 3 minutes or until smooth. Pour filling over batter in pan. Spoon preserves evenly on top. Bake 45 to 55 minutes or until crust is golden brown. Cool 20 minutes before removing sides of pan.

Meanwhile, stir together powdered sugar and lemon juice until smooth. Drizzle glaze over warm coffee cake. Serve warm or cold. Store in refrigerator.

Serves 16

Lemon Frosted Breakfast Ring

2	(8-ounce) cans refrigerated crescent rolls	¼	cup sugar
		1	teaspoon cinnamon
3	tablespoons butter, melted	½	teaspoon mace
1	teaspoon lemon juice	1	teaspoon lemon zest

Topping

2	tablespoons plus 1 teaspoon lemon juice	1½	cups powdered sugar
		¼	cup chopped nuts
1	tablespoon lemon zest		

Preheat oven to 350 degrees. Unroll dough and separate into triangles. Combine butter and lemon juice and brush over triangles. Mix sugar, cinnamon, mace and zest. Sprinkle 1 teaspoon of mixture over each triangle. Roll each triangle into a crescent shape and place in a greased tube pan. Bake 30 minutes. Remove from pan.

Meanwhile, prepare topping. Combine lemon juice and zest and powdered sugar and drizzle over hot baked bread. Sprinkle with nuts.

Serves 8

Saints' Sticky Buns

2	(10-ounce) cans refrigerated flaky biscuits	1	cup brown sugar, firmly packed
		2	tablespoons water
½	cup margarine or butter	½	cup chopped pecans

Preheat oven to 350 degrees. Cut biscuits in half crosswise to form semi-circles. Melt margarine in a saucepan or in a bowl in the microwave. Add sugar, water and nuts and stir well. Pour half the mixture into a tube pan. Place half the biscuits in the pan, rounded side down. Pour remainder of sugar mixture over biscuits. Use remaining biscuits to form a top layer, rounded side down.

Bake 20 to 25 minutes. Cool slightly before turning pan onto a serving dish to remove buns.

Serves 8

Mini Cinnamon Rolls

2 (8-ounce) cans refrigerated crescent rolls

½ cup butter, melted

½ cup granulated sugar

2 teaspoons cinnamon

¼ cup raisins (optional)

1 cup powdered sugar

2 tablespoons apple juice or milk

Preheat oven to 350 degrees. Unroll dough and separate each roll into 4 rectangles. Press seams together to remove perforations. Brush rectangles with butter. Mix granulated sugar, cinnamon and raisins and sprinkle over rectangles. Roll each rectangle, starting at short end. Refrigerate until chilled.

Cut each roll into 5 slices and place, cut-side down, in an ungreased 9x13-inch baking pan. Bake 20 to 25 minutes or until golden brown. Mix powdered sugar and apple juice or milk to make a glaze. Drizzle glaze over warm rolls.

Makes 40 mini rolls

Strawberry Turnovers

1 pint strawberries, chopped

6 tablespoons strawberry jam

Zest of 1 lemon

12 slices thin, soft white bread, crusts removed

6 tablespoons butter, melted

Powdered sugar and sour cream for garnish

Preheat oven to 400 degrees. Combine strawberries, jam and zest in a bowl. Flatten bread slices with hand or a rolling pin. Mound a heaping tablespoon of strawberry mixture in center of each slice. Fold bread over to form a triangle. Brush both sides with melted butter and place on a baking sheet. Bake about 10 minutes, turning once half-way through, or until golden. Dust with powdered sugar. Serve with sour cream on the side.

Serves 12

For a "PBJ" snack, spread center of each bread slice with 1 teaspoon peanut butter before adding strawberry mixture.

Peachy Breakfast Loaf

1	(16-ounce) can sliced peaches in light syrup	⅓	cup milk
2½	cups flour	1	egg
¾	cup granulated sugar	3	tablespoons vegetable oil
3½	teaspoons baking powder	⅓	cup chopped walnuts
½	teaspoon allspice	¼	cup brown sugar, firmly packed
¼	teaspoon salt		

Preheat oven to 350 degrees. Drain peaches, reserving syrup. Set aside 5 peach slices for garnish, if desired. Puree remaining peach slices. Add enough of reserved syrup to puree to equal 1¼ cups.

In a large bowl, blend peach puree with flour, granulated sugar, baking powder, allspice, salt, milk, egg and oil. Beat 30 seconds or until ingredients are just moistened. Pour batter into a greased 9x5-inch loaf pan. Mix walnuts and brown sugar and sprinkle over batter.

Bake 70 minutes or until a toothpick inserted in the center comes out clean. Cool 10 minutes before removing from pan. Garnish with reserved peach slices. If preparing ahead, wrap and refrigerate loaf for up to 3 days. Garnish just before serving.

Makes 1 loaf

Moon River Melt Aways

2	cups flour	1	cup chopped pecans, plus
1	cup butter, softened		extra for topping
1	cup cottage cheese		(optional)
½	cup butter, melted	1	cup powdered sugar
1	cup granulated sugar	2	tablespoons milk
4	teaspoons cinnamon		

Combine flour, softened butter and cottage cheese into a dough; cover and refrigerate overnight.

When ready to bake, preheat oven to 350 degrees. Divide dough into quarters. Roll out each quarter with a rolling pin. Brush with ½ cup melted butter and sprinkle with a mixture of granulated sugar and cinnamon. Top with pecans. Cut dough into triangles. Roll triangles, starting with long end, into crescents and place on a baking sheet. Bake 12 to 15 minutes. Combine powdered sugar and milk to make a glaze. Drizzle glaze over rolls. Sprinkle with more pecans, if desired.

Makes 2 dozen

Instead of cutting into triangles, roll dough jelly-roll fashion and refrigerate until chilled. Slice and place on a baking sheet, cut side down. Bake as above.

Georgia Apple Pancakes

2	apples, unpeeled and	1	cup milk
	grated or finely chopped	¾	cup brown sugar, firmly
2	eggs		packed
1	teaspoon cinnamon	½	cup vegetable oil
2	cups pancake mix		

Preheat an electric skillet to about 325 degrees, or on medium-high heat.

Combine all ingredients except oil. Mix until smooth. Brush skillet with vegetable oil. Drop about 2 tablespoons of batter for each pancake onto skillet. Cook 2 minutes or until top is covered with bubbles. Turn and cook on other side. Drain on paper towels.

Serves 4

Orange Toast

½ cup butter, softened

½ cup sugar

1½ tablespoons orange zest

1 loaf thin white bread

Preheat oven to 325 degrees. Combine butter, sugar and zest. Spread evenly over both sides of bread slices and place on a baking sheet. Bake 15 to 20 minutes or until lightly browned. Cut each slice into 3 strips or into 4 triangles.

Makes 60 sticks or 80 triangles

Place coated bread on a baking sheet and freeze. Remove and place in plastic zip-top bags and return to freezer until ready to bake.

Our all-time favorite story about biscuits comes from The Savannah Cookbook: Since 1933 *by Harriet Ross Colquitt. A Northern visitor was seated at a fine Southern table when the biscuits were passed with instructions from the hostess, "Take two and butter them while they're hot." This visitor followed instructions to the letter, but just as he had finished buttering his biscuit, and was ready to take a bite, he would be stopped. "Don't eat that, it's cold! The hot ones are just coming in," said his hostess. Being polite, the visitor gave up his buttered biscuit for another hot one, which he then buttered, and which was then taken away from him, and so on. He never got to taste the biscuits. (So remember, never give up your biscuit!)*

Sweet Potato Biscuits

2	cups self-rising flour	1	cup cooked and mashed sweet potatoes
¼	cup sugar		
3	tablespoons shortening	⅓	cup milk
2	tablespoons butter		Softened butter for topping

Preheat oven to 400 degrees. Combine flour and sugar in a medium bowl. Cut in shortening and butter with a pastry blender until mixture resembles coarse meal. Add potatoes and milk and mix until dry ingredients are just moistened.

Turn dough out onto a lightly floured surface and knead 4 to 5 times. Roll dough to ½-inch thickness. Cut with a 2-inch biscuit cutter and place biscuits on lightly greased baking sheets. Bake 15 minutes or until golden brown. Remove from oven and brush tops with softened butter.

Makes 12 biscuits

One large sweet potato should yield about 1 cup mashed.

Sausage Pinwheels

1	(8-ounce) can refrigerated crescent rolls	8	ounces bulk sausage, cooked, crumbled and drained

Preheat oven to 375 degrees. Unroll dough and press seams together to remove perforations. Sprinkle sausage on top. Roll up jelly-roll fashion and pinch ends to seal. Cut into ½-inch slices and place on a baking sheet. Bake 8 to 10 minutes or until golden brown.

Makes 18 pinwheels

Grated Cheddar cheese can also be added with the sausage.

Bacon-and-Cheese Biscuits

1½	cups all-purpose flour	1	cup grated sharp
2½	teaspoons baking powder		Cheddar cheese
¼	teaspoon salt	¼	cup chopped onion
½	cup shortening	½	cup milk
12	slices bacon, cooked and crumbled		

Preheat oven to 425 degrees. Combine flour, baking powder and salt in a mixing bowl. Cut in shortening with a pastry blender until crumbly. Stir in crumbled bacon, cheese and onion. Add milk and stir until dry ingredients are just moistened.

Roll dough into a 9x8-inch rectangle, then cut into smaller 3x1-inch rectangles and place on a lightly greased baking sheet. Bake 12 minutes or until light brown.

Makes 2 dozen

Biscuits today are so much easier to make than years ago. Old timey receipts for "beaten biscuits" called for the dough to be beaten with an iron or marble pestle, until it blistered and separated. This took somewhere between three to five hundred "licks."

Flaky Dinner Biscuits

1	(8-count) package refrigerated buttermilk biscuits	½	cup butter, melted Poppy seeds

Preheat oven to 350 degrees. Cut biscuits in half crosswise and place on a baking sheet. Pour butter over biscuits and sprinkle with poppy seeds. Bake according to biscuit package directions. Remove from oven and cool 3 to 5 minutes, giving biscuits time to absorb butter. Serve.

Makes 16 biscuits

Line a tube pan with cut biscuits and pour butter over top. Sprinkle with sesame seeds. To serve, place a small bowl of honey in center of biscuit ring for dipping.

Savannah cooks are in agreement that the preparation of a perfect Southern biscuit is a gift of grace.

Lady and Sons Cheese Biscuits

2	cups self-rising flour	⅓	cup Crisco shortening
1	teaspoon baking powder	¾	cup grated Cheddar cheese
1	teaspoon sugar	1	cup buttermilk

Preheat oven to 350 degrees. Mix flour, baking powder and sugar in a bowl with a fork. Cut in shortening until mixture resembles cornmeal. Add cheese. Add buttermilk all at one time and mix until dry ingredients are just moistened. Do not overmix.

Drop batter by tablespoonfuls, or by using an ice cream scoop, onto a well-greased baking sheet. Bake 12 to 15 minutes. Serve with garlic butter, or for breakfast, with honey or honey butter.

Makes 8 large biscuits

Lady and Sons Garlic Butter

½	cup butter, melted	2	cloves garlic, crushed

Combine butter and garlic in a saucepan. Cook over medium heat until butter absorbs garlic. Brush over top of warm biscuits. Refrigerate leftovers.

Savannah Sour Cream Muffins

1	cup butter, softened	1	cup sour cream
2	cups self-rising flour		

Preheat oven to 350 degrees. Mix all ingredients together with a fork. Spoon batter into nonstick muffin tins. Bake 25 to 30 minutes or until light brown.

Makes 12

For variety, flavor muffins with chopped fresh dill, basil or thyme.

Paula H. Deen is the owner and proprietor of The Lady and Sons Restaurant, one of the most celebrated southern-cooking restaurants in Savannah. If you need the definition of Southern Cooking, you need only to stop in the Lady and Sons for a meal. "These biscuits have become one of our signature items at the Lady and Sons Restaurant. Everyone really looks forward to us bringing them out, whether it be after they are seated or while they are waiting in line" Paula Deen, from The Lady and Sons: Savannah Country Cookbook.

Hush Your Mouth Hush Puppies

1½	cups cornmeal	2	tablespoons vegetable oil
½	cup all-purpose flour	⅓-½	cup minced onion, or
1	teaspoon salt		2 green onion tops,
1	teaspoon baking powder		minced
½-¾	cup milk		Vegetable oil for frying
1	egg, beaten		

Sift cornmeal, flour, salt and baking powder together into a large bowl. Combine ½ cup milk, egg, 2 tablespoons oil and minced onion in a separate bowl. Mix milk mixture with dry ingredients, adding up to ¼ cup more milk if needed. Batter should be able to drop from a spoon.

Heat 2 to 3 inches of oil in a skillet or deep fat fryer to 375 degrees. Drop rounded teaspoonfuls of batter into hot oil. Fry 3 minutes or until golden brown. Remove from oil with a slotted spoon and drain on paper towels. Be sure oil returns to cooking temperature between batches. Serve hot with tartar sauce.

Makes about 2 dozen

One most unusual account about hush puppies is that they originated in 1727, in New Orleans. They were developed by a group of French nuns who called them "croquettes de maise." From there hush puppies were said to have spread throughout the South. While this is possible, it is not likely. Probably, everyone was simply being polite.

Tartar Sauce

1	cup mayonnaise	1	tablespoon capers,
3	tablespoons dill pickle,		chopped
	chopped		Red pepper
3	tablespoons onion,		Salt
	chopped		Lemon juice

Mix mayonnaise, dill pickle, onion and capers until well blended. Add red pepper, salt and lemon juice to taste. Chill well before serving. Can be kept in refrigerator for up to 2 weeks.

For a variation, mix 1 cup mayonnaise with ½ cup chopped dill pickle, ¼ teaspoon garlic powder and ¼ teaspoon black pepper.

Crab Fritters

1	cup biscuit mix	1	egg, beaten
¾	teaspoon salt	2	tablespoons fresh lemon juice
⅛	teaspoon garlic powder		
½	teaspoon cayenne pepper	¼	teaspoon Worcestershire sauce
1	tablespoon chopped fresh parsley		
½	teaspoon lemon zest	1	pound fresh crabmeat, drained and picked over
¼	cup milk		Vegetable oil for frying

Combine biscuit mix, salt, garlic powder, cayenne pepper, parsley and lemon zest in a large bowl. Make a well in center of mixture. Mix milk, egg, lemon juice and Worcestershire sauce. Pour milk mixture into well in dry ingredients and stir until just moistened. Mix in crabmeat.

Heat 2 to 3 inches of oil in a Dutch oven or deep fryer to 375 degrees. Drop teaspoonfuls of batter into hot oil a few at a time. Fry 30 seconds or until golden brown, turning once. Serve immediately with Creole Sauce, Pineapple Jalapeño Dipping Sauce or Creole Rémoulade Sauce.

Creole Sauce

Stir together ½ cup Creole mustard, ¼ cup mayonnaise, 1 teaspoon lemon juice, ½ teaspoon hot pepper sauce and ¼ teaspoon black pepper.

Pineapple Jalapeño Dipping Sauce

Peel, core and cut 1 whole pineapple into chunks. Combine pineapple with 1 diced jalapeño pepper, ½ cup brown sugar and ½ cup water in a saucepan. Cook and stir over medium heat until pineapple is softened. Cool slightly, then puree in a blender. Serve at room temperature. Store for up to several days in refrigerator. Also good as a salsa with pork tenderloin.

Creole Rémoulade Sauce

¼ cup lemon juice

¼ cup tarragon vinegar

¼ cup Creole mustard

¼ cup horseradish

¾ cup ketchup

1¼ cups mayonnaise

½ cup minced green onion

½ cup finely chopped celery

¼ teaspoon garlic powder

¼ teaspoon hot pepper sauce

¼ teaspoon dried oregano

¼ teaspoon dried basil

2 tablespoons paprika

Combine lemon juice and vinegar in a blender. Add mustard and horseradish and blend. With blender on low, add ketchup, mayonnaise, onion, celery, garlic powder, pepper sauce, oregano, basil and paprika. Chill before serving. Delicious with boiled shrimp.

Makes about 2 cups

Pecan Cornbread

4	tablespoons unsalted butter	1¼	cups all-purpose flour
1-1½	cups buttermilk	1	teaspoon baking soda
1	extra large egg, beaten	1	teaspoon baking powder
½	teaspoon vanilla	2	tablespoons sugar
1	tablespoon dark rum	¾	teaspoon salt
¾	cup fine stone-ground cornmeal	½	cup coarsely chopped pecans, toasted

Preheat oven to 350 degrees. Melt butter in an 8-inch cast-iron skillet over high heat. Swirl pan to coat sides with butter and pour excess butter into a large mixing bowl; cool. When cool, whisk buttermilk, egg, vanilla and rum into butter in bowl. In a separate bowl, combine cornmeal, flour, baking soda, baking powder, sugar, salt and pecans. Mix well and add to milk mixture. Stir with a wooden spoon just until moistened. Pour batter into buttered skillet and place in oven. Bake 30 minutes or until firm and golden brown and until a toothpick inserted near the center comes out clean. Cool 3 minutes before inverting onto a round serving platter. Cut into wedges and serve with Whipped Orange or Tangerine Butter.

Serve 8

Broccoli Cheese Corn Muffins

6	ounces cottage cheese	1	(10-ounce) package frozen chopped broccoli, thawed and drained on paper towels
½	cup butter or margarine, melted		
4	eggs, well beaten	1	large onion, diced
1	teaspoon salt	1	(7-ounce) package corn muffin mix

Preheat oven to 400 degrees. Combine cottage cheese, butter, eggs and salt. Stir in broccoli, onion and muffin mix until just moistened. Do not overmix. Spoon batter into greased muffin tins. Bake 20 to 25 minutes.

Makes 12

Whipped Orange or Tangerine Butter

Orange Butter

½ cup butter, softened

2 tablespoons orange juice concentrate

2 tablespoons powdered sugar

1½ tablespoons orange zest

Tangerine Butter

½ cup butter, softened

2 tablespoons fresh tangerine juice

2 tablespoons honey

1½ teaspoons tangerine zest

For either option, combine all ingredients in a food processor. Blend until smooth. Transfer to a small serving bowl and chill until ready to serve.

Makes ¾ cup

These butters can be served with biscuits, muffins, pancakes, waffles or crêpes.

The Southern preference for cornbread over wheat bread is said to have developed during the War Between the States, when Union blockades kept wheat from the Southern region. Since corn, which originated in Mexico three to four thousand years ago, had been cultivated for some time by the Southern Colonists, this was no real hardship.

Jalapeño Cornmeal Muffins

1	egg, room temperature	½	teaspoon salt
½	cup butter, melted	2	tablespoons sugar
¼	cup vegetable oil	1-3	tablespoons seeded and minced jalapeño pepper
1	cup milk, warmed	2	tablespoons diced green onion (optional)
1	cup cake flour		
⅔	cup yellow cornmeal		
1	tablespoon baking powder		

Preheat oven to 400 degrees. Whisk together egg, butter and oil in a large bowl until well blended. Stir in milk. In a separate bowl, combine flour, cornmeal, baking powder, salt and sugar. Mix well. Add dry ingredients, jalapeño and onion to milk mixture. Stir until just blended.

Spoon batter into muffin tins lined with foil muffin liners, filling three-fourths full. Bake 15 to 20 minutes or until edges of muffins are slightly golden and a knife inserted into the center comes out clean. Serve hot or cool on racks.

Makes 12 muffins

DeSoto Cornbread Pie

1	cup butter, softened	½	cup grated Monterey Jack cheese
½	cup sugar	½	cup grated mild Cheddar cheese
4	eggs	1	cup all-purpose flour
1	(4-ounce) can chopped green chiles	1	cup yellow cornmeal
1	(16-ounce) can cream-style golden corn	4	teaspoons baking powder
		¼	teaspoon salt

Preheat oven to 300 degrees. Cream butter and sugar. Add eggs, 1 at a time, mixing well between additions. Mix in chiles, corn and cheeses. In a separate bowl, combine flour, cornmeal, baking powder and salt. Add dry ingredients to corn mixture and blend well. Pour batter into a greased and floured 9x13-inch baking dish. Bake 1 hour. Serve warm or at room temperature.

Serves 8 to 10

Spinach Cheese Bread

1	loaf French bread	1	egg, beaten
	Butter, softened	1	(10-ounce) package frozen
	Garlic salt		chopped spinach,
1	(8-ounce) package grated		thawed and drained
	mozzarella cheese		Parmesan cheese
1	(8-ounce) package grated		
	Cheddar cheese		

Preheat oven to 350 degrees. Cut bread in half lengthwise. Spread butter over cut side of both halves. Sprinkle with garlic salt and place on a baking sheet.

In a mixing bowl, combine mozzarella and Cheddar cheeses, egg and spinach. Spread mixture over bread halves. Bake 30 minutes. Sprinkle with Parmesan cheese during last 10 minutes. Serve hot.

Serves 10

Substitute a 12-ounce package of drained artichoke hearts for the spinach.

Zucchini Nut Bread

3	eggs, beaten	3	cups flour
1	cup oil	1	teaspoon salt
2½	cups sugar	1	teaspoon baking soda
2	cups peeled and grated	1	teaspoon baking powder
	zucchini	1	tablespoon cinnamon
1	tablespoon vanilla	½	cup chopped nuts

Preheat oven to 325 degrees. Combine eggs, oil, sugar, zucchini and vanilla in a mixing bowl. Mix thoroughly. Add flour, salt, baking soda, baking powder, cinnamon and nuts. Beat well. Transfer batter to greased loaf pans. Bake 1 hour. Freezes well.

Makes 2 loaves

A 20-ounce can of drained crushed pineapple can also be added to the batter.

Garlic Cheese Spread

For a quick garlic cheese spread, combine an 8-ounce package of softened cream cheese, a 10-ounce jar of Cheese Whiz and garlic powder to taste. Mix until well blended. Serve with sliced or torn French bread.

French Loaf with Italian Oil

Combine ½ cup extra-virgin olive oil, 1 large minced clove of garlic, 10 finely chopped basil leaves and freshly cracked black pepper to taste in a bowl. Mix well. Serve with a large loaf of French bread torn into bite-size pieces.

Bay Street Brown Bread

3	cups whole wheat flour	1	teaspoon salt
½	cup sugar	1	cup raisins
¾	cup light molasses	¾	cup coarsely chopped
2	cups sour milk		walnuts
2	teaspoons baking soda		

Preheat oven to 325 degrees. Combine all ingredients in order listed in a large mixing bowl. Turn mixture into two greased 9x5-inch loaf pans. Bake 35 minutes.

To sour milk, pour 1 tablespoon lemon juice or white vinegar into a glass measuring cup. Fill cup with room temperature milk. Stir and let stand 10 minutes.

Makes 2 loaves

Strawberry Honey Butter

1	pint strawberries, hulled	1	teaspoon fresh lime juice
3	tablespoons honey	¾	cup unsalted butter,
1	teaspoon sugar		slightly softened

Puree strawberries in a food processor or blender and strain through a fine sieve. Place strained berries in a medium saucepan. Add honey, sugar and lime juice. Bring to a boil. Cook and stir 3 minutes or until thickened. Cool to room temperature.

Combine cooled mixture and butter in a medium bowl. Cover and let stand 1 hour, or store in refrigerator for up to 2 days or freezer for up to 2 months. Serve with scones, croissants or rolls.

Makes about 1 cup

For Orange Honey Butter, substitute 1 tablespoon orange juice and the zest of 1 orange for the strawberries.

What did Eli Whitney, inventor of the cotton gin, say to his wife?

"Keep your cotton picking hands off of my gin."

(Old Georgia joke)

Honey should not be refrigerated. Place the jar in hot water if it crystallizes. This will dissolve the crystals. Before measuring honey, oil measuring cup or spoon and honey will slide out.

Eggs and Cheese

The *First* Newspaper in the Colony

"The Georgia Gazette" was the *first* newspaper in the Colony.
It was *first* published on April 7, 1763, by an enterprising young Scot named Johnson
(or Johnston). Johnson soon set up shop, and at 25, he was able to start publishing a
newspaper. "The Georgia Gazette" soon carried advertisements for 32 different merchants.
However, The Stamp Act of 1765, also included taxation on newspapers. Johnson closed down
"The Georgia Gazette" and it re-emerged as "The Royal Georgia Gazette" (possibly to avoid
some taxation). Although he strove to fairly present both sides as the War for American
Independence brewed, Johnson was considered loyal to the Crown. James Johnson "fled"
Savannah in 1782. Still thought to have been a Loyalist, he was "forever banned" from
the State of Georgia. Friends and family pled his case, and he returned to Georgia. By 1783,
he was the appointed printer - again. He soon began publishing "The Gazette of the
State of Georgia." The newspaper ceased upon his death in 1802.

Spirited Savannah

The fair city of Savannah may be the only one to have flourished under a curse. About 1818, a young physician and publisher, Dr. John M. Harney, had started a newspaper, which he called "The Georgian." Reception for "The Georgian" went from bad to worse. Bitterly, Harney sold the newspaper in 1820, but not before having his say about the demise of Savannah. At that time, Savannah had suffered set backs in shipping, due to a national depression in 1819. It had also survived the great fire and yellow fever epidemic of 1820, with heavy casualties. These events notwithstanding, Harney published a vengeful "poem" on the last day of his newspaper. The final words of this "Curse on Savannah" were, "I leave you, Savannah, a curse that is far the worst of all curses - to remain as you are!" Today, almost 270 years after Savannah was founded, 22 of her original 24 squares have been, or are being restored, with considerable historical accuracy. People come from all over the world to see this most beautiful National Historic Landmark, which has strived - to remain as it was. Thus, a curse became a blessing instead.

"The Yes You Can Show Off Cheese Soufflé"

Julia Child once said that if you can do cakes, you can do soufflés. Granted, she was not talking about cake mixes. What you really need to know about soufflés is yourself. If you are the tiptoe, delicate type, a soufflé is too nerve-wracking. If you are a shoot from the hip type, a soufflé is too sensitive.

However...if you like a bit of a challenge, read on for some soufflé secrets.

1. Soufflés can be prepared up to two hours before baking. Keep covered and cool, not cold.

2. Cheese needs to be strong flavored. American = Cheddar or European = Swiss or Gruyère.

3. Preparation is done either slowly or quickly, no middle ground.

4. Egg whites must be fresh, stiff-peaked and shiny.

5. Add one or two extra peaked egg whites to the cheese mixture before folding the rest of the egg whites.

6. Soufflé dish must be no more than 6 or 7 inches in diameter.

7. Have a contingency plan. (A back-up microwaveable casserole is nice!)

Here's a bit of the showy part. Before baking, arrange foil around the outside of the soufflé dish three inches above the rim, for a collar. Secure with pins and butter the inside. Also showy but easier, is a "top hat". Just before baking, make an inner circle with a spoon, 1 inch deep, and 1 inch from the edge of the soufflé dish.

Now you have an hour to recover. Keep a "so-what-if" attitude. If it falls, it's a good appetizer, cut into pieces. If it's too runny, it isn't a bad spread, re-mixed in the processor with some extra butter. If either happens, quickly pour wine and slowly drink it.

Praline French Toast

1	(1-pound) loaf French bread	1	cup milk
8	eggs or 2 cups egg substitute	2	tablespoons sugar
1	cup half-and-half or evaporated milk	1	teaspoon vanilla
		¼	teaspoon cinnamon
		¼	teaspoon nutmeg
			Dash of salt

Praline Topping

1	cup butter, softened	2	tablespoons light corn syrup
1	cup light brown sugar, firmly packed	½	teaspoon cinnamon
1	cup chopped pecans	½	teaspoon nutmeg

Cut bread into 20 (1-inch thick) slices. Arrange slices, overlapping, in two rows in a well-greased 9x13-inch deep baking dish. In a large bowl, combine eggs, half-and-half, milk, sugar, vanilla, cinnamon, nutmeg and salt. Whisk until blended but not too bubbly. Pour mixture evenly over bread, spooning mixture between slices. Cover with foil and refrigerate overnight.

When ready to bake, preheat oven to 350 degrees. Combine all praline topping ingredients in a medium bowl. Spread topping over bread. Bake 40 minutes or until puffed and lightly golden. Serve with maple syrup or honey.

Serves 6

This recipe should be made ahead and refrigerated overnight.

Excellent breakfast for a large group.

Maple Syrup

When buying pure maple syrup, be sure to read the labels since many contain large amounts of cane and little maple syrup. Finer grades of maple syrup are light in color, and contain more flavor than the darker grades.

Baked Pineapple Pancakes and Sausage

3	eggs	3	tablespoons margarine, melted
1½	cups milk		
1¾	cups sifted flour	1	cup crushed pineapple, drained
4	teaspoons baking powder		
1½	tablespoons sugar	1	pound brown and serve sausage patties
1½	teaspoons salt		

Preheat oven to 450 degrees. Beat eggs until light and fluffy. Add milk. In a separate bowl, sift together flour, baking powder, sugar and salt. Add dry ingredients to egg mixture and beat until batter is smooth. Fold in margarine and pineapple. Pour into a greased 10x15x1-inch baking pan. Arrange sausage on batter. Bake 20 minutes. Cut into squares and serve hot.

Serves 8

This recipe can be prepared ahead and refrigerated overnight.

Saints' Sunrise Sausage and Eggs

8	ounces sharp Cheddar cheese, sliced	1	cup sour cream
		1	pound hot bulk sausage, cooked and drained
¾	teaspoon dry mustard		
¾	teaspoon paprika	10	eggs
1	teaspoon salt	8	ounces sharp Cheddar cheese, grated
½	teaspoon black pepper		

Preheat oven to 325 degrees. Arrange cheese slices to cover the bottom of a 10x6x2-inch baking dish. Combine mustard, paprika, salt, pepper and sour cream. Spread half of mixture over cheese. Sprinkle evenly with crumbled sausage. Break eggs on top of sausage. Spread remaining sour cream over eggs. Sprinkle with grated cheese. Bake 30 to 40 minutes or until eggs are firm.

Serves 6

Sliced, hard-cooked eggs can be used in place of raw eggs.

Savannah is the birthplace of many celebrities of world renown. Johnny Mercer, the brilliant songwriter, grew up in Savannah, and always had a house to come home to...on the Moon River. Flannery O'Conner was born in Savannah, though she spent her years as a writer in Milledgeville. Conrad Aiken, poet and writer, was one Savannahian who won a Pulitzer Prize. Journalist Albert Scardino is another. There is Charles Coburn, the actor, and Ted Turner, a gentleman of many enterprises. Two Supreme Court Justices, James M. Wayne a century ago, and now Clarence Thomas, round out this list of Savannah celebs.

Fresh Mushroom, Bacon and Egg Puff

4	cups day-old white or French bread cubes	¼	teaspoon onion powder
			Dash of black pepper
2	cups grated Cheddar cheese	10	slices bacon, cooked and crumbled
10	eggs, lightly beaten	½	cup sliced fresh mushrooms
4	cups milk	½	cup chopped tomato
1	teaspoon dry mustard		
1	teaspoon salt		

Arrange bread cubes in a well-greased 9x13-inch baking dish. Sprinkle with cheese. Beat together eggs, milk, mustard, salt, onion powder and pepper in a large bowl. Pour mixture evenly over cheese. Sprinkle with bacon, mushrooms and tomato. Cover and refrigerate overnight.

When ready to bake, preheat oven to 325 degrees. Bake, uncovered, for 1 hour, 15 minutes or until set. Tent with foil, if necessary, to prevent overbrowning.

Serves 8 to 10

Baked Egg in Herbed Tomato

1	firm, ripe tomato	1	slice white bread, toasted and buttered, crust removed
	Salt and pepper to taste		
1	teaspoon finely chopped onion	1	egg
¼	teaspoon chopped fresh parsley	1	tablespoon grated Swiss or Cheddar cheese
2	teaspoons finely chopped ham	¼	teaspoon basil

Preheat oven to 400 degrees. Cut a thin slice from stem end of tomato and scoop out seeds. Season inside of tomato with salt and pepper. Mix onion, parsley and ham and spoon into tomato. Place tomato on buttered toast in a small baking dish. Break egg into tomato. Sprinkle with cheese and basil. Bake 12 minutes or until egg is set and cheese is melted and browned.

Serves 1

It is interesting to note that many of those in Savannah's St. Patrick's Day parade will be seen in their Irish Greens on March 17, and then be seen in their kilts and tartans at the Savannah Scottish Games (the 2nd weekend in May).

A little Gaelic note: the word "Scotch" is only used to describe eggs fried with sausage, whiskey (the elixir of life), and in the US, a brand of cellophane tape. All else is Scottish.

Revivals and reunions have always played a major role in the lives of Southern families. In days gone by, the arrival of summer brought about plans for revivals, camp meetings and the much-anticipated "dinner on the grounds." Social halls were emptied of their folding chairs and tables as the men of the church set them up outside in the shade of the live oak trees. Proper planning was essential for the ladies so as to be able to have the platters of fried chicken, fresh vegetables, and red rice ready the moment the benediction was over. No outside meal would ever be considered ready until the plates of chilled deviled eggs (sometimes called stuffed eggs) were in place. No matter how many platters of these were prepared, there never seemed to be enough.

Ham Devils

6	hard-cooked eggs	3	tablespoons finely chopped cooked ham
2	tablespoons mayonnaise		
2	tablespoons cream cheese, softened	2¼	teaspoons chopped fresh dill
1	teaspoon prepared mustard	½	teaspoon caraway seeds
1	teaspoon lemon juice		Fresh dill sprigs for garnish

Slice eggs in half lengthwise. Carefully remove yolks, reserving white shells. Mash yolks. Stir in mayonnaise, cream cheese, mustard and lemon juice until smooth. Mix in ham, dill and caraway seeds. Spoon mixture into egg white shells. Garnish with dill sprigs.

Makes 1 dozen

Country Breakfast Pie

1	pound bulk sausage, cooked, crumbled and drained	¼	cup chopped green bell pepper
1½	cups grated Swiss cheese	¼	cup chopped red bell pepper
1	(9-inch) deep-dish pie crust	2	tablespoons chopped onion
4	eggs	1	cup light cream
			Sliced tomato (optional)

Preheat oven to 375 degrees. Mix sausage and cheese and sprinkle in pie crust. Lightly beat eggs in a mixing bowl. Add bell peppers, onion and cream to eggs. Pour mixture into pie crust. Top with tomato slices, if using. Bake 40 to 45 minutes. Cool on a rack 10 minutes.

Serves 6 to 8

Scotch Eggs

10	ounces bulk sausage	1	egg, beaten
1	onion, finely chopped		Bread crumbs
4	hard-cooked eggs, peeled		Vegetable oil for frying
	Flour		

Combine sausage and onion in a bowl. Dust eggs with flour. Press sausage mixture around each egg to cover, keeping the shape of the egg. Dip coated eggs in beaten egg, then roll in bread crumbs. Fry eggs in hot vegetable oil for 7 minutes. Drain on paper towels. Serve eggs sliced in half with a salad.

Serves 4

Also good for Easter morning.

Crab-Cheese Puff

6	slices white bread, crusts trimmed and cut into small cubes	4	tablespoons butter, melted
		3	eggs
1	pound crabmeat, or 2 (6-ounce) cans, drained	2	cups milk
		½	teaspoon salt or to taste
1	(8-ounce) package Old English processed cheese, chopped or 1 cup grated Cheddar cheese	½	teaspoon dry mustard or to taste

Preheat oven to 350 degrees. Layer bread cubes, crab and cheese in greased 2-quart casserole dish. Top with melted butter. Beat eggs, milk, salt and mustard together and pour over layers. If making ahead, cover and refrigerate until ready to bake. Bake 1 hour or until golden and puffy.

Serves 4

Serve as a brunch dish without the crab, with broiled tomatoes and link sausage.

The Savannah Scottish Games celebrated its 25th anniversary in 2001. One of the highlights of the Games throughout the South was a Scotch egg from Hamish, "The Frying Scotsman." As Hamish had passed on just before the Savannah 25th anniversary, a special tribute was given to him at the Scottish Games, as well as at the Ceildh ("Kay-lee," song and dance fest) in the evening. This illustrates quite well the deep connection which the Scots (in particular, the Highlanders) have for one another, and for their Gaelic heritage.

Crab Quiche

¼	cup minced green onion	4	eggs
3	tablespoons butter	1	cup light cream
1½	cups crabmeat	1	pie crust
¼	teaspoon salt	1	egg white, beaten
	Pinch of white pepper	½	cup grated Gruyère
3	tablespoons dry sherry		cheese

Preheat oven to 375 degrees. Sauté onion in butter until tender but not browned. Add crab, cook and stir 2 minutes. Sprinkle with salt and pepper. Add sherry. Increase heat and bring to a boil for a moment, then remove from heat and cool slightly. Beat together eggs and cream. Gradually add crab mixture. Adjust seasonings as desired. Brush pie crust with egg white. Pour egg mixture into crust. Sprinkle with cheese. Bake 25 to 30 minutes or until quiche is puffed and browned.

6 to 8 servings

Hangtown Fry

1	pint oysters	¼	cup beer
3	tablespoons chopped onion	¼	teaspoon salt
		¼	teaspoon Tabasco sauce
4	tablespoons butter or margarine	¼	teaspoon garlic salt
6	eggs	4	slices bacon, cooked and crumbled

Drain oysters and pat dry with paper towels. Sauté onion in butter in a large heavy skillet until transparent. Add oysters and cook just until edges begin to curl. Remove skillet from heat. In a mixing bowl, beat eggs with beer, salt, Tabasco sauce, garlic salt and bacon. Pour egg mixture over oysters in skillet. Return to low heat and cook, stirring constantly, until eggs are set.

Serves 6

Quiche is one of those great foods that can be easily modified. A quiche is a pastry shell filled with eggs, milk, seasonings, and you determine the other ingredients. Quiches can also be served as an appetizer when you fill individual pastry shells, quichettes. You can create vegetarian, seafood, or meat and cheese variations.

When slicing hard-boiled eggs, wet the knife to keep the egg yolks from crumbling.

Hash Brown Brunch Pie

1	pound bulk pork sausage	8-10	eggs
½	(16-ounce) package frozen hash brown potatoes, thawed	¾	cup half-and-half Salt and pepper to taste

Preheat oven to 350 degrees. Brown sausage in a skillet, stirring to crumble. Transfer sausage to a plate, reserving fat in skillet. Add potatoes to skillet and cook until softened. Transfer potatoes to a deep-dish pie pan using a slotted spoon. Mold potatoes in pan to form a crust. Arrange sausage over potatoes.

Combine eggs, half-and-half, salt and pepper in a mixing bowl. Beat until frothy. Pour mixture over sausage. Bake 25 to 30 minutes or until set.

Serves 6

Sundance Eggs Enchiladas

4	flour tortillas	2	medium tomatoes, peeled, seeded and chopped
8	eggs		
2	teaspoons water	1	(4-ounce) can chopped green chiles, drained
¼	teaspoon salt		
1	tablespoon butter or margarine	1	cup grated Monterey Jack cheese
½	cup chopped green onion	4	tablespoons taco sauce Sour cream (optional)

Preheat oven to 350 degrees. Wrap tortillas in foil. Bake 5 minutes or until warm. (For crispier tortillas, fry each in a small amount of oil, turning frequently, until golden brown.)

Meanwhile, combine eggs, water and salt in a medium bowl. Beat well. In a large skillet, melt butter. Add egg mixture and cook, stirring occasionally, until eggs are almost set. Remove from heat. Place warm tortillas on a large ungreased baking sheet. Divide egg mixture, onion, tomatoes, chiles and cheese among tortillas. Roll up tortillas. Bake 5 to 10 minutes or until cheese melts and enchiladas are very warm. Top each with 1 tablespoon taco sauce and sour cream.

Serves 4

For an Easy Cheesy Soufflé with extra flavor in half the time: use 1 (11-oz) can Cheddar Cheese Soup, 1 cup sharp (or extra sharp) shredded cheddar cheese, and four eggs separated.

Mix soup and cheese in a heavy saucepan and cook, on low, until cheese is melted. Remove from heat and set aside. Beat egg yolks until they are thick and lemon colored. Now, slowly add the cheese mixture to the beaten egg yolks, stirring constantly. Beat egg whites until stiff peaks form, and then gently fold the cheese and egg yolk mixture into the egg whites. Pour into an ungreased, 2-qt. soufflé dish or a deep casserole dish. Bake in a slow oven (preheated 300 degrees) for one hour or until an inserted knife comes out clean. Serve immediately. Serves four to six people who will be sure that you are a gourmet chef.

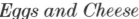

Georgia Ramble

8	ounces extra-sharp Cheddar cheese, grated	1	teaspoon Worcestershire sauce
4	ounces chopped pimento, drained	3	tablespoons onion, minced
			Tabasco sauce, to taste

Combine cheese, pimento, Worcestershire sauce, onion and Tabasco in a food processor until well blended. Chill and serve with crackers.

This "kicked-up" version of pimento cheese can be stored in the refrigerator for up to 2 weeks.

Broccoli Brunch Casserole

8	slices white bread, cubed	2	cups cubed ham
¾	cup butter, melted	4	eggs
1	(8-ounce) package grated sharp Cheddar cheese	2	cups milk
2	cups chopped broccoli, cooked and well drained	1	teaspoon salt
		½	teaspoon black pepper

Toss bread cubes with butter until evenly coated. In a greased 9x13-inch casserole dish, assemble the following layers: half the bread cubes, half the cheese, half the broccoli, all of ham, remaining broccoli, remaining cheese and remaining bread cubes. In a mixing bowl, beat eggs with milk, salt and pepper. Pour mixture over layers. Cover and refrigerate at least 2 hours or overnight.

When ready to bake, preheat oven to 350 degrees. Bake 1 hour or until puffy and nicely browned.

Serves 6

This dish must be prepared ahead. It is a great recipe for using leftover holiday ham. Perfect for a luncheon or light supper.

Pimento Cheese

"Ask any Southerner to name the most nostalgic preparations of his or her youth and I guarantee that pimento cheese will be listed right along with fried chicken, turnip greens, grits and pecan pie."
James Villas,
My Mother's Southern Kitchen, 1994.

Once a concoction associated only with Southern cooking and homemade mayonnaise, pimento cheese conjures up memories of childhood sandwiches on soft white bread yet it now appears to have made the transition onto the appetizer or luncheon menu as well.

Vegetables

The *First* Art Museum

The Telfair Academy of Arts and Sciences is the *first* art museum in the Southeast. "Telfair," as it is called, was originally the home of Alexander Telfair, one of Savannah's foremost "Merchant Princes" and planters. Designed by William Jay, the house was completed in 1820, and is a grand example of the Neoclassical Regency style. Upon Alexander Telfair's death in 1832, the house was inherited by his sisters, Mary and Margaret, both of whom were among the *first* patrons of the arts in Savannah. In 1886, Mary Telfair's vision was implemented, when in accordance with her will, the "Telfair Academy of Arts and Sciences" was opened to the public. It continues under the auspices of the Georgia Historical Society, which was organized in 1839.

Spirited Savannah

Mary Telfair's will specifically prohibited "amusements" of any sort, such as eating, drinking, or smoking at both Hodgson Hall and the Telfair Museum. Once, when inclement weather sent guests inside Hodgson Hall, along with their "amusements," far more than a simple thundershower ensued. Strange winds blew through closed rooms, glasses shattered and mysterious voices were heard. Any of the prohibited "amusements" now take place in the newer annex at Hodgson Hall, with few exceptions. As to the Telfair Museum, it is agreed by many that Mary Telfair is still very much in residence, albeit in spirit. Glimpses of Mary and her guests, the sounds of a harp where there is none and the opening and shutting of doors by someone unseen, have all been reported on a fairly regular basis. Even the security alarms have been triggered for reasons unknown. Above all else though, Mary Telfair's portrait must remain in the dining room. This is to avoid any further damage to the museum, as was done when the portrait was moved once before.

"The Veritable Art of Southern Vegetables"

Vegetables are so important to Southern cooking that the meat is sometimes an afterthought or left out altogether. This is especially true during the summer season when we fairly immerse ourselves in vegetables. When such an abundance is available, we bring the presentation and preparation of vegetables to a high art. This can range from the most elaborate gourmet medleys, to fresh vegetables simply sliced and served... with just a little salt, because it would be a crime to do anything else while they are "so in season."

It is this fine designation, "so in season," that explains our particular relationship with vegetables – very particular. We live within an agrarian region, with a warm climate and a long growing season. We're spoiled, and we know it. We know how the vegetables are supposed to look, feel, smell, and taste. We'll sound off if something isn't right, as though someone is trying to pull a fast one on us (or on the grocer, if we're fond of him.) "You know these would not be so anemic if those people hadn't been in such a hurry to make money on them…."tsk."

"Those people" applies to the unknown gardener, about whom we are naturally suspicious. These are the same people who have been trying to sell us hydroponics for years. While we are glad that modern technologies have made most vegetables available year round, they are still not up to "in season" standards to us. Something within Southerners cannot be completely satisfied unless vegetables are brought in fresh, straight from the garden (the produce stand is a very close second here.) A sprinkling of soil still on their surfaces is like a seal of approval. Now these most perfect garden vegetables are fresh and beautiful enough to grace our tables artfully. They have also been tended well enough to be assuredly delicious.

Sautéed Asparagus

½	cup butter	2	pounds asparagus, trimmed
1	teaspoon garlic powder		
½	teaspoon seasoning salt	¾	cup freshly grated Parmesan cheese
	Salt and pepper to taste		

Melt butter in a large saucepan over medium-low heat. Stir in garlic powder, seasoning salt, salt and pepper until well blended. Add asparagus and toss to coat. Sauté 5 minutes or until crisp-tender. Sprinkle with cheese and remove from heat. Toss to allow cheese to melt. Serve immediately.

Serves 4 to 6

Bodacious Baked Beans

1	pound kielbasa sausage, sliced	1	tablespoon Worcestershire sauce
1	pound ground beef	1	tablespoon prepared mustard
½	cup chopped onion	⅔	cup ketchup
2	(28-ounce) cans baked beans	10	slices bacon, cooked and crumbled
¼	cup molasses		
½	cup brown sugar, firmly packed		

Preheat oven to 350 degrees. Brown sausage in a skillet. Remove sausage and set aside. Add beef and onion to skillet and cook until browned; drain fat. Combine beef mixture, sausage, beans, molasses, sugar, Worcestershire sauce, mustard, ketchup and bacon in a large casserole dish. Bake, uncovered, for 30 minutes.

Serves 10

Original drawings done by the mystic poet Khalil Gibran for his 1923 work, The Prophet, *are part of the Telfair collection. These fragile pencil drawings are on display intermittently. Mary Haskell, Khalil Gibran's patroness, was a Savannahian in her later years.*

Southern Baked Beans

No Southern Bar-B-Q is complete without baked beans. One reason baked beans are so popular is that there are so many ways to prepare them. Whether with or without meat, pineapples, and even nuts, any version will be a hit at your next get-together.

Streak-O-Lean Snappies with Pecan Butter

2	pounds fresh green beans	1	(1-inch thick) chunk
1	medium onion, finely		streak-o-lean (lean salt
	chopped		pork) cooking meat
			Salt and pepper to taste

Pecan Butter

½	cup butter	Salt to taste
⅔	cup coarsely crushed	
	pecans	

Rinse beans in cold water and drain. Pinch off ends, snap beans into 1½-inch pieces and place in a large pot. Add onion, cooking meat, salt, pepper and enough water to cover by 1 inch. Bring to a boil. Reduce heat to low. Cover and simmer slowly for 45 minutes.

Shortly before beans are done, make pecan butter. Melt butter in a small, heavy skillet over medium heat. Add pecans and stir until pecans are coated. Cook and stir 10 minutes or until golden brown. Season with salt. Drain beans and spoon pecan butter on top.

"Snappies" is a Southern term that originally applied to pole beans with tough strings that had to be removed before the beans were snapped for cooking. Although real string beans are often hard to find these days, even in the South, many still refer to all green beans as "snappies" and enjoy them only after they are simmered and flavored with cooking meat for at least 45 minutes to 1 hour. Southern pecan butter is not a "butter" at all, simply crushed pecans that are glazed and used to enhance a variety of vegetables and broiled or grilled fish. It's exquisite.

Green Bean Bundles

5	(16-ounce) cans whole green beans	1	(8-ounce) bottle Catalina salad dressing
1	pound bacon		

Preheat oven to 350 degrees. Drain green beans into a colander 1 can at a time. Divide each can into 5 bundles of beans. Cut bacon in half crosswise. Wrap each bundle with a slice of bacon and secure with a toothpick. Arrange bundles in a 9x13-inch casserole dish. Pour dressing over bundles, coating each bundle well. Bake 35 minutes. Remove from oven and drain off grease. Broil bundles for a few minutes until bacon crisps.

Serves 12

Cayenne Green Beans

6	ounces bacon	3	tablespoons white vinegar
1	onion, minced	3	tablespoons butter
2	pounds fresh green beans, washed and tips removed		Salt and pepper to taste
1	cup boiling water	1	teaspoon cayenne pepper

Cook bacon in a skillet until crisp. Drain bacon and crumble, leaving drippings in skillet. Add onion to drippings and sauté until tender. Add green beans to skillet and sauté over medium heat for 2 minutes, stirring frequently. Add boiling water to pan and cover. Steam, shaking pan occasionally, for 15 minutes or until beans are tender; do not overcook. Add vinegar and stir. Add butter, salt and peppers. Transfer to a serving dish. Toss gently and sprinkle with bacon.

Serves 6

Bagna Calda Dipping Sauce

2 cups butter, divided

1½ bulbs garlic, minced

2 (2-ounce) cans anchovies, chopped

1 pint whipping cream

Melt 1 cup butter in a large skillet over medium-low heat. Add garlic and sauté until opaque; do not brown. While stirring constantly, add remaining 1 cup butter and anchovies. Cook 20 minutes or until anchovies have cooked together. Slowly add cream. Cook, stirring constantly, until warm. Serve as a dipping sauce for cooked cabbage, raw broccoli, cauliflower and red or green bell pepper slices. Serve with French bread.

Make 1 quart

Chewing fresh parsley helps to cleanse the palate of a strong garlic flavor.

125

Chili Rellenos

5 (4-ounce) cans whole
green chiles, seeded

2 (8-ounce) packages
grated Cheddar cheese

1 pound Monterey Jack
cheese, grated

1 (12-ounce) can
evaporated milk

4 eggs, separated

3 tablespoons flour

Salt and pepper to taste

2 (8-ounce) cans
tomato sauce

Preheat oven to 325 degrees.
Flatten chiles. Starting with
chiles, layer chiles and cheeses
in a 3-quart casserole dish.
Beat milk and egg whites
together in a bowl. In a
separate bowl, beat egg yolks.
Add flour, salt, pepper and
milk mixture to yolks. Pour
over layers in dish. Bake
1 hour. Pour tomato sauce
over casserole and bake
30 minutes longer or
until bubbly.

Serves 8

Butter Beans

2	tablespoons butter	¼	teaspoon freshly ground
½	cup diced onion		black pepper
1	teaspoon minced garlic	1	smoked chicken neck
4	cups fresh butter beans		bone or 4 ounces white
	(about 1½ to 2 pounds)		meat chicken
6	cups chicken broth		

Heat butter in a large, heavy saucepan over medium heat. Add onion
and garlic and sauté 2 to 3 minutes or until onion is translucent. Add
beans and broth. Bring to a simmer over medium heat, skimming off
foam as it forms. Add pepper and neck bone. Cook, uncovered, 50 to 55
minutes. Remove neck bone. The broth will have reduced to about
1 cup. Reduce heat and mash some of the beans with a whisk or spoon
to thicken remaining broth.

Serves 4

**Frozen beans can be used. Reduce cooking time by 25 minutes and
reduce chicken broth to 4 cups.**

**If beans are to be added to another recipe and cooked again, reduce
cooking time to 20 minutes.**

Steamed Broccoli in Olive Nut Sauce

½	cup butter	¼	cup black olives, sliced
½	cup slivered almonds	1	teaspoon lemon pepper
3	tablespoons lemon juice	3	pounds fresh broccoli, cut
2	cloves garlic, crushed		into stalks or florets

Melt butter in a skillet. Add almonds, lemon juice, garlic and olives
and sauté. Remove from heat and let stand 1 hour for flavors to blend.
Steam broccoli until tender and place in a serving dish. Reheat olive
nut sauce and pour over broccoli. Serve immediately.

Serves 8

Nut sauce may be made ahead and refrigerated overnight.

Bacon-Tomato Butter Beans

3	slices bacon, chopped	4	cups fresh or frozen butter beans, thawed
1	medium onion, finely chopped	2	tablespoons minced fresh parsley
1	small green bell pepper, chopped	1	teaspoon salt
3	cloves garlic, minced	1	teaspoon black pepper
1	bay leaf	1	teaspoon Worcestershire sauce
3	medium tomatoes, chopped	½	teaspoon hot pepper sauce
4	cups chicken broth		

Cook bacon in a Dutch oven until crisp. Add onion, bell pepper, garlic and bay leaf. Sauté until vegetables are tender. Stir in tomatoes and cook 3 minutes. Stir in broth and beans. Bring to a boil. Reduce heat and cover. Simmer, stirring occasionally, for 30 minutes. Uncover and simmer 20 minutes longer, stirring often. Add parsley, salt, pepper, Worcestershire sauce and hot pepper sauce. Cook, stirring often, for 5 minutes. Discard bay leaf before serving.

Serves 6

Broccoli-Stuffed Tomato Cups

6	medium tomatoes	½	cup mayonnaise
	Salt and pepper	2	tablespoons chopped onion
1	(10-ounce) package frozen chopped broccoli	2	tablespoons Parmesan cheese
1	cup grated Swiss cheese		Green onion fans (optional)
1	cup soft bread crumbs		

Cut off tops of tomatoes and scoop out pulp, leaving shells intact. Sprinkle inside of tomato shells with salt and pepper. Invert shells on a wire rack to drain for 30 minutes. Cook broccoli according to package directions, omitting salt; drain well.

Preheat oven to 350 degrees. Combine broccoli, Swiss cheese, bread crumbs, mayonnaise and onion. Stuff mixture into tomato shells. Sprinkle Parmesan cheese on top. Bake 30 minutes. Arrange tomatoes on a serving platter and garnish with onion fans.

Serves 6

In Savannah, you can always find fresh vegetables and fruit at the open-air farmer's market and suburban produce stands. Local farmers bring their fresh produce straight from the fields and you can take home bushels full, or a hand full, of your favorites. Savannahians know that they can always find the freshest of everything at Davis Produce, known as the "Home of the Killer Tomato." Locals also know not to go there on Monday – they are closed – and if you are looking for silver queen corn, don't go on Wednesday because they have sold it all on Tuesday.

New South Succotash

1	teaspoon olive oil	2	cups washed, stemmed and julienned fresh spinach
½	cup diced red onion		
1	teaspoon minced garlic		
½	cup diced red bell pepper	1	cup creamed chicken gravy
1½	cups cooked fresh yellow corn kernels		
		½	cup chicken broth
2	cups cooked butter beans		Salt and freshly ground black pepper to taste
20	large shrimp, peeled and deveined		

Heat oil in a heavy saucepan over medium heat. Add onion, garlic, bell pepper and corn and sauté 2 to 3 minutes or until onion is translucent. Mix in beans. Add shrimp, spinach, gravy and broth. Simmer and stir until shrimp are pink and begin to curl. Season with salt and pepper. Serve immediately.

Serves 4

This makes an excellent accompaniment to grilled fish or chicken. The chicken gravy gives it depth and helps to bring the flavors together.

Festive Carrot Ring

1 pound carrots, sliced

1 cup cracker crumbs

1 cup milk

¾ cup grated sharp Cheddar cheese

1 cup butter, softened

¼ cup grated onion

1 teaspoon salt

¼ teaspoon black pepper

⅛ teaspoon cayenne pepper

3 eggs

Cooked peas and fresh parsley for garnish

Preheat oven to 350 degrees. In a saucepan, cook carrots in water until tender. Drain and mash thoroughly and measure to equal 2 cups. Combine 2 cups mashed carrots with cracker crumbs, milk, cheese, butter, onion, salt and peppers. Beat eggs until light and fold into carrot mixture. Pour into a well-greased 1½-quart ring mold. Bake 40 to 45 minutes. Invert onto a warm platter and fill center with cooked peas. Garnish outside of ring with parsley.

Serves 8 to 12

Double Orange Carrots

10	medium carrots, sliced diagonally	½	teaspoon ground ginger
		½	cup orange juice
2	tablespoons sugar	4	tablespoons butter or margarine
2	teaspoons cornstarch		
½	teaspoon salt		

Cook carrots just until tender. Drain and keep warm. In a small saucepan, combine sugar, cornstarch, salt, ginger and orange juice. Cook and stir over medium heat until thickened. Boil 1 minute. Stir in butter. Pour mixture over hot carrots and toss to coat.

Serves 6

Sautéed Cabbage

1	large head cabbage		Salt and pepper to taste
4-6	tablespoons butter	¼	teaspoon seasoning salt

Cut cabbage into quarters, removing outer dark green leaves and core. Rinse cabbage with cold water and drain. In a large skillet, melt butter over medium-high heat. Add damp cabbage and toss to coat. Add salt, pepper and seasoning salt. Cover skillet and simmer 7 to 10 minutes or until crisp-tender.

Serves 6 to 8

If not serving with Bagna Calda Dipping Sauce (page 125), add extra flavor by adding 3 to 4 slices of bacon, chopped, to butter and cook until half done.

Colonial Corn Pudding

½	cup butter, softened	4	eggs, well beaten
2-3	tablespoons self-rising flour	1	teaspoon salt
2	cups milk		Dash of white pepper
1	cup half-and-half	2	tablespoons sugar (optional)
4	cups frozen shoepeg or niblet corn, thawed and drained		

Preheat oven to 350 degrees. Melt butter in a large skillet. Stir in flour until blended. Add milk and half-and-half and stir until smooth. Cook, stirring constantly, for 15 minutes or until creamy. Remove from heat and stir in corn. Cool. Add eggs, salt, pepper and sugar. Mix thoroughly and transfer to a greased 9x13-inch casserole dish. Bake 30 to 40 minutes or until set and top begins to brown. Let stand 10 minutes before serving.

Serves 8 to 10

By the 1860's, a large portion of Savannah's population was of Irish descent. Our Irish pride would lead you to expect Irish stew to be served on St. Patrick's Day. This is not always the case. In Savannah, the entrée of the day is quite often Irish Corned Beef Brisket (pg 181) and cabbage. It is added to the menu of local restaurants for that day only and can be enjoyed as it is served off many tailgates and tables of spectators of the parade.

Hoppin' John (peas, rice and a bit of pork) is served on New Years' Day for luck. Some Southerners also have some greens and cornbread. In this, they say the peas stand for coins, the greens for cash and the cornbread for gold. All agree that Hoppin' John brings luck for the coming year. Troops overseas often requested that black-eyed peas, dried or canned, be sent in their Christmas package, so they could have them on New Years.

Hoppin' John

1	(16-ounce) package dried black-eyed peas	2	tablespoons garlic salt
½	pound ham hocks	2	tablespoons basil
10	cups water	2	tablespoons dried chopped tarragon
1	teaspoon black pepper	1	medium onion, chopped
2½	teaspoons salt	½	cup celery, chopped
2	teaspoons crushed red pepper	1	dash Tabasco
		1	cup rice, uncooked

In a 5-quart pot, combine all ingredients, except rice, with 8 cups of water. Cook on high uncovered until boiling. Reduce heat to medium-low, cover and cook for 1 hour and 15 minutes, stirring occasionally. Add remaining 2 cups of water and 1 cup of rice. Cover and cook on medium heat for 40 minutes, stirring often until rice is tender.

Serves 8 to 10

Serve with chopped raw onions and collard greens, especially on New Year's Day.

Eggplant Fritters

1	eggplant	1	teaspoon salt
2	eggs		Dash of black pepper
1	teaspoon baking powder		Vegetable oil for frying
½	cup all-purpose flour		Sugar or paprika
½	cup milk		(optional)

Cook eggplant in boiling water until tender. Peel, chop and remove seeds. Mash pulp well. In a bowl, combine eggs, baking powder, flour, milk, salt and pepper. Mix in eggplant pulp. Drop mixture by rounded teaspoons into 3 to 4 inches of hot oil. Fry until golden brown. Drain on paper towels. Sprinkle with sugar or paprika, if desired, and serve warm.

Serves 6

Substitute 2½ to 3 cups mashed zucchini or summer squash for the eggplant.

Big Mama's Minced Greens

1	tablespoon olive oil	16	cups washed, stemmed
1	cup coarsely chopped		and coarsely chopped
	yellow onion		mustard, turnip or
1	tablespoon minced garlic		collard greens
¾	cup finely diced country	½	cup chicken broth
	ham		White pepper to taste

Heat olive oil in a large pot over medium heat. Add onion and garlic and sauté 2 minutes or until translucent. Add ham and sauté 3 minutes. Add greens in batches and cook over medium heat, stirring occasionally, until wilted. As greens wilt, there will be room to add more greens. Add broth and cook 10 minutes or until greens are tender but still dark green. Season with white pepper.

Serves 6

Caramelized Vidalia Onion with Corn and Bacon

4	ears fresh corn	2	tablespoons light
6	slices bacon, chopped		molasses
2	medium sweet onions, cut	¼	teaspoon salt
	into thin strips	¼	teaspoon black pepper

Cut corn kernels from cob, set aside. Cook bacon in a heavy skillet until crisp. Remove bacon and crumble, reserving 1 tablespoon drippings in skillet. Add onions to drippings and cook, stirring often, for 15 minutes or until onion is a caramel color. Add corn and cook 8 minutes, stirring often. Stir in molasses, salt and pepper. Transfer to a serving dish. Sprinkle with bacon.

Serves 6

Greens

The greens which are most popular in the South are turnips and collards. People from all walks of life enjoy these greens, particularly turnip greens. While turnips are grown for their tuber (the turnip) in most places, they are grown for their leaves in the South. Turnip greens are a little less nutritious than collards, but are more palatable to most people. Collards are actually a kind of cabbage, developed from European wild mustard greens. Stewed greens may be made entirely ahead of time and reheated. Artichoke relish as well as peppers in cider vinegars are the traditional accompaniments with "greens," as is the favorite, cornbread.

In 1990, the Vidalia onion was named Georgia's Official State Vegetable. Vidalia onions have an international reputation as the world's sweetest onion. Their mild flavor is due to the unique combination of soils and climate in the 20-county production area. It used to be that Vidalias were available only during a brief season of April until June, but today, growers are keeping Vidalias in cold storage with great success, extending the time of year they are available.

Vidalia Onion Tart

1	(9-inch) pie crust	1	(8-ounce) package grated
2	large Vidalia onions,		sharp Cheddar cheese
	thinly sliced (about	½	teaspoon salt
	2 cups)	¼	cup whipping cream

Preheat oven to 400 degrees. Bake pie crust for 10 minutes. Arrange half the onion slices in baked crust. Top with half the cheese. Make a second layer with remaining onions and cheese. Sprinkle with salt and drizzle cream over the top. Bake 25 minutes or until cheese is lightly browned. Cool slightly on a wire rack before serving.

Serves 8 to 10

Vidalia Onion Casserole

½	cup butter or margarine	6-8	ounces Cheddar cheese,
4	medium Vidalia onions,		grated, plus extra for
	sliced		topping
12	saltine crackers, crushed		Salt and pepper to taste
1	(10¾-ounce) can	2	eggs
	condensed cream of	½-1	cup milk
	mushroom soup		

Preheat oven to 350 degrees. Melt butter in a large skillet. Add onions and cook 12 to 15 minutes or until tender and transparent. Saving some for topping, sprinkle cracker crumbs in a greased 9x13-inch casserole dish to line bottom and sides. Layer cooked onions, soup and cheese in dish. Lightly season onion layer with salt. Beat together eggs, milk, salt and pepper and pour over layers. Sprinkle with reserved crumbs and extra cheese. Bake 30 to 45 minutes or until browned and bubbly.

Serves 6 to 8

Spinach and Artichoke Tomato Cups

Tomato Cups

2	large firm tomatoes	2	green onions, sliced
	Salt and pepper to taste	2	ounces cream cheese, softened
4	slices bacon, cooked and crumbled	2	tablespoons sour cream
1½	cups chopped canned artichoke hearts, packed in water, drained	2	tablespoons butter, softened
		2	teaspoons basil
		½	cup Parmesan cheese
1	cup frozen chopped spinach, thawed and squeezed dry		

Topping

2	tablespoons bread crumbs	2	tablespoons chopped slivered almonds
2	tablespoons butter, melted		

Preheat oven to 350 degrees. Halve tomatoes, scoop out and discard pulp. Sprinkle tomato shells with salt and pepper. Combine bacon, artichoke, spinach, onion, cream cheese, sour cream, butter, basil and Parmesan cheese in a food processor. Process until well blended. Stuff mixture into tomato shells.

Combine all topping ingredients and mix well. Sprinkle over tomato halves and place halves on a lightly greased baking dish. Bake, uncovered, for 10 minutes.

Serves 4

Creamed Dilly Peas and Carrots

¾ cup water

1 cup sliced carrots (2 medium)

¼ cup butter

1 tablespoon cornstarch

1 cup half-and-half

1 (10-ounce) package frozen tiny peas, thawed and drained

2 tablespoons chopped green onion

½ teaspoon salt

½ teaspoon dried dill

⅛ teaspoon black pepper

Bring water to a full boil in a 2-quart saucepan. Add carrots. Cover and cook over medium heat 8 to 10 minutes or until carrots are crisp-tender. Drain and set aside. In same saucepan, melt butter. Stir in cornstarch until smooth. Add carrots, half-and-half, peas, onion, salt, dill and pepper. Cook over medium heat, stirring constantly, for 8 to 10 minutes or until mixture comes to a full boil. Boil and stir 1 minute.

Serves 5

Praline Acorn Squash

2 medium acorn squash

2 tablespoons butter or margarine

¼ cup coarsely chopped pecans

¼ cup brown sugar, firmly packed

¼ teaspoon cinnamon

Cut squash in half lengthwise and remove strings and seeds. Place squash, cut-side down, in a 9x13-inch microwave-safe dish. Microwave on high power for 15 to 17 minutes or until tender. Let stand 5 minutes. Turn squash and gently mash insides, leaving shells intact. Dot with butter and sprinkle with a mixture of pecans, sugar and cinnamon. Microwave on high for 2 minutes or until sugar melts. Serve hot.

Serves 4

Tastes like sweet potatoes with pecans.

Cheesy Squash and Tomato Casserole

12	small yellow squash, sliced	1	(8-ounce) package Velveeta cheese, cubed
1	onion, finely minced	1	(14½-ounce) can tomatoes, drained and mashed, or 1 cup diced fresh
	Pinch of dried basil		
	Dash of garlic powder		
⅛	teaspoon freshly ground black pepper	¼	teaspoon salt
3	tablespoons corn oil	2	tablespoons sugar
1	teaspoon salt		

Preheat oven to 350 degrees. Sauté squash, onion, basil, garlic powder and pepper in oil in a skillet. Stir well, cover and simmer until vegetables start to soften. Remove from heat and add salt and cheese. Stir until cheese melts. Pour into an 8x8-inch casserole dish. In same skillet, quickly heat tomatoes, salt and sugar. Pour over squash. Bake 30 minutes.

Serves 6 to 8

A favorite for Easter lunch or dinner parties. It's rich, so serve with a simple entrée.

Squash Boats Florentine

10	medium yellow squash, uniform in size	½	cup Parmesan cheese
1	small onion, finely chopped	⅔	cup bread crumbs
2	eggs, beaten		Salt and pepper to taste
4	tablespoons butter, melted	1	(10-ounce) package frozen chopped spinach, drained
1	cup grated Cheddar cheese		

Preheat oven to 350 degrees. Cut off ends of squash and cut in half lengthwise. Scoop out pulp and reserve, leaving shells intact to make "boats." Cook reserved pulp and onion until tender in just enough water to cover. Drain completely and mix well with eggs, butter, cheeses, bread crumbs, salt and pepper. Stir in spinach. Add more bread crumbs if mixture is too watery. Place squash boats in greased 9x13-inch casserole dishes. Spoon bread crumb mixture into boats. Bake 30 to 40 minutes.

Serves 10

An excellent choice for a buffet luncheon.

Substitute a 10-ounce package frozen chopped broccoli for the spinach. Also, stuffing for boats can be your favorite squash or broccoli casserole recipe.

Summer Squash and Cherry Tomatoes in Basil Butter

1 pound yellow squash, thinly sliced

8 ounces cherry tomatoes, halved

2 tablespoons Basil Butter

Basil Butter

1 shallot, minced

3 cloves garlic, minced

¾ cup minced fresh basil

½ cup butter, softened

Freshly ground black pepper to taste

Sauté squash and tomatoes in Basil Butter in a medium skillet for 10 minutes or until tender. Serve with extra Basil Butter on the side.

To make Basil Butter, combine all ingredients in a food processor. Process until smooth and refrigerate until solid.

Serve 6

Deep South Tomato Pie

4	tomatoes, sliced	1	cup grated Cheddar cheese
⅓	cup chopped green onion		
	Basil to taste	1	cup grated mozzarella cheese
1	deep dish pie crust, baked	1	cup mayonnaise
	Salt and pepper to taste		

Preheat oven to 350 degrees. Layer tomato slices, onion and basil in baked pie crust. Season with salt and pepper. Mix cheeses and mayonnaise and spread over top of tomatoes. Bake 30 minutes or until lightly browned.

Serves 8

Tomato and Artichoke Bake

3	tablespoons butter or margarine	2	ripe tomatoes, each cut into 8 wedges
2	(14-ounce) cans artichoke hearts, drained		

Crumb Topping

½	cup dry crumb-style herb-seasoned stuffing	2	tablespoons butter or margarine
¼	cup freshly grated Parmesan cheese	¼	teaspoon salt

Preheat oven to 350 degrees. Melt butter in a 9-inch square baking pan in oven for 5 to 6 minutes. Stir in artichokes and tomatoes.

In a small bowl, combine all crumb topping ingredients. Sprinkle topping over vegetables. Bake 25 to 30 minutes or until heated through.

Serves 6

Who in their right mind would have taken a pie shell, sliced tomatoes, mayonnaise, onions, and cheese, and of all things – baked it? Miss Lucille Wright, well-known Savannah caterer of Midnight... memory, traditionally served her tomato pie at both sophisticated luncheons and elegant dinner parties. This Savannah summertime dish has grown to be a regional favorite.

Zucchini Milano

1	cup water	1	tablespoon minced fresh basil
2	teaspoons salt		
8	medium zucchini, sliced ¼-inch thick	1	tablespoon minced fresh oregano
8	slices bacon, diced		Black pepper to taste
1	large onion, chopped	1	(15-ounce) can tomato sauce
1	clove garlic, minced		
4	slices bread, cubed	¼	cup Parmesan cheese
2	cups grated mozzarella cheese		

Preheat oven to 350 degrees. Combine water and salt in a saucepan and bring to a boil. Add zucchini and cook 3 to 5 minutes or until just tender. Drain and place zucchini in a large mixing bowl.

In a skillet, cook bacon until crisp. Remove bacon and drain, reserving drippings in skillet. Sauté onion and garlic in drippings until softened. Drain and add to bowl with zucchini and bacon. Mix in bread, mozzarella cheese, basil, oregano, pepper and tomato sauce. Spoon mixture into a 9x13-inch baking dish. Top with Parmesan cheese. Bake 20 minutes or until bubbly.

Serves 10

If you do not have fresh herbs, substitute 1 teaspoon Italian seasoning for the basil and oregano.

Pecan Zucchini Casserole

6 cups sliced zucchini

½ cup mayonnaise

4 tablespoons butter

1 egg

3 tablespoons sugar

Salt and pepper to taste

Topping

2 tablespoons butter, melted

½ cup dry herb stuffing

½ cup pecans

Preheat oven to 350 degrees. Cook zucchini in water until tender. Drain and place in a 2-quart casserole dish. In a mixing bowl, combine mayonnaise, butter, egg, sugar, salt and pepper. Add mixture to zucchini and mix well.

To make topping, combine melted butter and stuffing. Spread over casserole. Bake until slightly browned. Top with pecans. Bake at 400 degrees for 20 minutes.

Serves 8

Swiss Vegetable Mélange

1 (16-ounce) bag frozen broccoli, carrot and cauliflower mix, thawed and drained

1 (10¾-ounce) can condensed cream of mushroom soup

1 cup grated Swiss cheese, divided

⅓ cup sour cream

¼ teaspoon black pepper

1 (4-ounce) jar chopped pimiento, drained (optional)

1 (2.8-ounce) can French fried onions, divided

Preheat oven to 350 degrees. Combine vegetables, soup, ½ cup cheese, sour cream, pepper, pimiento and ½ can of onions. Pour into a 1-quart casserole dish. Cover and bake 30 minutes. Top with remaining cheese and onions. Bake, uncovered, 5 minutes longer.

Serves 6

Fresh Summer Vegetables on the Grill

Your choice of:

Sliced green tomatoes
Sliced rutabaga
Sliced squash
Sliced zucchini
Peeled and sliced sweet potatoes

Sliced onions, Vidalia if available
Quartered red or green bell peppers
Garlic-flavored or plain olive oil spray

Place vegetables in a 9x13-inch casserole dish. Spray with oil spray until well coated, using garlic-flavored for most vegetables, but plain on the sweet potatoes.

When ready to grill, place vegetables on a grill over medium heat. Vegetables such as potatoes and rutabaga will take longer to cook and should be added to grill first. Grill until done; do not overcook.

Chilled Vegetable Marinade

1	cup olive oil, or other vegetable oil	1-2	tablespoons Italian seasoning
½-¾	cup sugar	2	teaspoons dry mustard
½-¾	cup white wine vinegar	1	teaspoon salt
		½	teaspoon black pepper

Combine all marinade ingredients and pour over vegetables. Chill overnight. Serve cold, or grill or sauté vegetables.

Makes enough marinade for 12 cups of vegetables.

Poultry

The *First* Plantations

The *first* plantations in Georgia evolved from the original 500-acre land grants given to the Colony's Trustees. Many had evocative names, such as Silkhope, Mulberry Grove, Beaulieu, and Wormsloe (Welsh for Dragon's Lair). Of these, only Wormsloe and Bethesda remain. Wormsloe, owned by Noble Jones, now belongs to his descendants (except for acreage given to the State of Georgia in 1973). Bethesda, founded by Rev. George Whitefield, is still in operation as a home for boys. Cotton was experimental in 1764, when eight bales were sent to England. In 1767, John Earle planted the *first* crop of long fibered, Sea Island cotton. Cotton became King soon enough, adding to the cycle of slavery. This cycle ended only when Savannah surrendered to Sherman in 1864, 130 years after the founding of Georgia.

Spirited Savannah

Among the oldest plantations in Georgia is Grove Point, built on a land grant from 1757. Legend has it that Grove Point was a favorite spot for Blackbeard (Edward Teach). Blackbeard, for whom one of Georgia's islands is named, is said to have left buried treasure on the grounds (somewhere). An overseer with a limp (perhaps a former pirate), lived at Grove Point with his mistress. While the spirit of the overseer seems to still be active, the spirit of his mistress, "The White Lady," has not been seen since around 1900. Another lady, probably mistress of the house from the Victorian era, is the foremost spirit in residence at Grove Point. She often lets her presence be known, appearing in a long dress with her hair down on her shoulders. Renovation disturbs this lady somewhat, and workmen are eager to finish their tasks before dark! She is also fond of gliding through walls and closed doors, much to the surprise of guests.

"Death and Dying Chicken Casseroles"

Every fine Southern cook we know has a signature chicken casserole, which she can practically assemble in her sleep. Whatever the life transformation, out comes the casserole to be shared in a ceremonial or celebratory manner. Generally, this is the casserole brought when someone has slipped the mortal coil, is sick, has had surgery, or is overwhelmingly swamped for reasons beyond their control. Care has to be taken in the last case, as the casserole recipient may be scared into thinking things are worse than they are.

The "death and dying" chicken casseroles are so individualized that they are often known only by the name of the cook who makes it. This is helpful for coordinating food for someone's serious condition, as well as providing a sense of security for all concerned. One downside of this is that these casseroles can become associated with sad or dramatic events, and aren't prepared very often otherwise. Husbands and children, on merely seeing the ingredients for these signature casseroles, invariably ask, "What happened?" or "Who died?" Family members have even been known to say sneaky things such as, "I wish something would happen so you'd make that chicken casserole of yours."

These casseroles are sometimes served at covered dish suppers where most of the people there won't know that it's one of the signature casseroles. Efforts are made to refrain from commenting in front of newcomers and non-Southerners, in general. "Lord, this casserole reminds me of the night Old Judge Johnny Walker lost his car keys...and the big toe on his right foot, too...when he tripped over the railroad tracks...in the pouring rain. Wasn't that after the Georgia Florida game?"

"Yes, and we lost that year."

"Oh well, then... that explains it."

Honey Pecan Fried Chicken

6	cups buttermilk	¾	teaspoon garlic powder
10	boneless, skinless chicken breasts, pounded ½-inch thick	½	teaspoon cayenne pepper
		2	cups butter
		1	cup honey
2½	cups self-rising flour	1	cup chopped pecans
1½	teaspoons salt		Vegetable oil

Pour buttermilk into a large bowl. Add chicken, cover and refrigerate 1½ hours. Combine flour, salt, garlic powder and cayenne pepper in a shallow dish. Drain chicken and dredge in flour mixture, shaking off excess. Let chicken stand 20 minutes at room temperature.

Melt butter in a small heavy saucepan over low heat. Stir in honey and bring to a boil. Add pecans and simmer 15 minutes. Meanwhile, add oil to a large heavy skillet to ½- to ¾-inch in depth. Heat oil to 375 degrees. Add chicken and fry, in batches, about 7 minutes on each side or until golden brown and cooked through. Drain on paper towels. Arrange chicken on a serving platter. Pour honey glaze on top and serve immediately.

Serves 6 to 8

Honey-Lime Grilled Chicken

½	cup honey	4	boneless, skinless chicken breast halves
⅓	cup soy sauce		
¼	cup lime juice		

Combine honey, soy sauce and lime juice in a plastic zip-top bag or shallow glass dish. Add chicken and turn to coat. Seal or cover and refrigerate 30 to 45 minutes. Grill chicken, uncovered, over medium heat for 6 to 7 minutes on each side or until juices run clear.

Serves 4

Mulberry Grove was the home of Caty Greene, widow of Nathaniel, sponsor of Eli Whitney, and "Vamp of Savannah," according to Russell and Hines in Savannah: A History of Her People Since 1733. *Observers of both sexes considered her "a refreshingly liberated woman. She possessed honest candor, and bravery...not hypocrisy or pretense." She counted, among her admirers, George Washington and "Mad" Anthony Wayne (of Revolutionary fame, as well as a Savannah lawyer), a Georgia politician, and a Marquis. She finally married her caretaker at Mulberry Grove, who was 10 years younger than she was.*

For double-flavored fried chicken, try this tip shared by an incomparable cook who is expected to be 90 about the time this book is published. She says to save all skimmed off chicken fat drippings and well-strained oil, in which chicken has been fried. When frying chicken again, add these to fresh oil to deepen the flavor. If you are expecting to fry a number of chickens in a short period of time, you can keep this mixture in the refrigerator for a few weeks. Freeze any surplus you may create and thaw it out when you have used the batch in the refrigerator. Her family swears they have to fight for her chicken at social gatherings!

Southern Fried Chicken

1	(3-pound) frying chicken, cut into pieces	1	teaspoon salt, plus extra for seasoning
1	cup milk or buttermilk	½	teaspoon white pepper
1	cup flour		Vegetable shortening

Soak chicken pieces in milk for 30 minutes. Combine flour, salt and pepper in a medium brown paper bag. Drain chicken, but do not dry. Season chicken liberally on both sides with salt. Add chicken to paper bag and close top. Shake to evenly coat all pieces. Remove chicken and shake to remove excess.

Heat shortening in a large skillet. Hold on high heat for a few minutes until fat is crackling hot. Carefully place chicken into skillet, side by side, fleshy-side down. Cook quickly for a few minutes, making sure pieces have a firm, but very light brown crust on the bottom. Turn chicken and continue to cook over high heat for 1 minute longer. Reduce heat to low and cover skillet. Cook 10 to 15 minutes or until cooked through. Remove cover and increase to high heat. Turn each piece as the bottom turns very crisp and golden but not too brown. Cook top surface of chicken over high heat for a few minutes to restore crispness and golden color. Drain chicken on paper towels.

Serves 4

Deep Fried Turkey

1	turkey	5	gallons peanut oil or enough to cover
	Salt to taste		
	Cayenne pepper to taste		

Clean and thoroughly dry turkey, inside and out. Season inside and out with salt and cayenne pepper. Add peanut oil to a pot large enough to hold a turkey without oil overflowing. Heat oil to 325 to 350 degrees. Put bird in pot slowly, being careful not to splash the oil. Fry about 4 minutes per pound. Test for doneness at the thigh joint.

This method of cooking produces such moist meat, you may never bake your Thanksgiving bird again. This only works for turkeys up to 12 pounds.

Jamaican Jerk Raspberry Chicken

4	pounds chicken pieces	2	cups hickory chips
2	tablespoons olive oil		Raspberry glaze
3	tablespoons Jamaican Jerk Rub		

Rub chicken with oil and sprinkle with Jamaican Jerk Rub. Cover and refrigerate 4 to 6 hours.

Soak hickory chips in water 30 minutes. Prepare grill by piling charcoal or lava rocks on each side of the grill, leaving center empty. Drain chips and place on a square of heavy-duty aluminum foil. Fold foil to seal. Cut several slits in top of packet and place packet on one side of coals. Place drip pan between coals. Place rack on grill. When grill reaches 350 to 400 degrees, arrange chicken over coals and cook, covered, for 10 to 15 minutes on each side. Move chicken over drip pan and grill, covered for 5 to 6 minutes on each side, brushing often with Raspberry Glaze.

Serves 8

Raspberry Glaze

2	tablespoons butter	1	tablespoon olive oil
½	medium Vidalia onion, diced	2	tablespoons dry red wine
½	(18-ounce) jar raspberry preserves	1½	teaspoons red wine vinegar
1½	teaspoons Jamaican Jerk Rub	1	tablespoon lemon juice

Melt butter in a saucepan over medium-high heat. Add onion and sauté until tender. Stir in preserves, Jamaican Jerk Rub and oil. Cook, stirring often, for 5 minutes or until preserves are melted. Stir in wine and vinegar. Bring to a boil. Reduce heat and simmer 15 minutes. Add lemon juice.

Jamaican Jerk Rub

⅓ cup freeze-dried chives

1 tablespoon fine grain sea salt

1 tablespoon onion powder

1 tablespoon dried onion flakes

1 tablespoon garlic powder

1 tablespoon ground ginger

1 tablespoon dried thyme

1 tablespoon light brown sugar, firmly packed

1 tablespoon cayenne pepper

2 teaspoons ground allspice

2 teaspoons coarsely ground black pepper

2 teaspoons ground coriander

1 teaspoon ground cinnamon

½ teaspoon ground nutmeg

½ teaspoon ground cloves

Combine all ingredients in a blender. Process until ground and well blended. Store extra rub in an airtight container.

143

Cranberry Chicken

6 pounds boneless,
skinless chicken
breast halves

1 (1-ounce) package
onion soup mix

1 (8-ounce) bottle
Catalina salad dressing

1 (16-ounce) can whole
cranberry sauce

Preheat oven to
350 degrees. Place chicken
in a 9x11-inch casserole
dish. Combine soup mix,
salad dressing and cranberry
sauce and pour over chicken.
Bake for 1 hour or until
chicken is done. Serve
with white rice.

Serves 4 to 6

Barbecued Chicken Bundles

8	boneless, skinless chicken breast halves	16	slices bacon
4	ounces Cheddar cheese, cut into 8 (1x1x½-inch) cubes	1	cup barbecue sauce

Preheat grill to medium heat. Make a slit in each chicken breast to form a pocket. Place 1 cheese cube in each pocket. Roll each breast into a bundle and wrap with 2 slices of bacon. Secure bacon with toothpicks. Grill chicken bundles, turning every 15 minutes, for 30 to 40 minutes or until chicken is fork tender. If crisp bacon is desired, place bundles directly over heat, turning 2 to 3 times, during final 10 minutes of cooking. Baste with barbecue sauce during last 10 minutes of cooking.

Serves 8

For moister chicken, place an aluminum pan of water on the grill. Bundles can be made ahead and refrigerated until ready to use.

Bourbon Barbecue Sauce

4	tablespoons butter	½	cup pure maple syrup
¼	cup canola or corn oil	⅓	cup unsulphered dark molasses
2	medium onions, minced		
¾	cup bourbon	2	tablespoons Worcestershire sauce
⅔	cup ketchup		
½	cup cider vinegar	½	teaspoon salt
½	cup fresh orange juice	½	teaspoon black pepper

Melt butter with oil in a saucepan over medium heat. Add onions and sauté 5 minutes or until golden. Mix in bourbon, ketchup, vinegar, orange juice, syrup, molasses, Worcestershire sauce, salt and pepper. Reduce heat to low and cook, stirring frequently, for 40 minutes or until mixture thickens. Prepare at least 1 day ahead for best flavor. Store sauce in refrigerator for up to 2 weeks. Serve sauce warm. Excellent with grilled or smoked chicken. Pour heated sauce over meat for a great crowd pleaser.

Makes about 3 cups

Chicken Breasts with Mustard and Cream

1½-2	pounds boneless, skinless chicken breasts	4	ounces fresh mushrooms, thickly sliced
¼	teaspoon salt	½	cup dry white wine
⅛	teaspoon black pepper	¾	cup whipping cream
3	tablespoons unsalted butter	3	tablespoons Dijon mustard
2	tablespoons vegetable oil	2	tablespoons chopped fresh parsley
2	tablespoons chopped shallots or green onion		

Pat chicken dry with paper towels. Sprinkle with salt and pepper. In a skillet, sauté chicken in butter and oil on 1 side for 6 minutes or until light golden. Turn chicken and reduce heat. Sauté chicken 5 minutes or until just tender. Cover skillet and cook 2 to 3 minutes longer to steam. Transfer chicken to a warm platter. Remove all but 2 tablespoons fat in skillet. Add shallots to skillet and sauté about 1 minute. Add mushrooms and sauté until lightly golden. Add wine and bring to a boil. Cook until reduced and slightly thickened. Reduce heat and add cream. Cook until warm and thick. Stir in mustard. Adjust seasonings as needed. Place chicken in sauce and add parsley. Serve when thoroughly warmed.

Serves 4

This is nice served with wild rice. A good recipe to serve to company.

Sherman sent this now-famous telegram to Abraham Lincoln, the first instance of a city being presented to a President. The telegram read:

"Savannah, Georgia, December 22, 1864

To his Excellency, President Lincoln,

Dear Sir,

I beg to present you as a Christmas Gift, the City of Savannah with 150 heavy guns and plenty of ammunition; and also about 25,000 bales of cotton.

W. T. Sherman, Maj. Genl."

Classic Crêpes

2 cups flour

¼ teaspoon salt

2 cups cold water

4 eggs

1 tablespoon oil

1 tablespoon butter, melted

Softened butter

Sift together flour and salt in a mixing bowl. Slowly beat in water with a wooden spoon to prevent lumps. Whisk in eggs, one at a time, until thoroughly blended. Add oil and melted butter and whisk until smooth. Preheat a crêpe pan or a small skillet. Brush with softened butter. Ladle about 2 tablespoons of batter into the pan. Tip pan quickly to spread batter evenly over the surface. Brown lightly and then turn with a spatula to brown on other side. Stack cooked crêpes between foil squares. Keep warm if using immediately. If using later, cool, wrap tightly and refrigerate or freeze.

Makes 20 to 24

Crêpes Bellisimo

Cream Sauce

4	cups whipping cream	½	teaspoon salt
¾	cup freshly grated Parmesan cheese	⅛	teaspoon white pepper

Filling

4	tablespoons butter	½	cup cream sauce
⅓	cup chopped green onion	1	egg, beaten
1	clove garlic, minced	⅛	teaspoon black pepper
1	cup finely chopped mushrooms		Pinch of nutmeg
1	(10-ounce) package frozen spinach, cooked and drained	½	teaspoon salt
		16	crêpes
2	cups cooked and coarsely chopped turkey or chicken	¼	cup freshly grated Parmesan cheese

To make cream sauce, bring cream to a boil in a medium saucepan. Reduce heat to low and simmer 5 minutes. Remove from heat and add cheese, salt and pepper. Return to low heat and stir constantly until cheese melts. Set aside.

For filling, melt butter in a large skillet. Add onion and garlic and cook over medium heat until softened but not browned. Add mushrooms and cook over medium-high heat until softened. Stir in spinach and cook over low heat until all liquid has evaporated. Remove from heat and stir in chicken, ½ cup of the cream sauce, egg, pepper, nutmeg and salt. Mix well and set aside.

Preheat oven to 350 degrees. To assemble crêpes, spread 3 tablespoons of cream sauce in the bottom of a 9x13-inch baking dish. Divide filling evenly among crêpes. Roll crêpes and arrange, seam-side down, in baking dish. Pour remaining cream sauce over crêpes. Sprinkle with Parmesan cheese. Cover and bake 15 minutes. Uncover and broil 1 minute if needed to brown top.

Serves 8

This entire dish can be prepared a day in advance and refrigerated. Bake just before serving. Excellent entrée for luncheons or dinners. Even men love these crêpes!

Spinach-Stuffed Chicken Breasts

1	clove garlic, minced	2	tablespoons chopped sun-dried tomatoes in oil, rinsed
2	cups chopped fresh spinach, or ¼ cup chopped frozen, thawed	1	teaspoon chopped fresh rosemary
1	cup cooked instant rice	2	boneless, skinless whole chicken breasts
½	cup grated low-fat Monterey Jack cheese	1	cup chicken broth
¼	cup pine nuts, toasted (optional)	1	tablespoon cornstarch
		2	tablespoons water

Spray a medium skillet with cooking spray. Add garlic and cook over medium heat for 1 minute. Add spinach and cook 2 to 3 minutes or until wilted. Place spinach in a strainer and press lightly to remove excess moisture. Combine spinach with rice, cheese, pine nuts, tomatoes and rosemary in a medium bowl. Flatten each chicken breast to about ¼-inch thick by pounding between 2 pieces of wax paper. Divide spinach mixture between chicken breasts and roll, tucking in edges to cover filling. Secure with toothpicks. Spray a large nonstick skillet with cooking spray. Add chicken rolls and brown over medium-high heat. Add broth. Cover and simmer 10 to 15 minutes or until meat is tender. Dissolve cornstarch in water and add to skillet. Cook until sauce thickens. To serve, slice chicken into 1-inch thick slices. Top with sauce.

Serves 4

Chicken with Linguine and Artichoke Hearts

1 (6-ounce) jar marinated artichoke hearts, liquid reserved

2 tablespoons olive oil

1 medium onion, chopped

1 cup fresh snow peas

2 cups chopped cooked chicken or turkey

6 slices bacon, cooked and crumbled

1 tablespoon snipped fresh oregano, or 1 teaspoon dried

¼ teaspoon black pepper

1 (8-ounce) container sour cream

6 ounces dry linguine or spaghetti, cooked and drained

Drain liquid from artichoke hearts into a 10-inch skillet. Halve artichoke hearts and set aside. Add oil to artichoke liquid. Add onion and snow peas and cook until tender. Stir in artichoke hearts, chicken, bacon, oregano and pepper. Cook and stir until hot. Remove from heat and stir in sour cream. Toss sauce mixture with hot linguine.

Serves 4

Georgia Country Captain Chicken

1	cup flour		1	cup vegetable oil
	Dash cayenne pepper		1	cup slivered almonds,
½	teaspoon black pepper			toasted
½-1	teaspoon salt		½-1	cup raisins or currants
1	(3½ to 4-pound) chicken,			(optional)
	cut into pieces			

Sauce

1	large Vidalia or other		1	(28-ounce) can tomatoes
	sweet onion, finely		½-1	teaspoon curry powder or
	chopped			dried rosemary
1	clove garlic, minced		1½	teaspoons minced fresh
1	large bell pepper,			parsley
	chopped		½	teaspoon dried thyme
1-1½	cups hot water		½	teaspoon dried basil

Combine flour, peppers and salt in a medium bowl. Dredge chicken pieces in flour mixture. Brown chicken quickly in hot vegetable oil. Remove chicken and drain on paper towels. Pour cooking oil into a small bowl and set aside. Transfer drained chicken to a greased baking dish.

Preheat oven to 350 degrees. In same skillet, prepare sauce. Add 3 to 4 tablespoons of reserved used cooking oil. Add onion, garlic and bell pepper and sauté until softened and golden brown. Add water, tomatoes, curry powder, parsley, thyme, basil and 1 to 2 tablespoons more of cooking oil. Bring to a slow boil and cook gently for 3 to 5 minutes. Adjust seasonings as needed. Spoon sauce over chicken. Bake 1 hour or until chicken is tender. Transfer chicken to a serving platter. Sprinkle with almonds and raisins. Serve with white rice and sauce on the side to spoon over the top of all.

Serves 6

Sherman stayed at the home of a wealthy British cotton factor named Charles Green. This was to prevent any Savannahians from having Sherman stay at their home. It is also said that Green hoped to keep his own cotton, by offering his home to Sherman. The cotton was confiscated by the Union anyway, and Sherman paid Green rent, as required, because Charles Green was still a British subject.

Chicken with Crescent Rolls

1   **(8-ounce) can refrigerated crescent rolls**

4   **ounces Cheddar cheese, grated**

1   **whole frying chicken or 2½ to 3 pounds chicken breast, cooked, deboned and chopped**

White Sauce

4   **tablespoons butter**
6   **tablespoons flour**
1   **cup whole milk**

½   **cup chicken broth**
     Salt and pepper to taste

Separate crescent dough into four rectangles and pinch seams together. Sprinkle cheese on top and roll into cylinders. Refrigerate 1 hour.

To make white sauce, melt butter in a saucepan. Blend in flour until smooth. Stir in milk. Cook and stir over medium heat until thickened. Season with salt and pepper.

Preheat oven to 375 degrees. Place chopped chicken in a 9-inch square casserole dish. Cover with white sauce. Cut crescent cylinders into 7 slices each and arrange in a single layer on top. Bake, uncovered, for 30 minutes.

Serves 4

Turkey Sandwiches with Cranberry Relish

1   **(8-ounce) jar cranberry-pecan chutney or relish**

1   **loaf sliced pumpernickel bread**

2   **pounds honey-glazed barbecued deli turkey, thickly sliced**

Spread chutney over half the bread slices. Layer turkey about ¼-inch thick on top. Top with remaining bread. Cut into fourths. Refrigerate until ready to serve. To serve, place sandwich quarters on dry curly lettuce leaves on a glass raised cake plate. Cover sandwiches to prevent drying.

Serves 8

Despite Sherman's estimate, there were 38,000 bales of cotton, which were ordered burned, by the Confederates and the Central of Georgia Railroad. Charles Miller, a stock manager, probably saved Savannah by not following orders. This was due to a high wind, which he felt would carry the flames too far and set the city ablaze.

Hot Chicken Crunch

2 cups chopped celery

3 cups chopped cooked chicken

½ cup slivered almonds

1 cup mayonnaise

½ cup grated sharp Cheddar cheese

2 teaspoons lemon juice

½ teaspoon salt

¼ teaspoon black pepper

1 (10¾-ounce) can condensed cream of chicken soup

1 cup crushed Cheddar cheese crackers

Preheat oven to 350 degrees. Combine celery, chicken and almonds in a bowl. In a separate bowl, combine mayonnaise, cheese, lemon juice, salt, pepper and soup. Mix well. Stir in chicken mixture. Pour mixture into a 1½-quart casserole dish. Sprinkle with cracker crumbs. Bake 30 minutes or until bubbly.

Serves 8

Spectacular Chicken and Wild Rice Casserole

3	cups chopped cooked chicken breast	1	(2-ounce) jar sliced pimiento
1	(6-ounce) box long grain and wild rice mix, prepared	1	medium white onion, chopped
1	(10¾-ounce) can condensed cream of celery soup	1	(7-ounce) can sliced mushrooms
1-2	(16-ounce) cans French-cut green beans, drained	1	cup mayonnaise
		1	(8-ounce) can water chestnuts, sliced

Preheat oven to 350 degrees. Combine all ingredients in a large bowl. Transfer to a greased 9x13-inch glass baking dish. Bake 25 to 30 minutes.

Serves 6 to 8

If freezing for later use, freeze before baking.

Poppy Seed Chicken

1	(3-pound) chicken, cooked, deboned and chopped	2-3	tablespoons poppy seeds, divided
			Salt and pepper to taste
1	(8-ounce) container sour cream	4	tablespoons butter, melted
1	(10¾-ounce) can cream of chicken soup	½	cup cracker or bread crumbs

Preheat oven to 350 degrees. Combine chopped chicken, sour cream, soup and half the poppy seeds. Season with salt and pepper. Pour mixture into a greased casserole dish. Drizzle butter on top and sprinkle with crumbs and remaining poppy seeds. Bake 30 minutes.

Serves 6 to 8

Triple Layered Chicken and Stuffing Casserole

6	chicken breasts with bones	1	(10¾-ounce) can
1	medium onion, chopped		condensed cream of
	Sliced mushrooms to taste		celery soup
2	teaspoons butter		Salt and pepper to taste
1	(10¾-ounce) can	1	(14-ounce) package dry
	condensed cream of		cornbread stuffing mix
	chicken soup		

Cook chicken in boiling water. Cool chicken, reserving broth. Cut meat into large chunks and place in a lightly greased 2-quart casserole dish. Sauté onion and mushrooms in butter in a skillet until slightly cooked. Add soups and 2 cups of reserved chicken broth to skillet. Season with salt and pepper. Stir until smooth and pour over chicken.

Preheat oven to 375 degrees. Prepare stuffing according to package directions, using remaining reserved broth as needed for preparation. Spread stuffing over casserole. Bake 30 to 40 minutes.

Serves 8 to 10

Baked Chicken Reuben

4	boneless, skinless whole	4	slices white cheese,
	chicken breasts		halved
¼	teaspoon salt	1¼	cups bottled Thousand
	Black pepper to taste		Island dressing
1	(16-ounce) can		Sandwich buns, toasted
	sauerkraut, drained		

Preheat oven to 325 degrees. Place chicken in a greased baking dish. Sprinkle with salt and pepper. Top with sauerkraut and cheese slices. Pour dressing evenly over cheese. Cover with foil and bake 1½ hours. Serve hot on toasted buns.

Serves 4

If you have a taste for turkey and dressing, but it's not Thanksgiving, try this simply delicious chicken and stuffing casserole. When served with cranberry sauce, a vegetable and rolls, your family will think it must be November. This dish works as well as chicken soup to nourish the body and soul.

"Noble Wymberly Jones, the son of Noble Jones was called the 'Morning Star of Liberty' because of his brilliant and daring services during the Revolution."

Ron Freeman from Savannah: People, Places, and Events

Chicken Artichoke Burritos

2	onions, thinly sliced	1	(8-ounce) package cream
½	cup butter		cheese, softened
1	(1-ounce) package dry	8	(8-inch) flour tortillas
	fajita seasoning	1	cup grated mozzarella
4	boneless, skinless chicken		cheese
	breast halves, cooked	3-4	cups grated Mexican
	and shredded		white cheese
1	(6-ounce) jar marinated	1½	cups chopped Roma
	artichokes, drained and		tomatoes
	chopped		

Preheat oven to 350 degrees. Sauté onions in butter in a skillet until tender. Stir in seasoning and remove from heat. Add chicken and artichokes and mix well. Spread cream cheese over 1 side of each tortilla. Spread chicken mixture over cream cheese and sprinkle with mozzarella cheese. Roll tortillas and arrange, seam-side down, in a greased baking dish. Sprinkle with Mexican cheese and tomatoes. Cover with foil and bake 20 to 25 minutes or until heated through. Serve with sour cream and/or guacamole.

Serves 8

Burritos can be prepared up to 1 day in advance and refrigerated, then baked just before serving.

Apple Cheese n' Turkey Grill

8 slices cinnamon swirl raisin bread, divided

8 (1-ounce, ¼-inch thick) slices smoked turkey

2 medium apples, each cored and cut into 4 (¼-inch) rings

4 (4x4x¼-inch) slices colby cheese

4 tablespoons butter or margarine, divided

Place 4 slices of bread on a baking sheet. Top each with 2 slices of turkey, 2 apple rings and 1 slice of cheese. Place remaining slices of bread on top. Melt 2 tablespoons butter in a 10-inch skillet until sizzling. Place 2 sandwiches in skillet and cook over medium heat, turning once, for 3 to 5 minutes on each side or until bread is browned and cheese is melted. Transfer to a platter and keep warm. Repeat cooking procedure, using remaining 2 tablespoons butter, with remaining 2 sandwiches. Cut sandwiches diagonally and serve.

Serves 4

Seafood

The *First* Lighthouse

The Tybee Lighthouse was the *first* on the South Atlantic Coast.
In 1733, Oglethorpe inspected Tybee Island for a spot to build a daylight aid to navigation, marking the Savannah port entrance. In 1736, the *first* tower was built of wood, with a brick foundation. At 90 feet, it was the tallest building of its kind in America. Since it was too close to the shore, it fell in a 1741 storm. The second Tybee Lighthouse, built in ten months and made of wood, was 90 feet tall with a stone foundation. Still too close to shore, it fell in a 1768 storm. The third Tybee Lighthouse (well inland this time) was completed by 1773, with a 100-foot tower. In 1866, more height was added to the lower 60 feet (undamaged in "The War"). Extensive restorations on "Tybee Light" were completed in 1999. It now stands 154 feet tall, and can be sighted at 18 miles out. It is one of the few lighthouses to still have its original support buildings, as well as a unique painted pattern.

Spirited Savannah

Fort Pulaski, on Cockspur Island, is the site of many a ghostly experience, especially on a full-moon night. Even more ghostly are the events which arose from April 10 and 11, 1862. This is when Fort Pulaski fell to the Union guns. Today in Confederate Col. Charles Olmstead's old quarters, some believe his haunted spirit replays those hellish hours and days. After thirty hours of shelling from the new, rifled cannon, Fort Pulaski was in danger of being completely destroyed, along with nearly 400 confederate troops. With most of his cannons out of commission and walls breeched exposing the gunpowder magazine, Col. Olmstead made the fateful decision to surrender the fort.

Upon giving his sword to Union Major James Halpine, Olmstead said, "I yield my sword, but I trust I have not disgraced it." This decision would haunt Olmstead always. Some had harshly criticized him for not fighting to the death (to strengthen sympathy for the Confederate Cause). About 130 years after the surrender, a member of the Halpine family returned Olmstead's sword to Fort Pulaski. Hopefully, this gracious gesture will help give Col. Charles Olmstead peace at last.

"Fare to Middens for Oyster Roasts"

Native American shell "middens" give evidence that oyster roasts are not new to the Low Country. Large piles of shells, dating from around 3,000 B.C., are found throughout this area. With fish and animal bones, and an occasional arrow point, or pottery fragment, these "middens" are simply dumps from a culture long gone. It is interesting to speculate on what type "middens" modern Low country residents may create. How will these be analyzed when they are uncovered in the future?

Will a fragment of brown glass and the fragile, unraveling finger from a glove, ever convey the taste of having a cold beer in one hand, and a steaming oyster in the other? Could a flat-bladed, blunt-tipped knife, so perfect for wrestling the delicious oyster from its shell, be mistaken for something ceremonial? Could they ever describe an oyster roast accurately? Probably not, for they would miss so much. They would miss waiting for the metal sheets to become luminous with heat. They couldn't feel the anticipation as bushels of oysters are poured on top, then covered with wet, sturdy croaker sacks. They couldn't hear the hissing as the *first* oysters pop open and the juices hit the hot metal. Sadly, they couldn't taste the sweet-hot seafood sauce, with horseradish bringing tears to the eyes. Nor, could they enjoy the delicate lemon flavored butter. Most of all, they couldn't share in that special Southern tradition, always available to rich and poor alike, harvested from our waterways.

Boiled Blue Crab

3	ounces Old Savannah crab boil seasoning	1½	gallons water
1	medium onion, sliced	⅓	cup salt
1	lemon, quartered	24	live male blue crabs

Place seasoning, onion and lemon in cheesecloth and tie shut. Place water in a large pot. Add cheesecloth and salt. Cover and bring to a boil. Plunge crabs, head first, into boiling water. Cover and cook 15 minutes or until crabs are bright red; drain. Serve with lemon butter, garlic butter or Creole sauce.

Serves 4 to 6

Cleaning Your First Cooked Blue Crab

Divide and conquer is the key, so don't get discouraged on your first attempts.

1. To get to the cooked meat, first twist off crab legs and claws intact. Crack claws, and remove meat with a small cocktail fork.

2. Invert the crab, and pry off the apron or "tail flap," and discard it. Turn crab right side up again.

3. Insert thumb under shell by apron hinge; pry off the top shell, and discard it.

4. Pull away the inedible gills, the gray feathery structures, or "dead man" fingers as they are locally known; discard them along with the internal organs and the yellowish material called the fat. Break the body and remove the meat from the pockets. Take your time, don't leave any behind!

Ingredients for your first crab boil.
- *Live blue crabs*
- *A large pot with lid*
- *Long handle tongs*
- *Plenty of cold beer*
- *Paper towels*
- *Good friends*

Always begin with frisky, live male crabs. In the low country, we harvest only male crabs to ensure species longevity. Males are determined by their thin, pointed "tail flap" or apron. Female aprons are wider more like a "V" shape...Go figure! Discard any dead crabs before cooking since bacteria in crab multiplies quickly and may kill other crabs in your container. Use long tongs to handle the crabs. A pinch from a blue crab is no laughing matter!

"The ultimate delight in seafood" is the well-deserved reputation of the soft-shell crab in Savannah. Contrary to some beliefs, they are not a separate breed, but our familiar blue crab at the molting stage. Crabs outgrow their shells, burst out of the old ones, and grow new ones. For the few hours after the "buster" crab has shed its old shell, the crab's shell is soft. This is the "magic stage" prized by crabbers and gourmets alike. To clean the soft-shell crab, place it on a cutting surface. Lift the shell and remove the gills on the left and right sides of the top of the crab. These are known as the "dead man's fingers." Remove the internal organs and trim off the eyes.

Steamed Blue Crab

¼	cup plus 2 tablespoons Old Savannah seasoning	3	tablespoons pickling spice
¼	cup plus 2 tablespoons coarse salt	2	tablespoons celery seeds
			White vinegar
3	tablespoons cayenne pepper		Water
		12	blue crabs

Combine seasoning, salt, pepper, pickling spice and celery seeds; set aside. Combine water and vinegar in a very large pot with a lid in equal amounts to a depth of 1 inch. Place a rack in pot over liquid. Bring to a boil. Arrange half the crabs on the rack. Sprinkle with half the seasoning mixture. Top with remaining crabs and sprinkle with remaining seasoning mixture. Cover pot tightly and steam 20 to 25 minutes or until crabs are bright red. Rinse well with cold water and drain. Serve with lemon butter or garlic butter.

Fried Soft Shell Crabs

½	cup buttermilk	1	teaspoon dried thyme
2	eggs	1	teaspoon dried oregano
1½	cups flour, plus extra for dusting	1	teaspoon dried basil
1½	teaspoons baking powder	1¼	cups beer
2	teaspoons salt	1	tablespoon Worcestershire sauce
2	tablespoons sugar		Canola or peanut oil
2	teaspoons black pepper	6-8	soft shell crabs, cleaned

Beat buttermilk and eggs in a large bowl. In a separate bowl, combine flour, baking powder, salt, sugar, black pepper, thyme, oregano and basil. Slowly whisk half the flour and herb mixture into the buttermilk mixture, whisking to a smooth paste. Add remaining flour and herb mixture and whisk until smooth. Slowly add beer, whisking until smooth. Whisk in Worcestershire sauce.

Fill a deep fat fryer or deep frying pan three-fourths full with oil. Heat oil to 340 degrees. Dust crabs with flour and shake off excess. Holding crabs by the back fins, immerse in batter, then carefully immerse in hot oil. Cook 2 crabs at a time so crabs have room to float to the surface. Fry 5 to 6 minutes or until golden brown. Place on paper towels to drain and hold in a 325 degree oven while frying the rest. Serve with lemon wedges and tartar sauce or honey mustard dip.

Serves 4

Crab Au Gratin Casserole

1-1½ pounds mushrooms, sliced
½ cup butter, divided
½ cup flour
1 (10-ounce) can chicken broth
1½ cups light cream
Salt and pepper to taste
1-1½ pounds crabmeat
1½ cups grated mild or medium Cheddar cheese
Bread crumbs
Butter

Preheat oven to 350 degrees. Sauté mushrooms in 2 tablespoons butter in a skillet for about 5 minutes. In a saucepan, melt 6 tablespoons butter. Blend in flour. Add broth, cream, salt and pepper. Layer sautéed mushrooms, sauce, and crabmeat in a 6-cup casserole dish. Sprinkle cheese and bread crumbs on top. Dot with butter. Bake 30 minutes.

Serves 4 to 6

Casserole can be frozen before baking. Bake frozen casserole at 300 degrees for 45 minutes.

Savannah Deviled Crab Casserole

½ green bell pepper, chopped
1 medium onion, chopped
½ cup margarine
2 cups crabmeat
1 tablespoon Worcestershire sauce
Dash of Tabasco sauce or to taste
3 tablespoons Shedds Old Style sauce
¾ cup bread crumbs
1 teaspoon baking powder
Salt and pepper to taste
1 tablespoon ketchup
1 teaspoon water

Preheat oven to 375 degrees. Sauté bell pepper and onion in margarine until softened but not browned. Mix in crab, Worcestershire sauce, Tabasco sauce, Shedds sauce, bread crumbs and baking powder. Season with salt and pepper and transfer to a casserole dish. Mix together ketchup and water and spread over top of casserole. Bake 30 minutes.

Serves 4 to 6

Microwave Crab Mornay

½ cup butter
¾ cup finely chopped green onion
½ cup finely chopped parsley
2 tablespoons flour
1½ cups half-and-half
8 ounces Swiss cheese, grated
1 tablespoon white wine
½ teaspoon salt
½ teaspoon cayenne pepper
1 pound lump crabmeat
Seasoned bread crumbs

Melt butter in a large microwave-proof glass bowl. Add green onion and parsley and cook on high for 3 to 5 minutes. Blend in flour and half-and-half. Cook on high for 3 minutes or until mixture thickens. Stir in cheese and cook on high for 1 to 2 minutes or until cheese melts. Add wine, salt and pepper. Stir well. Gently fold in crabmeat. Spoon mixture into shells or small ramekins and sprinkle with bread crumbs. Broil until lightly browned and bubbly. If serving as a hot dip, spoon into a chafing dish and serve with crackers or baguette slices.

Serves 6

Martha Nesbitt's Crab Cakes

1	green onion, finely chopped	1	tablespoon Dijon mustard
1	clove garlic, minced	1	egg
2	tablespoons finely chopped red bell pepper	½	teaspoon minced parsley
3	tablespoons butter, divided	1	cup bread crumbs, divided
	Cayenne pepper to taste	1	pound white or claw crabmeat, picked through
3	tablespoons whipping cream	¼	cup Parmesan cheese
		2	tablespoons oil

Sauté onion, garlic and bell pepper in 1 tablespoon butter for 3 minutes or until softened. Add cayenne pepper, cream and mustard. Mix well. Stir in egg, parsley and ½ cup bread crumbs. Gently fold in crab. Form mixture into 8 patties, each about ½-inch thick. Combine remaining ½ cup bread crumbs and cheese and pat mixture onto both sides of patties. Refrigerate 2 hours or until firm.

Preheat oven to 400 degrees. Heat oil and remaining 2 tablespoons butter in a heavy or electric skillet. Sauté crab cakes in hot oil mixture for about 3 minutes on each side. If baking, place crab cakes on a baking sheet and drizzle oil/butter mixture on top. Bake at 400 degrees for 7 to 10 minutes. Serve with Lemon Dill Sauce.

Makes 8 cakes

Lemon Dill Sauce

1	cup mayonnaise	1	tablespoon minced fresh parsley
¼	cup buttermilk		
2	tablespoons chopped fresh dill	2	teaspoons lemon juice
		1	tablespoon lemon zest
		1	small clove garlic, minced

Combine all ingredients and chill. Mixture thickens as it chills. Place a dollop beside crab cakes and pass extra on the side.

This recipe is excellent for a plated appetizer since instead of frying a few at a time, it can be prepared in the oven and all served at the same time, yet tastes as good as fried.

Martha Giddens Nesbitt is an award-winning food and lifestyle author and food editor for the "Savannah Morning News and Evening Press." *In her credits for* Savannah Entertains, *Martha stated,* "Although I do not consider myself a great cook, I am shamefully good at asking great cooks for their recipes and techniques," *and for that, we thank her. Martha Giddens Nesbitt lives south of Savannah on the Isle of Hope.*

Low Country Shrimp Boil

½	cup butter
½	cup salt
	Tabasco sauce to taste
4-5	pounds new potatoes, quartered
16	ears fresh corn, broken in half, or 18 small frozen ears
4-5	pounds Roger Wood Lumber Jack smoked sausage, cut into 2 to 3-inch pieces
6	pounds shrimp in shells

Fill a 10- to 12-quart pot, or 2 smaller ones, half full with water. Add butter and salt and bring to a boil. Add Tabasco sauce and potatoes and boil 10 minutes. Add fresh corn and boil 5 minutes, or 10 minutes for frozen corn. Add sausage and boil 5 minutes. Add shrimp and boil 3 to 5 minutes or until shells begin to separate from shrimp; do not overcook. Drain and serve from a large bowl or dump mixture onto newspaper spread on a table. This recipe works well for outdoor cooking on gas burners. Serve with squeeze butter and Cocktail Sauce.

Serves 12 to 14

If necessary, due to a guest's seafood allergy, cook shrimp separately for 3 to 5 minutes in a pot of boiling salted water. Add 10 minutes on to cooking time of pot with potatoes, corn and sausage.

Cocktail Sauce

1	cup ketchup
2	tablespoons Worcestershire sauce
2	tablespoons lemon or lime juice
2	tablespoons prepared horseradish
	Salt and pepper to taste
	Tabasco sauce to taste

Combine all ingredients and refrigerate until ready to serve. Best made ahead to allow flavors to blend.

Serving sizes per pound – and count per pound:

Jumbo 18-20
4 per serving

Large 21-25
6 per serving

Medium 26-35
7 per serving

Small 35+
10 per serving

White Dipping Sauce

1½ cups mayonnaise

¼ cup prepared horseradish

3 tablespoons lemon juice

2 tablespoons Worcestershire sauce

1 teaspoon salt

1 teaspoon onion juice, or 1 tablespoon minced onion

1 teaspoon minced fresh parsley

¼ teaspoon hot pepper sauce

1 clove garlic, minced

Combine all ingredients. Cover and refrigerate 8 hours. Serve with peeled, steamed or boiled shrimp and garnished with parsley.

Makes 2 cups

Boiled Shrimp

Here are three favorite ways to cook shrimp.

1. Boil 1 qt. water with 1 T. salt. Add unpeeled shrimp, stir and boil 2 to 5 minutes until pink. Drain immediately.

2. Drop shrimp into a pot of salted, boiling water. Then return to a boil. Cover and remove from heat. Let shrimp stand 3 to 5 minutes (depending on size) or until shrimp turn pink. Remove and drain.

3. Pour 2 T. vinegar into pot. Over medium heat, add shrimp and stir constantly. As the shrimp heat, the water is drawn out so they do not burn. Continue stirring until shrimp turn pink. Remove and drain.

Saints' Creamy Shrimp with Mushrooms

1	pound shrimp, cooked, peeled and deveined	1	cup sour cream
	Salt and pepper to taste	5	tablespoons butter, softened
8	ounces fresh mushrooms, sliced	1	teaspoon soy sauce
3	tablespoons butter	¼	cup freshly grated Parmesan cheese
1	tablespoon flour	1	teaspoon paprika

Preheat oven to 400 degrees. Place shrimp in a greased shallow baking dish just large enough to hold shrimp in a single layer. Season with salt and pepper. In a skillet, sauté mushrooms in 3 tablespoons butter until browned. Transfer to a bowl and toss with flour. Add sour cream, softened butter and soy sauce. Season with salt and pepper. Pour sauce over shrimp. Sprinkle with cheese and paprika. Bake 10 minutes. Excellent served over pasta or rice.

Serves 4

To make as a casserole, cook pasta and place in a greased 9x13-inch baking dish. Add shrimp and sauce and bake as directed above.

Shrimp or Crawfish Fettuccine

1½	cups margarine	2	cloves garlic, minced
2	bell peppers, chopped	1	pint half-and-half
3	medium onions, chopped	1	pound Velveeta pepper cheese, grated
¼	cup flour		
¼	cup chopped fresh parsley	1	(1-pound) package medium egg noodles
2	pounds shrimp or crawfish tails		Parmesan cheese

Melt margarine in a large saucepan. Add bell peppers and onions and cook 15 minutes. Add flour, cook and stir 15 minutes longer to make the roux. Add parsley, shrimp and garlic. Cover and cook 15 minutes. Add half-and-half and pepper cheese. Cook 30 minutes.

Preheat oven to 350 degrees. Cook noodles and drain. Toss noodles with sauce and place in a large baking pan. Sprinkle with Parmesan cheese. Bake 15 to 30 minutes.

Shrimp with Tomato and Feta

½	cup chopped onion	2	teaspoons dried oregano
2	tablespoons extra virgin olive oil	1	pound medium shrimp, peeled and deveined
1	(28-ounce) can Italian-style plum tomatoes, drained and chopped	1	(4-ounce) package feta cheese, crumbled
⅓	cup dry white wine	2	tablespoons chopped fresh parsley

Sauté onion in oil in a large skillet over medium heat for 3 minutes. Add tomatoes, wine and oregano. Reduce heat to low and simmer 5 minutes or until thickened. Add shrimp, cook and stir 3 minutes or until shrimp are pink. Sprinkle with cheese. Simmer 1 minute. Stir in parsley. Serve over yellow or white rice.

Serves 4

Excellent for a dinner party - quick to prepare and cook. One of our favorites!

A roux is the thickening agent used for many southern gumbos and stews. A quick and easy roux can be done in a microwave. Whisk equal amounts of vegetable oil and flour in an 8-cup glass dish. Microwave on high for several minutes. Stir well. Keep microwaving until mixture has the color of a copper penny. Continue stirring. Watch carefully to avoid burning. Roux can be frozen and used later.

Shrimp and Artichoke Casserole

6½ tablespoons butter or margarine, divided

¼ cup plus ½ tablespoon flour

1 cup whipping cream

½ cup half-and-half

1 tablespoon Worcestershire sauce

3 tablespoons dry sherry

1 pound fresh mushrooms, sliced

1 (14-ounce) can artichoke hearts, drained and quartered

1½ pounds cooked shrimp, peeled and deveined

1 cup freshly grated Parmesan cheese

Preheat oven to 425 degrees. Melt 4½ tablespoons butter in a saucepan. Blend in flour until smooth. Stir in cream and half-and-half. Cook until thickened. Blend in Worcestershire sauce and sherry. Set aside. In a large skillet, sauté mushrooms in remaining 2 tablespoons butter. Spread mushrooms in a 3-quart casserole dish. Arrange artichokes and shrimp evenly over mushrooms. Pour sauce over top. Bake 20 minutes. Sprinkle with cheese and broil until top is lightly browned.

Serves 6

Shrimp Creole

¼	cup flour	1	cup water
¼	cup bacon grease	1	teaspoon black pepper
1½	cups chopped onion	½	teaspoon cayenne pepper
1	cup chopped green onion		Hot pepper sauce to taste
1	cup chopped celery	2-3	bay leaves
1	cup chopped bell pepper	1	teaspoon sugar
2	cloves garlic, minced	1	teaspoon Worcestershire sauce
1	(6-ounce) can tomato paste	1	tablespoon lemon juice
1	(16-ounce) can chopped tomatoes with liquid	4	pounds peeled and deveined shrimp
1	(8-ounce) can tomato sauce	½	cup chopped fresh parsley
		2-3	cups cooked rice

In a large heavy roasting pan, cook and stir flour and bacon grease to make a dark brown roux. Add onions, celery, bell pepper and garlic. Sauté 20 to 30 minutes or until softened. Add tomato paste and mix well. Add undrained tomatoes, tomato sauce, water, black and cayenne peppers, pepper sauce, bay leaves, sugar, Worcestershire sauce and lemon juice. Cover and simmer slowly for 1 hour, stirring occasionally. Add shrimp and cook 5 to 15 minutes or until shrimp are cooked. Add parsley just before serving. Serve over rice.

Serves 10

This dish is much better made ahead, preferably a day before serving. When reheating, bring only to a simmer; do not boil. This recipe freezes well and is good with chicken, too.

Chilled Shrimp in Jade Sauce

2	pounds (15 to 20 count) shrimp	1	tablespoon white sesame seeds
4	quarts water		

Jade Sauce

2	cups spinach leaves, washed and dried	2	tablespoons Chinese rice wine or dry sherry
¼	cup cilantro sprigs	2	tablespoons white vinegar
8	basil leaves	2	tablespoons dark sesame oil
1	green onion, chopped		
2	cloves garlic, chopped	2	teaspoons hoisin sauce
2	teaspoons minced fresh ginger	2	teaspoons sugar
		½	teaspoon Asian chili sauce
1	teaspoon orange zest	¼	cup freshly squeezed orange juice
1	tablespoon thin soy sauce (available at Asian markets)		

Shell shrimp; devein and butterfly deeply. Bring water to a boil. Add shrimp and cook 2 minutes or until shrimp turn white. Drain and transfer to a bowl of ice water until chilled. Pat dry and refrigerate until ready to use. Toast sesame seeds in an ungreased skillet over medium heat until golden.

To make sauce, combine all ingredients in a blender and liquefy. Toss shrimp with sauce and place on a serving platter or individual serving plates. Sprinkle with sesame seeds.

Serves 4 as an entrée or 8 as an appetizer

Sizzling Shrimp and Vegetable Sauté

¾ cup dry converted white rice

1½ cups water

2 tablespoons chopped fresh dill

2 teaspoons olive oil

1 cup sliced red onion

2 cups fresh broccoli florets

1 pound peeled and deveined medium shrimp

¾ cup sliced red bell pepper

1 tablespoon lemon juice

⅓ cup chili sauce

Prepare rice according to package using 1½ cups water and adding dill. Meanwhile, heat olive oil in a large skillet. Add onion and cook 1 minute. Stir in broccoli, shrimp, bell pepper and lemon juice. Cover and cook over medium-high heat, stirring occasionally, for 3 to 4 minutes or until shrimp are pink and vegetables are crisp-tender. Stir in chili sauce. Serve over cooked rice.

Serves 4

Scallop and Shrimp Fettuccine

3 cloves garlic, minced

¼ cup olive oil

¾ pound medium shrimp, peeled and deveined

½ pound medium scallops

2 tablespoons fresh basil, finely chopped

2 tablespoons minced fresh parsley

2 cups fish stock or clam juice

½ cup pine nuts

1 pound fettuccine pasta, cooked al dente and drained

Sauté garlic in oil for 1 minute. Add shrimp and scallops and cook 4 minutes. Add basil, parsley and fish stock. Simmer 10 minutes. Meanwhile, toast pine nuts in a separate skillet, shaking pan frequently, over low heat for 3 to 4 minutes or until evenly golden. Serve seafood mixture over fettuccine. Top with pine nuts.

Serves 4

Scallops on Spinach with Ginger Sauce

3	ounces fresh ginger, grated	1	cup whipping cream
1	medium onion, chopped	½	tablespoon butter
1	stalk celery, chopped	2	(10-ounce) packages fresh spinach
1	clove garlic, minced		Salt and pepper to taste
	Pinch of thyme	½	teaspoon nutmeg
2	tablespoons olive oil	16	scallops, halved
1	cup white wine		Carrot sticks for garnish
1	cup fish stock or clam juice		

Sauté ginger, onion, celery, garlic and thyme in oil in a saucepan over medium heat for 5 minutes. Add wine and cook 5 minutes over high heat. Add fish stock and cook 5 minutes on high. Reduce heat to low and add cream. Cook 10 minutes. Pour cream mixture into a blender and process. Strain sauce and return to saucepan; keep warm.

Melt butter in a large saucepan. Add spinach, salt, pepper and nutmeg and cook 2 minutes. Meanwhile, add scallops to sauce and cook 5 to 7 minutes or until scallops are tender. Arrange scallops over spinach on a serving platter. Pour sauce on top and garnish with carrot sticks.

Serves 4 to 6

Scallops and Mushrooms in Cream

2½	pounds scallops, rinsed and halved if large	1¾	cups whipping cream
		½	teaspoon salt
1¼	pounds fresh mushrooms, sliced	¼	teaspoon black pepper
		¾	teaspoon Worcestershire sauce
5	tablespoons butter		
2½	tablespoons flour		

Place scallops in a 3-quart saucepan. Cover with cold water and heat slowly to boiling. Remove from heat and drain immediately; set aside. Sauté mushrooms in butter in a large skillet for 5 minutes or until browned. Add flour and cook 5 minutes, stirring constantly. Gradually add cream, cook and stir until sauce thickens. Stir in scallops, salt, pepper and Worcestershire sauce. Serve on toast points for brunch or over rice for a dinner entrée.

Serves 6 to 8

If serving a crowd, you will have no difficulty in doubling this recipe. Either bay or sea scallops may be used depending on the season.

The first Miss Georgia pageant was held on Tybee Island in July of 1926. None of the contestants were allowed to wear swimsuits. The next pageant held at Tybee was in 1939, and the last in 1941.

"How To" Do A Savannah Oyster Roast

According to Charlie Russo of Russo Seafood, "whichever method you choose, you're in for some delicious eating."

A. Modern Method

1. Buy good, single shell oysters, make sure they have been washed.

2. Allow 8 to 10 people per bushel for oyster roast.

3. Get oyster knives, cocktail sauce, and saltines per guest.

4. The easy way to roast oysters is to do it the modern way by steaming.

The steaming method is accomplished by putting the oysters on a rack in the cooker with a couple of inches of water in the bottom. This method takes approximately 5 minutes; check oysters to make sure they are cooked to your satisfaction.

Barbecued Oysters with Hogwash

½	cup natural rice vinegar	1	small jalapeño pepper, seeded and minced
½	cup seasoned rice vinegar		
2	shallots, minced	1	small bunch fresh cilantro, coarsely chopped
3	tablespoons freshly squeezed and strained lime juice		
		2	dozen oysters, scrubbed

To make hogwash, combine all ingredients except oysters in a medium bowl. Refrigerate at least 1 hour before using.

When ready to cook, preheat a grill until very hot. Place oysters on grill and cook 3 minutes or until shells open. Use an oyster knife to detach oysters from top shells, then loosen top shells and discard. Spoon hogwash over oysters before serving.

Serves 3 to 4

Surefire Seafood Kebabs

¾	cup olive oil, divided	1	pound large shrimp, peeled and deveined
1	tablespoon white wine vinegar	1¼	pounds sea scallops
1	tablespoon fresh lime juice Zest of 1 lime	2-3	green or yellow bell peppers, cut into 1-inch pieces
1-2	tablespoons finely chopped fresh mint	32	cherry tomatoes
1-2	finely chopped fresh parsley	32	small mushrooms, stems removed
1	clove garlic, finely chopped	2	red onions, cut into 1-inch pieces
2	tablespoons grated fresh ginger		

Whisk together ½ cup oil, vinegar, lime juice, lime zest, mint, parsley, garlic and ginger in a large bowl. Add shrimp and scallops and stir to coat. Cover and refrigerate 2 to 3 hours.

If using bamboo skewers, soak in hot water for 30 minutes. When ready to cook, preheat grill. Drain shrimp and scallops, reserving marinade. Thread seafood onto skewers, alternating with bell peppers, tomatoes, mushrooms and onions. Brush kebabs with remaining ¼ cup oil. Grill kebabs 3 to 5 minutes or until done, turning frequently and basting with reserved marinade. Serve hot or at room temperature.

Serves 8

(Oyster Roast continued)

B. Old Fashioned Method

1. Dig a hole and make a fire inside the hole. After the coals are ready, place a sheet of metal on top of the coals. Place oysters on top of the metal sheet, spread the oysters out flat and cover with wet croaker sacks.

2. This method requires shoveling the oysters into place on the table and can't be done with many bushels.

Oysters Bienville

½	cup butter	½	cup half-and-half
1	cup finely chopped green or yellow onion	½	cup white wine
½	cup flour	1	teaspoon salt
2	cups chicken broth or fish stock, warmed	1	teaspoon white pepper
1½	pounds cooked shrimp, peeled and finely chopped	½	teaspoon cayenne pepper
8	ounces fresh mushrooms, finely chopped	6	pie pans filled with rock salt
3	egg yolks	3	dozen oysters on the half shell
		¼	cup bread crumbs
		½	cup Parmesan cheese
		⅛	teaspoon paprika

Preheat oven to 375 degrees. Melt butter in a 3-quart heavy saucepan. Add onion and sauté until tender. Slowly blend flour over low heat, stirring constantly, until lightly browned. Gradually stir in broth. Simmer over medium heat for 10 minutes or until the sauce is very thick. Stir in shrimp and mushrooms. Cook 5 minutes; then remove from heat. Whisk together egg yolks, half-and-half and wine. Very slowly pour a small amount of sauce into egg mixture, stirring constantly to avoid curdling. Stir egg mixture into sauce in saucepan. Season with salt, white pepper and cayenne pepper. Cook over low heat, stirring constantly, until thickened. Sauce must be very thick so that it will sit on top of oysters. Drain excess liquid from each oyster and place 6 oysters in their shells in each pan filled with rock salt. Bake 7 minutes. Remove pans from oven and increase oven to 400 degrees. Pour off any liquid that has accumulated in each oyster. Spoon sauce over each oyster. Combine bread crumbs, cheese and paprika and sprinkle over oysters. Bake 10 minutes or until tops are lightly browned. Serve immediately.

Serves 6

This can also be made into a pie. After cooking oysters, arrange shelled oysters in a baked pie crust. Spoon sauce over oysters. Top with bread crumb mixture. Bake at 400 degrees for 10 minutes.

Eating Raw Oysters

Eat raw oysters (in the shell)... on a cracker, topped with cocktail sauce, horseradish sauce, or a little lemon juice squeezed on top.

Flounder Ambassador

4	flounder fillets	½	cup whipping cream
⅛	teaspoon salt	¼	cup milk
⅛	teaspoon black pepper	1	tablespoon Dijon mustard
½	cup chopped fresh parsley	2	tablespoons Parmesan cheese
2	tablespoons butter		
2	tablespoons lemon juice	1	tablespoon fine dry bread crumbs
4	ounces fresh mushrooms, sliced	¼	teaspoon paprika
1	tablespoon all-purpose flour		

Preheat oven to 350 degrees. Arrange fillets in a lightly greased 12x8x1-inch baking dish. Sprinkle with salt, pepper and parsley. In a skillet, melt butter with lemon juice. Add mushrooms and sauté 2 to 3 minutes. Stir in flour until smooth. Gradually stir in cream and milk. Cook and stir over medium heat until thickened and bubbly. Stir in mustard. Spread cream sauce over fillets. Sprinkle with cheese, bread crumbs and paprika. Bake 30 to 35 minutes or until done.

Serves 4

On September 8, 1779, French war ships with 4,000 troops landed at Tybee, surprising the British. There, 1,500 American soldiers joined forces with the French. The fleet was led by count Charles Henri d'Etaing, who made a gallant, but doomed, frontal assault in an effort to free Savannah from the British. This "Siege of Savannah" was one of the bloodiest battles in the American Revolution. Casualties included the heroic Polish Count Casmir Pulaski and Sgt. William Jasper. Savannah remained under British rule until 1782.

Pecan Crusted Flounder with Hazelnut Sauce

1	cup ground pecans	½-¾	cup vegetable oil
1	cup bread crumbs	⅓	cup hazelnut liqueur
½	cup white wine	⅓	cup demi-glaze
	Juice of 1 lemon	3-4	tablespoons butter
2	(6-ounce) flounder fillets	2	teaspoons chopped
	All-purpose flour for		pecans
	dredging		

Combine ground pecans and bread crumbs in a shallow dish. In a separate dish, combine wine and lemon juice. Add fish to wine mixture and marinate 2 minutes. Remove fish from marinade. Dredge in flour, then dip in marinade and roll in pecan mixture. Sauté fish in oil over medium heat for 3 minutes on each side, turning only once. Remove and keep warm on a serving platter. Combine liqueur and demi-glaze in a skillet over medium heat. When warm, swirl in butter. Mix in chopped pecans and pour over fish.

Serves 2

In 1782, General "Mad" Anthony Wayne liberated Savannah. The Loyalists withdrew to Tybee Island to await English ships. Appropriately, the Loyalists had to sit, basically unsheltered and consumed by insects, for weeks along with their slaves.

Oglethorpe's much-married interpreter, Mary Musgrove, almost interfered with the building of the Tybee Lighthouse. Her trading posts ignored the ban on strong "spirits" and the workmen were nearly always drunk.

Salmon Bake with Pecan Crunch Coating

4	(4 to 6-ounce) salmon fillets	1½	tablespoons honey
⅛	teaspoon salt	¼	cup soft bread crumbs
⅛	teaspoon black pepper	¼	cup finely chopped pecans
2	tablespoons Dijon mustard	2	teaspoons chopped fresh parsley
2	tablespoons butter or margarine, melted		Fresh parsley sprigs and lemon slices for garnish

Preheat oven to 450 degrees. Season salmon with salt and pepper. Place fillets, skin-side down, in a lightly greased 9x13-inch pan. Combine mustard, butter and honey and brush over fillets. Mix bread crumbs, pecans and parsley. Spoon mixture evenly over fillets. Bake 10 minutes or until fish flakes easily when tested with a fork. Garnish with parsley and lemon slices.

Serves 4

To test a fish fillet for doneness, use a fork to prod fillet at its thickest point, preferably from underneath so the outer appearance remains intact. If the fillet flakes easily and has opaque, milky white juices, then it is properly cooked. If the fillet is translucent and has watery juices, it is not done. If it is dry and easily falls apart, it is overdone.

From 1829 to 1831, a young West Point graduate with the rank of lieutenant worked on the construction of Ft. Pulaski, near Tybee. He would later become a legend in his own time. His name was Robert E. Lee.

Legend has it that Sir Francis Drake once landed on Tybee. While that may be romantic, it is certain that early Spanish and French explorers (and a few pirates) did visit Tybee. Before that, native Americans (called Euchee) fished in Tybee's waters and hunted in its maritime forest.

Grilled Salmon Quesadilla with Cucumber Salsa

1	(8-ounce) salmon fillet	2	ounces goat cheese, crumbled
4	(8 to 10-inch) flour tortillas	2	fresh jalapeño peppers, seeded and sliced
1	cup grated Monterey Jack cheese		

Cook salmon on a covered grill for 5 to 6 minutes on each side or until done. Cool and flake with a fork. Spoon salmon evenly over half of each tortilla. Top with cheeses and pepper slices. Fold tortillas in half. Cook filled tortillas in a large, nonstick skillet over high heat for 1 minute on each side or until tortillas are slightly browned and cheese is melted. Cut each tortilla into 3 triangles and serve with Cucumber Salsa.

Serves 4

Cucumber Salsa

1	large cucumber, chopped	1	tablespoon finely chopped yellow bell pepper
1	clove garlic, minced		
1	tablespoon finely chopped poblano pepper	1	tablespoon finely chopped fresh cilantro
1	tablespoon finely chopped purple onion	1	teaspoon olive oil
1	tablespoon finely chopped red bell pepper	¼	teaspoon salt
		⅛	teaspoon black pepper

Combine all ingredients. Cover and chill.

Makes 1¼ cups

Margarita Salmon

1	teaspoon lime zest	1	clove garlic, crushed
½	teaspoon orange zest	4	(6-ounce) salmon steaks
3	tablespoons fresh lime or		(about 1 thick)
	lemon juice	8	ounces dry angel hair
1	tablespoon tequila		pasta
2	teaspoons sugar		Lime slices for garnish
2	teaspoons vegetable oil		(optional)
½	teaspoon salt		

Combine zests, lime juice, tequila, sugar, oil, salt and garlic in a large zip-top bag. Add fish and seal. Marinate in refrigerator for 20 minutes. Meanwhile, cook pasta according to package directions; drain and keep warm.

Preheat broiler or grill. Drain fish, reserving marinade. Place fish on a broiler pan or in a grill basket coated with cooking spray. Cook, basting occasionally with reserved marinade, for 7 minutes or until fish flakes easily when tested with a fork. Serve over pasta. Garnish with lime slices.

Serves 4

Both the Tybee Railroad and the Tybee Road allowed "day trippers" to enjoy the beauty of the island, especially from the late 1800s to the early 1900s. Dances were held at the beautiful and vast Tybrisia pavilion. By the 1920s and 30s, the Big Band sounds of Tommy Dorsey, Cab Calloway, Louis Armstrong and Duke Ellington were heard on Tybee. Whenever he could, Johnny Mercer loved to visit Tybee Island, as well.

Victory Drive used to run all the way from Savannah to Tybee. The entire route was planted with palm trees in memory of WWI veterans. Although much of the Tybee Road has changed, Victory Drive remains the longest palm-lined drive in the world.

Mahi Mahi or Grouper Polynesian

2	large mahi mahi or grouper fillets	1	cup crushed pineapple, drained
	Salt and pepper to taste	2	tablespoons chopped blanched almonds
2	tablespoons butter, melted	¼	teaspoon dried tarragon
1	cup cooked white rice	⅛	teaspoon dried dill
1	cup seasoned bread crumbs, plus extra for topping	⅛	teaspoon cayenne pepper
		2	slices bacon, halved crosswise

Preheat oven to 350 degrees. Season fillets with salt and pepper. Spread butter over bottom of a baking dish. Place 1 fillet in butter in dish. In a bowl, combine rice, bread crumbs, pineapple, almonds, tarragon, dill and cayenne pepper. Spoon mixture on fillet in baking dish, pressing mixture down to compact it. Top with second fillet. Press edges of fillets together and secure with toothpicks, if needed. Sprinkle with extra bread crumbs and a light dusting of cayenne pepper. Lay bacon pieces diagonally over fillets. Bake 40 to 45 minutes.

Serves 4 to 6

Meat and Game

The *First* Golf Club

The Savannah Golf Club (c. 1794) is the *first* in Georgia, with claims toward being the *first* in the nation. Until another golf club can produce evidence to the contrary, Savannah's claim to be the oldest will stand. What became the Savannah Golf Club is reported to have begun a few years before a course was laid out for play. Perhaps the most classically stylish aspect of the Savannah Golf Club is that they resumed play so shortly after the War Between the States, using Confederate redoubts for bunkers on the course. Fort Boggs, an earthenworks fortification, was a primary defense for the Confederates on the east side of Savannah and was located exactly where the Savannah Golf Club is now. Fore or Fire?

Spirited Savannah

At the turn of the 19th century, affairs of honor settled with dueling pistols had reached absurd levels. Duels often began at the Old City Hotel where self-important young men, with a few too many drinks under their belts, took offense far too easily. Despite laws against dueling, the challengers continued this practice. If an opponent refused to duel, posts in the newspaper often defamed the challengers. These posts called each other "liars," "scoundrels," "villains" and the like.

Far too often, though, the challengers and their seconds met in locations on the edges of Savannah, or in more remote areas. Savannahians went to Ft. Screven, South Carolina, and the Carolinians came to Tybee Island, by the Lighthouse. Perhaps most often, Hutchinson Island, in the midst of the Savannah River, was used for dueling. Even today, all of these places, as well as Ft. Wayne on River Street and behind the Colonial Cemetery, bear the taint of violence. Parts of Hutchinson Island are considered to be very haunted by unresolved spirits, some murdered, some killed in duels, some dumped there to die for unknown reasons.

"The Best of Bubba's Southern Barbeque"

Barbeque is a subject which tends to get all Southerners "fired up," even genteel Savannahians. From Southern barbeque by region, to barbeque by individual states in Dixie, on down to specific towns – and their favorite Bubba's Barbeque joint – everyone claims their barbeque to be the best. This applies to the kind of meat used, the methods of cooking, the methods of serving, the side dishes served with the barbeque, and most of all, The Sauce. No wine connoisseur in the world can match Bubba's ability to discern the most subtle nuances of difference in barbeque sauces. Furthermore, the secret barbeque sauce "receipt," handed down from generation to generation is a myth. Why? This is because Bubba has tasted his daddy's barbeque sauce, which was his granddaddy's sauce as well, you see? He knows what ingredients go into the sauce; but it is the taste which really tells him when the sauce is right. Even the most cultured Southern Gentlemen can become the best of Bubbas when engaging in this distinctly Southern ritual. As the barbeque process takes hours, with fires to be tended, and sauces to be made and applied – as well as the consumption of quantities of cold brew – there is plenty of time for Bubba to emerge. When he does, he is following a tradition so Southern as to have become symbolic of Dixie herself. (Confidentially, Georgia does have the best barbeque. Pork, of course, with that sweet-hot sauce we love in Savannah. Not that lukewarm, insipid mess they call a sauce in ...!)

Spinach and Ricotta-Stuffed Meatloaf

2	eggs, beaten, divided	1½	pounds ground beef
¾	cup soft bread crumbs	1	(10-ounce) package frozen
¼	cup finely chopped onion		chopped spinach,
¼	cup finely chopped green		thawed and well drained
	or red bell pepper	1	cup ricotta cheese
½	teaspoon garlic salt	¼	cup Parmesan cheese
¼	teaspoon black pepper	1½	teaspoons snipped fresh
1	(8-ounce) can tomato		basil or marjoram, or
	sauce, divided		½ teaspoon dried

Preheat oven to 350 degrees. Combine 1 beaten egg, bread crumbs, onion, bell pepper, garlic salt, black pepper and ¼ cup tomato sauce in a mixing bowl. (Reserve remaining tomato sauce for Chunky Tomato Sauce.) Add ground beef and mix well.

In a separate bowl, stir together remaining beaten egg, spinach, cheeses and basil. Pat one-third of meat mixture into the bottom of a 9x5x3-inch loaf pan. Spread half of spinach mixture on top. Repeat layers once and top with a final layer of meat mixture. Bake 1¼ hours or until meat is no longer pink and juices run clear. Remove from oven and let stand 5 minutes. Serve with Chunky Tomato Sauce.

Serves 6

Chunky Tomato Sauce

	Reserved tomato sauce	⅓	cup grated carrot
1	(7½-ounce) can tomatoes,	1	teaspoon sugar
	undrained and cut up	1½	teaspoons snipped fresh
⅓	cup chopped onion		basil or marjoram
⅓	cup chopped green or red	1	clove garlic, minced
	bell pepper	⅛	teaspoon black pepper

Combine all ingredients in a saucepan and bring to a boil. Reduce heat, cover and simmer about 10 minutes or until onion is tender.

The first horse race in Georgia took place in Savannah on June 26, 1740. It was a quick sprint of one-quarter mile, ending in a grassy square, which pleased the horses.

In 1755, Savannah was the first to have cattle exportation in Georgia. This allowed the fledgling colony to compete economically, in yet another way, with the Carolinas.

Individual Barbecued Beef Loaves

Probably, the first time baseball was played in Savannah was in about 1862, after Union troops had taken Ft. Pulaski. Photos of that time show a game in progress. Ft. Screven troops on Tybee Island also enjoyed organized baseball leagues. Today, Savannah is proud to claim "The Sand Gnats" as our very own baseball team.

½	cup ketchup	1	cup fine dry bread crumbs
⅓	cup cider vinegar		
3	tablespoons brown sugar, firmly packed	2	tablespoons finely chopped onion
1	teaspoon beef bouillon granules	½	teaspoon salt
		¼	teaspoon black pepper
1½	pounds lean ground beef	1	cup evaporated milk

Preheat oven to 350 degrees. To make a sauce, combine ketchup, vinegar, sugar and bouillon in a saucepan. Cook over medium heat, stirring constantly, until bouillon dissolves. Set aside.

Mix together beef, bread crumbs, onion, salt, pepper and milk until thoroughly blended. Shape mixture into 6 loaves and place in a lightly greased 11x7-inch baking dish. Spoon sauce over loaves. Bake 45 minutes. Serve immediately.

Serves 6

Double sauce ingredients if you like a lot of sauce. Prepare loaves ahead and keep a good supply on hand in the freezer.

Terrific Taco Ring

1	pound ground beef	1	medium green bell pepper	
1	(1¼-ounce) package taco seasoning mix	1	cup salsa	
1	cup grated Cheddar cheese	½	head lettuce, shredded	
2	tablespoons water	1	medium tomato, chopped	
2	(8-ounce) packages refrigerated crescent rolls	1	bunch green onions, chopped	
		½	cup chopped black olives Sour cream	

Preheat oven to 375 degrees. Cook beef in a skillet until browned; drain fat. Add taco seasoning and cheese and stir until cheese melts. Arrange crescent dough triangles in a circle on a 13-inch baking stone or pizza pan; place long edge of triangle to inside of circle, overlapping triangles at the base with points to outside, leaving an empty 5-inch diameter circle in the center. Use an ice cream scoop to spoon meat mixture over triangles. Fold outside points of triangle over meat and tuck under base at the center; filling will not be completely covered. Bake 20 to 25 minutes or until golden brown. Meanwhile, cut top off of bell pepper and remove seeds. Fill pepper with salsa. Place pepper in center of baked taco ring. Surround pepper with lettuce, tomato, onions and olives. Garnish each section of ring with a dollop of sour cream.

Serves 8

Refrigerated crescent rolls have become a staple for "quick and easy" supper preparations. Light, flaky and versatile, these rolls are often used in place of homemade dough. Using the same preparation as the Terrific Taco Ring, substitute cooked chicken and mozzarella cheese and fill the center with a Romano Spinach Salad (pg. 85). For an exciting breakfast presentation, substitute hot bulk sausage and Cheddar cheese and fill the center with scrambled eggs.

*It is said that
Northerners think
"Barbeque" is a verb
and Southerners think
"Barbeque" is a noun.
That is not quite right.
Southerners think
"Barbeque" is two
nouns and a verb.
Thus, it could be said
(but isn't, hopefully)
"We're fixin' to
barbeque some
barbeque at the
barbeque."*

Barbecued Spicy Southern Brisket

2	large onions, sliced	½	cup water
4	pounds beef brisket	¼	cup A-1 steak sauce
½	cup ketchup		Minced garlic to taste
½	cup chili sauce		Salt and pepper to taste

Preheat oven to 350 degrees. Place onions in the bottom of a roasting pan. Lay beef, fat-side up, on onions. Combine ketchup, chili sauce, water, steak sauce, garlic, salt and pepper and pour over meat. Roast, uncovered, for 1 hour. Baste and add water, if needed. Cover pan and roast 1 hour longer. Cool. Cut meat into thin slices and return to gravy in pan. Roast another hour.

Serves 6

Saints' Beef Stroganoff

4	tablespoons flour, divided	½	cup chopped onion
½	teaspoon salt	1	clove garlic, minced
1	pound beef sirloin, cut into ¼-inch strips	1	tablespoon tomato paste
4	tablespoons butter, divided	1	(10½-ounce) can condensed beef broth
1	(3-ounce) can sliced mushrooms, drained, or 1 cup fresh	2	tablespoons dry white wine
		1	(8-ounce) container sour cream

Combine 2 tablespoons flour and salt. Coat beef with flour mixture. Heat a skillet, then add 2 tablespoons butter. When melted, add beef to butter, in batches if necessary, and brown quickly on all sides. Add mushrooms, onion and garlic and cook until onion is tender. Remove meat and vegetables, reserving drippings in skillet. Add remaining 2 tablespoons butter. Blend in remaining 2 tablespoons flour. Add tomato paste. Stir in broth and wine. Cook and stir over medium-high heat until thick and bubbly. Return meat and vegetables to skillet. Stir in sour cream. Cook slowly until heated through; do not boil. Serve over hot, buttered noodles.

Serves 4 to 5

Irish Corned Beef Brisket

1	(3-pound) corned beef brisket	2	tablespoons pickling spices
2	tablespoons white or apple vinegar		

Place brisket and all of the liquid and spices from the brisket package in a large crockpot. Add enough water to cover along with vinegar and pickling spices. Cover crockpot and cook on high for 8 hours or until tender. Remove meat and place in a plastic zip-top bag, discarding cooking liquid. Refrigerate until meat is chilled. Slice thinly against the grain.

Serves 4 to 6

Marinated Beef Tenderloin

1	(4- to 6-pound) beef tenderloin	½	teaspoon Worcestershire sauce
1	cup ketchup	1½	cups water
2	teaspoons prepared mustard	2	(0.7-ounce) packages dry Italian salad dressing mix

Pierce beef and place in a plastic roasting bag. Combine ketchup, mustard, Worcestershire sauce, water and salad dressing mix and pour into bag. Marinate in refrigerator overnight, turning occasionally.

When ready to bake, preheat oven to 425 degrees. Drain marinade and reserve. Place meat on a rack in a pan. Bake 30 minutes or until a meat thermometer registers desired degree of doneness; 150 degrees for medium-rare, 160 degrees for medium. Baste beef occasionally with reserved marinade while baking. Oven heat can be reduced to 325 degrees after first 30 minutes if slower baking is desired.

Serves 6 to 8

Corned beef sandwiches, while enjoyed year round, are a favorite for every St. Patrick's Day picnic basket. Rye bread and Swiss cheese are the favored choices, spread with equal parts of sour cream, prepared mustard and mayonnaise. Cold, crisp kosher garlic pickles make the sandwich complete.

St. Patrick's Day celebrations in Savannah date from 1812. In that year, 13 Irish Protestants formed the Hibernian Society. This is the oldest Irish society in the United States. In 1813, the Hibernian Society marched in a private procession to the Independent Presbyterian Church.

Roquefort Stuffed Filet Mignon

6 (1½-inch thick) beef tenderloin filets

6 tablespoons Roquefort cheese

6 tablespoons roasted garlic

½ cup olive oil

½ cup red wine

1½ tablespoons chopped fresh basil

1½ tablespoons butter, melted

Salt and pepper to taste

Using a fillet knife, cut each filet lengthwise three-fourths of the way around center, being careful to not cut filet completely in half. Stuff each filet with 1 tablespoon cheese and 1 tablespoon roasted garlic. Combine oil, wine, basil, butter, salt and pepper. Marinate filets in oil mixture for 1 hour. When ready to grill, drain filets. Grill until done.

Serves 6

Beef Stew with Wine Sauce

4	pounds boneless beef chuck roast, cut into small pieces, or stew meat
	Garlic powder
2	(10¾-ounce) can condensed cream of mushroom soup
1	(1-ounce) package dry onion soup mix
¾	cup dry sherry
1	(8-ounce) can sliced mushrooms, drained
1	(20-ounce) package frozen sliced carrots

Preheat oven to 325 degrees. Place meat in a 9x13-inch casserole dish. Sprinkle lightly with garlic powder. Combine mushroom soup, onion soup mix, sherry and mushrooms. Pour mixture over meat and mix well. Cover and bake 3 hours. Add carrots during final 30 minutes of baking time.

Serves 6 to 8

Veal or Chicken Piccata

1	small yellow onion, chopped
4	green onions, chopped
2	cloves garlic, crushed
2	tablespoons olive oil
4	veal cutlets or boneless, skinless chicken breasts
½	cup flour
	Salt and pepper to taste
2	tablespoons butter
2	tablespoons dry sherry
2	tablespoons fresh lemon juice
1	tablespoon chopped capers
2	tablespoons chicken broth (optional)
8	thin lemon slices
2	tablespoons chopped fresh parsley

Sauté onions and garlic in olive oil just until tender; set aside.

Pound veal or chicken flat between 2 pieces of plastic wrap. Combine flour, salt and pepper in a shallow pan. Dredge meat in flour mixture. Sauté meat in butter for 2 to 3 minutes on each side or until lightly browned. Add sautéed onions and garlic to pan. Increase heat to high and add sherry, lemon juice and capers. Cook until mixture thickens to a gravy. Add chicken broth if gravy is too thick. Garnish with lemon slices and parsley.

Serves 4

Medallions of Veal with Shrimp and Chanterelles

8	thick veal chops	1	medium carrot, finely chopped
4	tablespoons unsalted butter, divided	16	large shrimp, peeled and deveined
1	pound chanterelle mushrooms		Brandy or cognac
	Salt and pepper to taste	⅓	cup veal or beef broth
1	clove garlic, pressed	½	cup whipping cream
1	tablespoon chopped fresh parsley	1	tablespoon chopped fresh tarragon
1	medium onion, finely chopped		

Remove bone and silver skin from veal chops. Wrap meat around rib-eye to form a "medallion" and secure with a toothpick. Cover and refrigerate.

Melt 1½ tablespoons butter in a large skillet. Add mushrooms and sauté over high heat. Add salt, pepper, garlic and parsley. Cover skillet and cook until mushrooms sweat. Uncover and cook until liquid evaporates. Transfer mixture to a bowl and wipe out skillet.

Add 1 tablespoon butter to skillet over medium heat. Add onion and carrot and sauté. Add shrimp and sauté 2 minutes. Add brandy and cook 8 minutes. Add mixture to mushrooms in bowl. Wipe out skillet.

Melt remaining 1½ tablespoons butter in skillet over medium heat. Season both sides of veal with salt and pepper. Add veal to skillet and cook 4 minutes on each side, pressing down with a spatula while cooking. Remove and keep warm. Deglaze skillet with broth. Add cream and cook over medium-high heat for a few minutes. Add veal and mushroom mixture to skillet and cook until heated through. Sprinkle with tarragon and serve.

Serves 8

From 1908 to 1911, Savannah became the foremost center for automobile racing. Three Grand Prix auto races were held in Savannah, capturing worldwide attention and hosting over 100,000 spectators. Entries came from Europe; specifically France, Germany, and Italy. The United States also sent in competitors to race 16 times (at about 65 to 80 mph) around a 25-mile long course, creating a 400-mile race. The start and finish line was on Victory Drive and the course ran south of Savannah, out to Isle of Hope and back. The American cars were usually defeated, but young auto buffs, such as Louis Chevrolet, were inspired to create better-engineered cars.

The most famous duel in Savannah was between Button Gwinnett, signer of the Declaration of Independence and General Lachlan McIntosh, hero of Bloody Marsh. Gwinnett, a politician, fancied himself a military commander and confused Georgia troops with orders that conflicted with McIntosh's. Matters escalated, a duel ensued, and each wounded the other in the thigh. Infection set in Gwinnett's leg and he was dead within a week. Lachlan McIntosh went northward to serve with General George Washington at Valley Forge. McIntosh is buried in the Colonial Cemetery not far from where Gwinnett is reputed to be buried.

Lamb Shanks with Red Zinfandel Mushroom Sauce

1	cup red Zinfandel wine
1	cup chicken broth
2	tablespoons oyster sauce
1	tablespoon soy sauce
2	teaspoons tomato paste
½	teaspoon Asian chili sauce
½	teaspoon sugar
1	tablespoon chopped fresh thyme
1	tablespoon cornstarch
	Salt and freshly ground black pepper
5	tablespoons unsalted butter, divided
8	large lamb shanks
2	small yellow onions, chopped
1½	pounds mushrooms, preferably a mixture of portobello, shiitake and button, stems discarded and sliced
4	cloves garlic, minced

Stir together wine, broth, oyster sauce, soy sauce, tomato paste, chili sauce, sugar, thyme, cornstarch, salt and pepper. Set aside.

Place a 12-inch skillet over medium heat. Add half the butter. When melted, add lamb shanks and brown on all sides. Remove shanks from pan. Add remaining butter and onions. Sauté until onions are golden. Add mushrooms and garlic and sauté 15 minutes or until mushrooms soften. Add wine mixture and bring to a simmer. Return shanks to sauce in skillet. Simmer 2 to 3 hours or until shanks are tender. Serve immediately, or cool and refrigerate until ready to serve. When ready to serve, reheat until very hot. Adjust seasonings as needed.

Serves 8

Pork Tenderloin in a Tomato Creole Cream Sauce

⅓	cup hoisin sauce	2	teaspoons hot pepper sauce
3	tablespoons plum sauce	1	teaspoon sugar
4	tablespoons oyster sauce, divided	½	teaspoon oregano
2	teaspoons Asian chili sauce	½	teaspoon thyme
1	pork tenderloin, trimmed	1	tablespoon unsalted butter
2	medium tomatoes, chopped	1	tablespoon olive oil
½	cup whipping cream	3	cloves garlic, finely minced
¼	cup dry vermouth or dry white wine	2	ounces goat cheese, crumbled

Combine hoisin sauce, plum sauce, 2 tablespoons oyster sauce and chili sauce. Rub mixture on pork and refrigerate 4 hours. When ready to cook, preheat grill over medium heat. Add pork and grill until a meat thermometer registers 160 degrees.

To make sauce, combine tomatoes, cream, vermouth, remaining 2 tablespoons oyster sauce, pepper sauce, sugar, oregano and thyme. Add butter and oil to a 12-inch skillet over high heat. Add garlic and sauté 5 seconds. Add tomato mixture and bring to a fast boil. Cook 1 minute or until sauce thickens slightly. Adjust seasonings as needed. Slice pork and transfer to heated dinner plates. Spoon sauce over pork and sprinkle with goat cheese.

Serves 4

In the early 1900s, the Atlantic Club and the Amfico Club on Tybee Island rather exclusively provided all the amenities needed for fishing, boating, swimming, or merely lazing in the sun. Tybee Island is the midpoint and stopover for the annual Worrell 1,000 Sail Boat Race, up the East coast. From Ft. Lauderdale, Florida, to Virginia Beach, Virginia, makes a 1,000-mile course of hard sailing. In 1999, Tybee Island entered a sailing team in the competition for the first time.

Rolled Stuffed Pork Roast

3-4 pounds pork shoulder roast, deboned	2 hard-cooked eggs, chopped
1-1½ teaspoons salt or to taste	1-1½ cups ricotta or small curd cottage cheese, drained
½-1 teaspoon black pepper or to taste	½-1 cup cooked wild rice (optional)
1 (10-ounce) package frozen leaf spinach, thawed and squeezed dry	1 large white onion, minced

Preheat oven to 350 degrees. Flatten pork roast, fat-side down. Roast must be flat enough to be rolled jelly roll fashion when stuffed; trim meat from center if needed. Season meat on both sides with salt and pepper. Gently combine spinach, eggs, cheese, rice and onion. Spread mixture in the center of the roast. There may be leftover stuffing mixture, depending on size of roast. Roll up meat, jelly roll fashion, and secure with strong string. Bake 1½ hours or until the roast is golden brown. Cut into thin slices across the roll.

Serves 6 to 8

Bread Stuffing Mixture: Combine 1½ cups toasted bread crumbs, ½ cup chopped, unpeeled apple, ⅓ to ½ cup grated Cheddar cheese, 2 to 3 tablespoons melted butter, 2 tablespoons orange juice, a dash of cinnamon and a dash of salt. Spread over pork and cook as directed above.

In the DAR Colonial Cemetery is a touching epitaph, written by Richard Henry Wilde for his brother, shot dead in a duel. Honored as a great American poem by Lord Byron, the *first* stanza has become famous.

"My life is like the Summer Rose,

That opens to the morning sky.

But ere the shades of evening close

Is scattered on the ground – to die."

Stovetop Pork Tenderloin

1½	pounds pork tenderloin, trimmed	2	tablespoons olive oil
	Minced garlic	1½	teaspoons butter
	Black pepper	1½	cups red wine

Season pork well with garlic and pepper. Heat oil and butter in a cast-iron skillet until sizzling. Add tenderloin and sear on all sides until crisp and browned. Add wine. Cover and simmer 5 to 10 minutes or until internal temperature reaches 160 degrees.

Serves 8

You won't believe how quick and easy this is until you try it. The flavor is excellent.

Pork Marinade

¼ cup soy sauce

2 tablespoons dry red wine

1 tablespoon honey

1 tablespoon brown sugar, firmly packed

1 clove garlic, minced

½ teaspoon cinnamon

1 green onion, minced

Mix all ingredients in a large plastic zip-top bag. Add pork to bag and marinate in refrigerator 2 to 24 hours.

Apple-Smothered Pork Chops

6	pork loin chops	3	tablespoons molasses
2	teaspoons salt, divided	3	tablespoons all-purpose flour
1½	teaspoons rubbed sage		
	Vegetable oil	2	cups hot water
3	tart apples, peeled, cored and sliced ¼-inch thick	1	tablespoon vinegar
		⅓	cup raisins

Preheat oven to 350 degrees. Season each chop with ¼ teaspoon salt and ¼ teaspoon sage. In a skillet, slowly brown chops on both sides in a small amount of oil. Place chops in a baking dish, reserving drippings in skillet. Arrange apple slices on chops. Pour molasses over apples. Sprinkle flour over drippings in skillet. Cook, stirring occasionally, until brown. Slowly add water and stir until smooth. Bring to a boil. Stir in vinegar, remaining ½ teaspoon salt and raisins. Cover dish and bake 1 hour.

Makes 6 servings

Highlander Whiskey Venison

4-5 pounds lean venison or beef roast, cubed

2 large Vidalia onions, sliced and separated

1 pound carrots, sliced, or baby carrots

1 large bell pepper, thinly sliced (optional)

1 tablespoon minced garlic

2 cups chopped potatoes (optional)

6-8 cups water

2 cups black coffee or strong tea

1 cup whiskey, divided

Salt and coarsely ground black pepper to taste

2 pounds fresh mushrooms with stems, quartered

¼ cup sifted flour (optional)

In a large heavy pot, or in a crockpot, combine meat, onions, carrots, bell pepper, garlic, potatoes, water, coffee, ½ cup whiskey, salt and pepper. Cook 2 hours or until meat is tender. Add mushrooms and remaining ½ cup whiskey. Adjust seasonings as needed. Cook 30 to 60 minutes longer. Thicken, if needed, with flour dissolved in a small amount of water. If desired, add more whiskey just prior to serving. Serve over rice if potatoes are not used.

Make about 1½ gallons

Sour Cream Venison

2	pounds venison, cut into 2-inch cubes	1	teaspoon salt
1	clove garlic, minced		Dash of black pepper
¼	cup shortening	1	bay leaf
1	cup diced celery	4	tablespoons butter or margarine
½	cup chopped onion	¼	cup all-purpose flour
1	cup diced carrot	1	cup sour cream
2	cups water		Parsley

Preheat oven to 350 degrees. Brown venison with garlic in shortening on all sides in a skillet over medium heat. Transfer to a shallow 2½-quart baking dish, reserving drippings in skillet. Add celery, onion and carrot to drippings in skillet and sauté 2 minutes. Stir in water, salt, pepper and bay leaf. Pour mixture over venison. Bake 30 minutes. Drain, reserving broth.

Melt butter in a skillet over low heat. Blend in flour until smooth. Add reserved broth and cook and stir until thickened. Stir in sour cream. Pour sauce over venison. Garnish with parsley. Serve over hot cooked noodles, if desired.

Serves 6 to 8

Dove or Quail Rice Magnifique

8	dove or 4 quail	¾	cup chopped fresh parsley
½-1	teaspoon salt, divided	1	cup dry wild and long-grain rice
½-1	teaspoon white or black pepper, divided	3	cups chicken broth
4	tablespoons butter		Dash of cayenne pepper or Tabasco sauce
1	cup grated carrot	2-4	slices raw bacon, quartered
1	cup sliced fresh mushrooms		
½	cup sliced green onion		

Preheat oven to 325 degrees. Season birds with some of salt and pepper and brown in butter. Set birds aside, reserving drippings in skillet. Add carrot, mushrooms, green onion and parsley to drippings in skillet and sauté. Add rice and stir well to mix. Stir in broth until blended and season with cayenne pepper and remaining salt and pepper. Pour mixture into a large greased casserole dish. Place birds on top. Sprinkle with raw bacon. Cover and bake 1 to 1¼ hours or until tender. Remove bacon before serving and sprinkle with fresh parsley.

Serves 4

This recipe also works well with 4 to 6 chicken breasts or 2 halved Cornish hens.

To make country fried, or "chicken" fried, steak: dredge meat in flour, then season with salt and pepper (garlic powder and onion powder, opt.) to taste. Let sit until flour has absorbed. Pat seasonings in gently, then dredge again. Repeat, ending with flour to seal in seasonings.

South Georgia Quail with Country Ham

The Savannah Yacht Club, founded on June 14, 1869, was first called the Regatta Association of the State of Georgia. From its ideal location on the Wilmington River, it helped host the 1996 Olympic Sailing Events at Priest's Landing.

2-3	tablespoons vegetable oil	12	slices "biscuit thin"
2-3	tablespoons butter		(¼- to ½-inch thick)
12	quail		cured country ham
	Salt and freshly ground	½	cup Madeira wine
	black pepper		

Preheat oven to 350 degrees. Heat oil and butter in a large skillet over high heat until sizzling. Season quail with salt and pepper. Add quail to skillet and quickly brown on all sides. Wrap each quail in a piece of ham and place in a 9x13-inch casserole dish. Pour wine over quail. Cover dish and bake 30 minutes. Transfer quail to a serving platter. If desired, cook liquid in dish over high heat for 10 minutes or until reduced by half. Pour sauce over quail and serve immediately.

Serves 4

This recipe works well for skinless quail because the ham acts as a protective coating to help keep the quail moist. Quail range in size according to age and diet, so cooking time may vary.

Grits, Rice, Pasta, and Potatoes

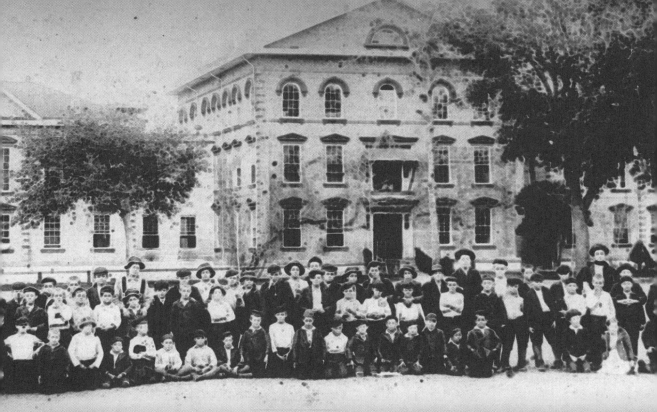

The *First* Orphanage

Bethesda is foremost among orphanages in America, as it is the oldest in continuous operation. Suggested by James Oglethorpe and Charles Wesley, it was founded in 1738, by Reverend George Whitefield. It is still on its original 500-acre trustee's land grant. Hardships in the new colony created many orphans and Whitefield made it his mission (for 32 years) to provide them with both refuge and spiritually based schooling. He wanted Bethesda (House of Mercy) to be away from "the wicked influence of the town," and he wanted it to be self-sufficient, which it was until the 1930's. Whitefield was a tireless fundraiser and an unparalleled orator. Lady Selina, Countess of Huntingdon, was moved to become one of Bethesda's greatest benefactors. Upon the deaths of Whitefield (1770) and Lady Huntingdon (1791), Bethesda began to endure a series of setbacks. Twice, it was destroyed by fire and moved temporarily several times. The Union Society Trustees took over stewardship of Bethesda in 1855, providing stability.

Spirited Savannah

It is most ironic that the very spirit which walks in the moonlight at Bethesda was never there while she lived. From England, Lady Selina, Countess of Huntingdon, sent her benevolent support. After she met Bethesda's founder, George Whitefield, she became deeply involved with its development. Workmen were sent from England to build additions, followed by the Countess' personal housekeeper. After a ruinous fire at Bethesda, Lady Selina sold her jewelry to finance repairs. Lady Selina sent a full-length life-sized portrait of herself to Bethesda which gave its own protection. During the Revolutionary period, British Redcoats saw this portrait of an English countess and moved on, without torching Bethesda. Called the "Mother Of Methodism" for her work with the Wesleys, Lady Selina also founded chapels in England, contributed to Princeton University, and had hoped to create "Indian Education." It is not known if Lady Selina's spirit visits the other places her charities funded but she is known to visit Bethesda. The Lady Huntington may be glimpsed on a clear, quiet evening walking along the path around Bethesda or near the amphitheater, both of which are named for her.

"Having It Out About Grits"

It is a puzzle that the same people who won't eat grits – at least not more than once – do relish such an indefinable dish as cream of wheat. Also, they persist in making disparaging remarks about "our" grits when they truly have no room to talk. Having heard one too many slanderous comments about grits, it is only reasonable, if not entirely hospitable, to return fire. Here it is!

Having tried cream of wheat, rather sportingly, there is only one thing to say. Cream of wheat is like something out of a Charles Dickens' novel. *Oliver Twist,* to be precise. "Please sir – don't make me have some more!" (Pardon the paraphrase.) Having defended grits for this long, there is no reason to give up now. Remember that Savannah only surrendered when she was out-gunned, with her back to the sea and a city to save. Grits are slightly less important than that. In defense of good grits, it is important that they be cooked according to the instructions. This is essential for our recipes using grits. (Please, not the microwave instant grits, either!) And no, "gourmet grits" is not an oxymoron. One of our most world famous restaurants, Elizabeth's on 37th, serves wonderful dishes made with grits.

Having gone this far, we will also say that stone-ground grits, like stone-ground cornmeal, is practically a sacred food in the South. Just don't confuse the two in preparation. These most authentic varieties may be ordered from Southern mills by the way of your local gourmet shop, or found while traveling in Dixie (this also impresses the "natives"). Having shared this much, our final piece of advice seems crucial. When traveling in the South, especially inland, please don't ask for cream of wheat. Potatoes are a safer choice, and if you really don't care for grits – please don't say so.

Savannah Cheese Grits with Breakfast Shrimp

2	cups milk	1½	cups grated sharp or
1	cup water		smoked Cheddar cheese
¾	teaspoon salt	2	eggs, beaten
1	cup quick-cooking grits	½	cup butter
¼	teaspoon garlic powder		Paprika for garnish
	Dash of hot pepper sauce		

Combine milk, water and salt in a 2-quart casserole dish. Microwave on high for 8 to 10 minutes or until boiling. Stir in grits. Microwave 2 to 3 minutes or until soft. Stir in garlic powder, pepper sauce, cheese, eggs and butter. Mix well. Microwave on high for 4 to 5 minutes or until thickened. Sprinkle with paprika.

Breakfast Shrimp

3	tablespoons butter	1	teaspoon or less salt
1	medium onion, chopped		Dash of hot pepper sauce
¼	green bell pepper, chopped	1	teaspoon Worcestershire sauce
2	tablespoons all-purpose flour	4-5	tablespoons ketchup
1	pound raw shrimp, peeled and deveined	2	tablespoons chopped fresh parsley
		½	cup whipping cream

Melt butter in a medium skillet over medium heat. Add onion and bell pepper and cook until tender. Stir in flour and cook and stir until bubbly. Cook 1 minute. Increase heat and add shrimp. Cook and stir 2 minutes or until shrimp are pink. Add enough water to cover shrimp. Cook and stir until mixture thickens slightly. Add salt, pepper sauce, Worcestershire sauce, ketchup and parsley and stir. Simmer about 5 minutes. Adjust seasonings as needed. Stir in cream. Heat thoroughly but do not bring to a boil. Serve immediately over plain or cheese grits.

Grits serves 8
Shrimp serves 4
Double ingredients for shrimp

Sliced andouille or Lumber Jack sausage can be added.

Savannah Red Rice

4 ounces bacon

½ cup chopped onion

½ cup chopped celery

¼ cup chopped green bell pepper

2 cups dry rice

2 (16-ounce) cans pureed tomatoes

1 teaspoon sugar

1 tablespoon salt

¼ teaspoon black pepper

2-3 dashes cayenne pepper

Preheat oven to 350 degrees. Cook bacon until crisp in a large skillet. Drain bacon and crumble, reserving drippings in skillet. Add onion, celery and bell pepper to drippings in skillet and sauté until tender. Add crumbled bacon, rice, tomatoes, sugar, salt and black and cayenne peppers. Mix well. Cook over medium heat for 10 minutes. Pour mixture into a greased 9x13-inch casserole dish and cover tightly. Bake 1 hour.

Serves 8 to 10

For a one-dish meal, slice and sauté smoked sausage, drain, and add with crumbled bacon.

Garlic Cheddar Grits

1 cup regular grits

4 cups water

1 tablespoon salt

½ cup butter

1 (6-ounce) roll garlic cheese spread

1 (8-ounce) package grated Cheddar cheese

2 tablespoons Worcestershire sauce

Paprika

Cooked and crumbled bacon (optional)

Chopped green onions (optional)

Preheat oven to 350 degrees. Cook grits in a large saucepan in water with salt according to package directions. Remove from heat and stir in butter, cheeses and Worcestershire sauce until cheeses melt. Pour mixture into a greased 2-quart casserole dish. Sprinkle with paprika. Bake 15 to 20 minutes. Top with bacon and onions and serve.

Serves 8 to 10

Grits Soufflé with Caramelized Onions and Roasted Red Peppers

Grits

4	cups milk	3	cups grated smoked
1	cup quick-cooking grits		Gouda or Cheddar
½	cup butter		cheese
½	teaspoon salt	3	eggs, well beaten
⅛	teaspoon cayenne pepper		

Caramelized Onions

5	large onions, thinly sliced	2	tablespoons sugar
¼	cup olive oil		

Roasted Peppers

3   whole red bell peppers

Preheat oven to 350 degrees. Bring milk to a boil in a large saucepan. Stir in grits. Reduce heat and continue to stir 3 to 4 minutes or until mixture thickens. Remove from heat. Stir in butter, salt, cayenne pepper and cheese. Beat in eggs with a whisk. Pour mixture into a well-greased 2½-quart casserole or soufflé dish. Bake, uncovered, for 1 hour or until well puffed and golden brown.

Sauté onions in oil in a large skillet until golden brown. Sprinkle with sugar and sauté until onions are well browned and crisp. Transfer to paper towels to drain excess oil. Set aside until ready to serve.

To make roasted peppers, preheat oven to 500 degrees. Place bell peppers on an ungreased baking sheet. Bake 25 minutes. Place hot peppers in a heavy-duty zip-top bag or paper bag. Close and allow to steam for 10 minutes. Remove from bag and peel away skin. Remove stems, seeds and ribs from inside of peppers. Slice peppers into thin slices.

When ready to serve, arrange onions and peppers over hot grits. Serve immediately.

Serves 6

Black Rice

3	cups black bean juice (from Spicy Black Bean Cakes recipe pg. 52)	2	tablespoons olive oil
		1	cup minced yellow onion
		1	teaspoon minced garlic
2	chicken bouillon cubes	2¼	cups dry converted rice
2	teaspoons ground cumin		Salt to taste

Preheat oven to 350 degrees. Combine bean juice, bouillon and cumin in a heavy saucepan. Bring to a boil over medium heat. Heat oil in a heavy stockpot over medium heat. Add onion and garlic and sauté 1 minute. Add rice and toss to coat with oil. Pour boiling bean juice over rice and stir. Bring to a boil. Cover stockpot and transfer to oven. Bake 20 to 30 minutes or until liquid is absorbed and rice is tender. Uncover stockpot and fluff rice with a fork. Season with salt.

Serves 6

Perfect Rice Pilaf

1½	cups dry rice	1	(1-ounce) package onion soup mix
2	cups water		
⅓	cup dry white wine	1	teaspoon dried basil
1	(10¾-ounce) can condensed chicken broth	⅛	teaspoon black pepper
		2	tablespoons lemon juice
		1	teaspoon butter

Preheat oven to 350 degrees. Combine all ingredients in a lightly greased 9x13-inch baking dish. Stir well and cover. Bake 1 hour, 15 minutes or until rice is tender and liquid is absorbed.

Serves 8

Pecan Wild Rice

2 cups dry long grain and wild rice mix

2 tablespoons butter

1 cup chopped green onions

1 cup finely chopped ham

1 cup chopped pecans

½ cup finely chopped fresh parsley

2 tablespoons white wine

Salt to taste

1 teaspoon white pepper

Prepare rice mix according to package directions. Melt butter in a large skillet. Add scallions, ham and pecans and sauté until ham is lightly browned. Add parsley, wine, salt and pepper. Cook and stir over medium heat for 5 minutes. Fold in rice and serve.

Serves 8

195

In 1785, the Assembly of Georgia voted to establish a public institute of higher learning. This resulted in the first charter in the US to be issued to a state university. Although Athens, Georgia, was chosen as the site for the University of Georgia, its inception was firstly in Savannah.

Another first for education in Georgia is The Massie School, in Savannah. It was the first public school in Georgia.

Curry Rice Pilaf

3	cups chicken broth	⅔	cup golden raisins
1½	cups dry long grain white rice	½	teaspoon turmeric
		½	teaspoon curry powder
¼	cup vegetable oil	3	tablespoons soy sauce

Bring broth to a boil in a 1-quart saucepan. Combine rice, oil, raisins, turmeric, curry powder and soy sauce in a separate medium saucepan. Add boiling broth. Cover and cook over low heat for 20 minutes or until all liquid is absorbed and rice is tender.

Serves 8

Our Grandmothers' Baked Macaroni and Cheese

½-¾	cup butter	2-3	tablespoons sifted all-purpose flour
3	cups whole milk		
1	cup half-and-half	2-2½	pounds sharp Cheddar cheese, grated
8	cups cooked elbow macaroni		
		3	eggs
½-1	teaspoon salt	½	teaspoon dry mustard (optional)
½-1	teaspoon black pepper		
			Softened butter (optional)

Preheat oven to 350 degrees. Melt butter in the oven in a large baking dish. Stir in milk and half-and-half. Warm liquid mixture, but do not allow to scald. Stir in macaroni, salt and pepper. Place in oven and "steam" macaroni in liquid for 15 to 20 minutes, stirring occasionally. Remove from oven and sift flour over macaroni. Stir until blended. Stir in cheese, saving a third of cheese for topping. Beat eggs and mustard until lemon colored and frothy. Pour over macaroni and stir to blend. Top with reserved cheese. Dot with softened butter. Bake, uncovered, for 45 minutes. Tent with foil during last 15 minutes if top is becoming too brown. Remove from oven and let stand 10 to 15 minutes before serving.

Serves 10 to 12

Pasta with Asiago Cheese and Spinach

3	cups boiling water	2	cloves garlic, crushed
4	ounces sun-dried tomatoes, packed without oil	1	(12-ounce) package cavatappi pasta, hot cooked and drained
2	tablespoons extra virgin olive oil	1	(10-ounce) bag fresh spinach, torn
⅛	teaspoon salt	¾	cup grated Asiago cheese
⅛	teaspoon freshly ground black pepper	½	cup finely grated fresh Parmesan cheese

Combine boiling water and tomatoes in a bowl and let stand 30 minutes. Drain, chop and place in a large bowl. Add oil, salt, pepper and garlic. Add hot cooked pasta and spinach. Toss gently. Sprinkle with cheeses and toss gently. Serve immediately.

Serves 8

Fusilli, penne or any medium-sized pasta can be substituted.

Pasta that is properly cooked is "al dente," completely tender but still firm. To accomplish this, bring 4 quarts of water to boil, add 2 tablespoons salt and drop in 1 pound of pasta. Some cooks add 1 teaspoon of olive oil to the water to keep the pasta from sticking together. Fresh pasta will be done when the water returns to a boil. Dried pasta takes generally 5 to 7 minutes and can take even longer when the pasta is large, such as lasagna. When cooking pasta, make more than you need. Drop the cooled pasta into a freezer container or bag. To reheat, drop the pasta into a pot of boiling water. Return the water to a boil and cook 1 minute. Drain and serve. You can also microwave in a microwave safe dish until hot.

Rigatoni with Olives, Arugula and Herbs

In 1864, Sherman's
troops asked an old
caretaker at
Bethesda's gates whose
place it was. The
caretaker replied that
it was the Union
Society. Surprised, but
believing there were
union sympathizers
there, the Yankees
rode on without
putting Bethesda to
the torch.

6	tablespoons extra virgin olive oil	½	cup minced fresh basil
1	tablespoon minced garlic	½	teaspoon freshly ground black pepper
¼	teaspoon dried red pepper flakes	1	(12-ounce) package rigatoni or other tubular pasta, cooked al dente
½	cup minced green olives		
2	tablespoons capers, rinsed, drained and minced	2	cups chopped fresh arugula
½	cup minced fresh parsley		Freshly grated Parmesan cheese

Heat olive oil in a large skillet over medium-low heat. Add garlic and pepper flakes and sauté 1 to 2 minutes or until garlic is soft but not browned. Add olives and capers and sauté 1 minute, stirring constantly. Stir in parsley and basil. Season with pepper. Combine olive sauce, pasta, arugula and cheese in a bowl. Toss to mix and serve immediately.

Serves 4

Rotini Swiss Twist

8	ounces bacon	1	(16-ounce) package rotini pasta, cooked and drained
1	large onion, thinly sliced		
1	(32-ounce) jar spaghetti sauce	¼	cup Parmesan cheese
		2	cups grated Swiss cheese

Cook bacon in a skillet until crisp. Drain and crumble bacon, reserving drippings in skillet. Add onion to drippings and sauté until softened. Add spaghetti sauce. In a large bowl, combine cooked pasta, cooked bacon, spaghetti sauce with onion and cheeses. Toss well.

Serves 4 to 6

Farfalle with Pesto and Tomatoes

3	cups packed fresh basil leaves (about 6 bunches)		Salt and pepper to taste
½	cup plus 2 tablespoons olive oil	1½	pounds farfalle (bow-tie) pasta
⅓	cup pine nuts	3	cups chopped, seeded plum tomatoes
3	large cloves garlic, chopped		Fresh basil sprigs (optional)
1¼	cups Parmesan cheese, divided		

To make pesto, combine basil, oil, nuts and garlic in a food processor. Blend until smooth. Transfer to a small bowl and mix in ¾ cup cheese. Season with salt and pepper. Cook pasta in a large pot of boiling salted water until al dente. Drain pasta, reserving ½ cup of cooking liquid. Return pasta to same pot. Add 1 cup of pesto and reserved ½ cup of cooking liquid. Toss to blend. Mix in tomatoes. Season with salt and pepper. Transfer to a serving bowl and sprinkle with remaining ½ cup cheese. Garnish with basil sprigs.

Serves 8

Accordion Garlic Potatoes

10	medium baking potatoes, peeled	2	cloves garlic, minced
			Salt and pepper to taste
1	cup butter, melted	6	ounces Parmesan cheese, freshly grated
3	tablespoons olive oil		

Preheat oven to 375 degrees. Thinly slice each potato crosswise three-fourths of the way through, carefully leaving bottom of potato intact. Combine butter, oil and garlic in a medium shallow bowl. Roll potatoes in butter mixture and place in a large shallow roasting pan. Pour remaining butter mixture over potatoes. Season with salt and pepper. Bake, basting frequently, for 1½ hours or until tender and golden. Sprinkle with cheese just before serving. Potatoes can be baked earlier in the day and reheated just before serving.

Serves 10

"Fried Up" Potatoes

For years, frugal Southerners have "fried up" mashed potatoes left over from dinner the night before. Shape potatoes into round, flat cakes and place on a large greased baking sheet. In a small bowl, whisk one egg with 2 tablespoons of water, brush the top of each cake with egg wash and bake the cakes until golden brown (20 to 25 minutes) These cakes are best served piping hot.

Creamy Garlic Mashed Potatoes

6	heads garlic, coarsely chopped	1	(8-ounce) package cream cheese, softened
¼	cup olive oil	1-2	cups hot chicken broth
6-8	large russet potatoes		Salt and pepper to taste

Preheat oven to 375 degrees. Spread garlic in a shallow baking sheet. Pour oil over garlic. Bake about 30 minutes or until garlic has softened and is golden brown. Transfer to a large bowl and set aside. Cut potatoes into 2-inch pieces. Steam potatoes on a rack over 1 inch of boiling water for about 30 minutes or until tender. Add potatoes to garlic in bowl along with cream cheese. Mix and mash, adding hot broth until desired consistency is reached. Season to taste with salt and pepper.

Serves 6 to 8

Delmonico Potatoes

8	medium potatoes, peeled and cubed	10	ounces sharp Cheddar cheese, grated
6	tablespoons butter	4	tablespoons butter
6	tablespoons flour	12	slices bacon, cooked and crumbled
2	cups half-and-half	1	bunch green onions, chopped
½	teaspoon garlic powder		
	Salt and white pepper to taste		

Preheat oven to 350 degrees. Cook potatoes until tender in boiling water; drain. Spread potatoes in a lightly greased 9x13-inch pan. In a medium saucepan, melt 6 tablespoons butter over medium heat. Whisk in flour and cook 1 to 2 minutes, stirring constantly. Slowly whisk in half-and-half and bring to a boil. Boil 1 minute. Remove from heat and add garlic powder, salt and white pepper. Pour sauce over potatoes. Sprinkle with cheese and drizzle with melted butter. Scatter bacon and green onions on top. Bake 30 minutes.

Serves 8 to 10

Piped New Potatoes

Combine 24 new potatoes and salt to taste with enough water to cover in a saucepan. Boil for 15 to 20 minutes or until tender but still firm and drain. Cut potatoes into halves. Carefully scoop out pulp with a melon baller, leaving shells intact and reserving pulp. Mix reserved pulp, 6 cloves of mashed roasted garlic, 2 tablespoons chopped fresh flat leaf parsley and salt and pepper to taste in a bowl. Add just enough buttermilk to make a piping consistency. Spoon mixture into a pastry bag fitted with a large star tip and pipe into the potato shells.

Sweet Potatoes with Delicious Differences

3	cups cooked and mashed sweet potatoes	¼	teaspoon salt
6	tablespoons butter, melted, divided	¾	cup raisins (optional)
		¼	cup self-rising flour
½	cup evaporated milk	½	cup light brown sugar, firmly packed
3	eggs, beaten		
1	cup granulated sugar	¼	cup chopped pecans

Preheat oven to 350 degrees. Mix potatoes, 4 tablespoons butter, milk, eggs, granulated sugar, salt and raisins. Pour mixture into a greased baking dish. For a topping, combine remaining 2 tablespoons butter, flour, brown sugar and pecans. Blend with a pastry blender to a coarse, crumb-like texture. Sprinkle topping over potato mixture. Bake, uncovered, for 15 to 20 minutes or until browned.

Serves 6

In place of above topping, try adding marshmallows over potato mixture or top with crushed ginger snap cookies drizzled with butter.

Thomas Jefferson, as everyone knows, was a creative genius. Among all his great inventions were a few for the kitchen. Jefferson brought home a "pasta machine" from Italy in 1787. From that, he created a "macaroni pie" which we now call Baked Macaroni and Cheese. He also brought us the recipe for "Potatoes, fried in the French Manner," which became our standby, French Fries.

Praline Sweet Potato Soufflé

6	pounds sweet potatoes			Zest of 1 lemon
1	tablespoon cane syrup			Juice of ½ lemon
⅓	cup nonfat sweetened condensed milk		¼	teaspoon cinnamon sugar
				Pinch of nutmeg
1	cup butter, softened		1	cup raisins
2	tablespoons granulated sugar		2	cups chopped pecans
2	tablespoons light brown sugar, firmly packed		8	ounces (about 6) large pralines, broken
	Juice of ½ orange			Italian Meringue

Preheat oven to 350 degrees. Bake sweet potatoes for 1 hour or until fork tender. Peel and place in a mixing bowl Add syrup, milk, butter and sugars. Mix well with electric mixer. Add orange juice, lemon zest and lemon juice. Blend thoroughly. Sprinkle with cinnamon sugar, nutmeg, raisins and pecans. Gently fold in pralines. Transfer mixture to a 2½-quart glass baking dish. Bake at 350 degrees for 20 minutes. Top with meringue. Broil 7 minutes or until meringue is golden brown.

Serves 12

Italian Meringue

1	cup superfine sugar		5	egg whites, room temperature
⅓	cup water		¼	teaspoon cream of tartar

Combine sugar and water in a small saucepan over low heat. Swirl pan over heat until sugar dissolves completely; do not stir. Increase heat and boil to soft-ball stage (235 to 240 degrees on a candy thermometer.) Scrape down inside wall of pan with a wet pastry brush to prevent sugar crystals from forming around sides.

In a mixing bowl, whip egg whites with an electric mixer on low speed until foamy. Add cream of tartar and increase to medium speed. Beat until soft peaks form. With mixer running, pour hot syrup in a thin stream over egg whites. Beat until whites are stiff and glossy. Spread meringue over sweet potato soufflé and broil as directed.

When George Whitefield died, it was a loss of great proportion. "In Savannah, upon the news of his death, 'all the black cloth in the stores was bought up,' as the town went into mourning."

Russell and Hines from Savannah: A History of Her People Since 1733

Meringue Cloud Cookies

Preheat oven to 200 degrees. Dollop spoonfuls of meringue onto parchment-lined baking sheets or pipe from a pastry bag using a star tip. Bake 2 hours or until crisp. Turn off oven and allow meringues to cool and completely dry out.

Cakes, Pies, Puddings, and Desserts

The *First* Church

Christ Church is called the "Mother Church" of Georgia. It was the *first* Anglican (Church of England) congregation in Georgia. The *first* service was held on February 12, 1733, the *first* day that the settlers landed. The present church is built on the original site and is also called Christ Episcopal Church. The Wesley brothers, co-founders of Methodism, encouraged by Oglethorpe, came to Georgia and John Wesley became minister of Christ Church. In 1½ years at Christ Church, John Wesley wrote and published the *first* English Hymnal in America and created the *first* Protestant Sunday School in the world. Christ Church had the *first* pipe organ in Georgia dated 1758. The Great Savannah Fire of 1796, destroyed Christ Church. It was built in its present style in 1838, burned again in 1898 and was rebuilt within the outer walls. It has a bell by Revere and Son.

Spirited Savannah

John Wesley, the founder of Methodism, had a significant interest in the supernatural. From his religious studies, he knew of angels, demons and ghosts. From his childhood experience with a house spirit named Jeffery, Wesley knew with certainty that ghosts could be very active. Old Jeffrey had made his presence known while the Wesley brothers were in their teens. Their mother, Susanna, ran her home like a tight ship and learned to incorporate Jeffrey in her usual activities. Susanna Wesley was only disappointed that spirits such as Jeffrey could not be more helpful to the living. Their father, Samuel Wesley, was often quite displeased with Old Jeffrey and is reported to have threatened the spirit with a gun. The only hint of the identity of Old Jeffrey was that this spirit made it quite clear that his loyalties were for the Stuart cause whenever Samuel prayed for King George. Smart Spirit.

"Dessert, Salvation, and the Church Social"

Anyone who doesn't know that "pride cometh before a fall" simply has to show up at a Church Social with a three layer chocolate cake, only to find another chocolate cake has already been cut. This is especially true when that other cake has 10 or 12 exactly matched ½ inch layers, each perfectly frosted with chocolate fondant! Dessert and coffee at our many cherished churches is truly a thing of beauty to behold. The desserts which emerge from Savannah's kitchens would bring many of the world's greatest pastry chefs to their knees in reverence; appropriately so. They would be hard-pressed to compete with a rich golden cake, iced with caramel. This classic has been created since Colonial days, with brown sugar, real butter and cream, in a black iron skillet. There are also pies with meringue so perfect that only an amber drop or two on the surface reveals that they were made where the humidity is quite often higher than the temperature.

Looking at these labors of love, most often presented in churches with histories of faith-testing trials of endurance and subsequent salvations, stirs something sacred deep inside. Savannah's oldest churches often host secular events, in addition to the regular services held for their specific faiths. These are welcoming and illuminating in their own right. This is also true for semi-secular or – perhaps semi-religious events – such as meetings for historic preservation and heritage societies. (These come fairly close to being considered Savannah's shared "religion." Thank God!)

Certainly, the impressive array of refreshments reflects a real appreciation for the comfort Savannah's many religions have had with each other for nearly three hundred years, give or take a few decades. Not to belittle the Pilgrims in any way whatsoever, but if Plymouth was primarily black and white, Savannah was a rainbow in comparison. She still is.

Butter Pecan Cream Cake

1	cup buttermilk	2	cups sifted all-purpose flour
1	teaspoon baking soda		
5	eggs, separated	1	teaspoon vanilla
½	cup butter or margarine	1-1½	cups finely chopped pecans
½	cup vegetable shortening or margarine		
2	cups sugar	1	(4-ounce) can flaked coconut

Icing

1	(8-ounce) package cream cheese, softened	1	(1-pound) package powdered sugar
½	cup butter or margarine	1	teaspoon vanilla

Preheat oven to 325 degrees. Combine buttermilk and baking soda; set aside. Beat egg whites until stiff. Cream butter, shortening and sugar until fluffy. Add egg yolks, one at a time. Add flour alternately with vanilla and buttermilk mixture. Add pecans and coconut. Fold in beaten egg whites until mixed. Pour batter into 3 well-greased and lightly floured 8-inch cake pans. Bake 25 to 30 minutes. Cool before icing.

To make icing, cream all ingredients together until spreadable.

Coconut Pecan Cake: Add 1 teaspoon coconut flavoring with vanilla to cake batter. Make a double recipe of 7-Minute Frosting. Fold 1 heaping cup of coconut into frosting. Frost all three layers, sprinkling top of each with extra coconut to taste and chopped pecans, if desired.

7-Minute Frosting

5 cups sugar

1 cup water

½ cup light corn syrup

½ teaspoon salt

4 egg whites

½ teaspoon cream of tartar

Combine sugar, water, corn syrup and salt in a heavy saucepan over medium heat. Boil 7 minutes or until mixture spins a long thread. In a mixing bowl, beat egg whites and cream of tartar with an electric mixer on high speed until stiff peaks form. While still beating, pour boiled mixture slowly over egg whites and beat until mixture loses its gloss. Spread over cake. If frosting becomes too stiff, add a small amount of warm water.

Makes enough for 3 to 4 cake layers

Caramel Cake

1	cup butter or margarine	1	tablespoon baking powder
2	cups sugar		
4	eggs	½	teaspoon salt
3	cups sifted cake flour	1	cup milk
		1	teaspoon vanilla

Caramel Icing

3¼	cups sugar, divided	1	cup canned evaporated milk
¼	cup water		
		½	cup margarine

Preheat oven to 350 degrees. Cream butter. Gradually add sugar, creaming until light and fluffy. Add eggs, one at a time, beating well after each addition. Sift together flour, baking powder and salt. Add dry ingredients to creamed mixture alternately with milk and vanilla, beating after each addition until smooth. Pour batter into 3 greased and floured 9-inch round cake pans. Bake 25 to 30 minutes. Cool in pan 10 minutes. Remove from pans and cool completely on racks before icing.

To make icing, heat ¼ cup sugar in a saucepan until light brown. Quickly stir in water. Add remaining 3 cups sugar and milk. Stir well. Cook over medium heat to soft-ball stage. Add margarine. Transfer to a mixing bowl and beat with an electric mixer until icing starts to harden. Spread over cooled cake.

Serves 12

Candied flowers make a beautiful garnish for any cake plate. There are a few tricks to candying flowers successfully. First, cut your flowers the day before you intend to candy them, leaving some stem on the flower. Place the cut ends of the stems in a small vase of water and refrigerate overnight. This will stabilize the flowers so they hold their shape. Dry weather makes more predictable candied flowers than humid.

Strawberry Pecan Cake

1	(18¼-ounce) package white cake mix	4	eggs
1	(3-ounce) package strawberry gelatin	1	cup frozen sliced strawberries with juice, thawed
1	cup vegetable oil	1	cup flaked coconut
½	cup milk	1	cup chopped pecans

Frosting

½	cup margarine, softened	½	cup frozen sliced strawberries, thawed and drained, juice reserved
1	(1-pound) package powdered sugar	½	cup flaked coconut
		½	cup chopped pecans

Preheat oven to 350 degrees. Combine cake mix and gelatin in a mixing bowl. Add remaining cake ingredients in order listed. Mix well with an electric mixer for 2 minutes. Pour batter into 3 greased and floured 9-inch round cake pans. Bake 25 to 30 minutes or until top springs back when lightly touched. Remove from pans and cool completely on wire racks before frosting.

To make frosting, cream margarine and sugar with an electric mixer. Add strawberries, coconut and pecans and mix well. If needed, thin with reserved strawberry juice.

Serves 12

Frosted cake should be stored in refrigerator until ready to serve.

Candied Flowers

1 egg white, lightly beaten

2 dozen violets and/or pansies, washed and dried

Granulated sugar

With a pastry brush, paint the flowers all over with the egg white. Sprinkle the flowers with plain granulated sugar, being careful not to let the petals stick together and place, stem down, on a small grid-type cooking rack to hold up the flower heads while they dry. This will take about 2 days. Store the candied flowers up to a year in paper candy cups in an airtight container. Makes 2 dozen.

Key Lime Cake

¾	cup vegetable oil	1	(18¼-ounce) package
¾	cup orange juice		lemon cake mix
5	eggs	¼	cup Key lime juice
1	(3-ounce) package lime	5-6	teaspoons powdered
	gelatin		sugar

Frosting

1	(8-ounce) package cream	1	teaspoon vanilla
	cheese, softened	1	(1-pound) package
4	tablespoons butter or		powdered sugar
	margarine		

Preheat oven to 325 degrees. Combine oil, orange juice, eggs, gelatin and cake mix in a mixing bowl. Beat until smooth. Pour batter into a greased and floured 9x13-inch baking pan. Bake 20 minutes or until done; do not overbake. Prick top all over with a fork. Combine lime juice and sugar, stirring until smooth. Drizzle mixture over cake. Cool completely.

To make frosting, beat cream cheese and butter until smooth. Beat in vanilla and sugar until creamy. Spread over cooled cake.

Serves 8 to 10

Key Lime Juice

Our most favorite key lime juice is Nellie and Joe's. If it is not available in your local stores, it may be ordered directly (see resources) from Key West. The distinctive tart flavor of this key lime juice has been used since 1968, for preparing classic Key Lime pies, cakes, and many tart desserts. It is also excellent as a marinade for seafood, meats, and poultry, and is an ideal bar ingredient for great mixed drinks. A real standby.

Hazel Franklin's Sour Cream Pound Cake

1	cup butter, softened	1	(8-ounce) container sour cream	
3	cups sugar			
6	eggs, separated	3	cups cake flour	
1	teaspoon vanilla	¼	teaspoon baking soda	

Preheat oven to 325 degrees. Cream butter and sugar. Beat in egg yolks, one at a time. Mix well. Add vanilla and sour cream and beat 2 to 3 minutes. Sift together flour and baking soda and mix into batter. Beat egg whites until stiff peaks form and fold into batter. Pour batter into a greased and floured tube cake pan. Bake 1 hour, 25 minutes.

For chocolate cake, add ¾ cup cocoa.

Traditional Southern Pound Cake

1½	cups butter, softened	1	teaspoon vanilla	
1	(8-ounce) package cream cheese, softened	1	tablespoon lemon extract	
3	cups sugar	6	eggs	
1	teaspoon butter flavoring	3	cups cake flour	

Preheat oven to 325 degrees. Cream butter and cream cheese with an electric mixer until smooth. Beat in sugar, one cup at a time, allowing mixture to blend thoroughly between additions. Add butter flavoring, vanilla and lemon extract. Beat in eggs, one at a time, beating well after each addition. Add flour, one cup at a time, scraping down sides of bowl as needed. Pour batter into a greased and floured tube cake pan. Bake 1 hour, 20 minutes or until a toothpick inserted in the center comes out clean. Cool in pan 10 minutes.

Serves 10 to 12

Hazel Franklin, a beloved TV chef, was the hostess of the first cooking show in Savannah. She was the inspiration for many Savannah cooks. Her personal touches to classic recipes have now been passed on to the next generation, with love.

To create a caramelized texture on the outside of baked sweets, spray the pan with a non-stick spray and sprinkle with sugar instead of dusting with flour.

Meme's Light Fruit Cake

1 cup butter, softened

1 cup sugar

6 eggs

2¾ cups cake flour, divided

8 ounces candied pineapple

12 ounces candied cherries

1 small piece candied citron

1 pound package golden raisins

4 cups chopped pecans

Juice of 1 lemon

Juice of 1 orange

1 teaspoon vanilla

Preheat oven to 275 degrees. Cream butter and sugar. Beat in eggs. Add 1¾ cups flour and mix until well blended. Combine pineapple, cherries, citron, raisins and pecans and dust with remaining 1 cup flour. Blend fruit mixture, juices and vanilla into batter. Pour batter into a greased and floured tube pan. Bake 1½ hours. Cool in pan 10 minutes before removing.

Peach Pound Cake

1	cup butter, softened	1	teaspoon vanilla
3	cups sugar	1	teaspoon almond extract
6	eggs	1	(10-ounce) package frozen
3¾	cups flour		peaches, thawed and
½	teaspoon baking powder		drained, or ¾ pound
1	teaspoon salt		fresh, peeled and diced
1	cup milk, cream or sour cream		

Preheat oven to 350 degrees. Cream butter and sugar. Beat in eggs, one at a time. Combine flour, baking powder and salt. Blend dry ingredients into creamed mixture alternately with milk. Add vanilla and almond extract. Stir in peaches. Pour batter into a greased and floured tube pan. Bake 1½ hours or until a toothpick inserted in the center comes out clean. Cool completely.

This cake is great with one of the following frostings:

Cream Cheese Frosting

1	(8-ounce) package cream cheese	1	(1-pound) package powdered sugar
½	cup butter, softened	1	teaspoon vanilla extract
		1	teaspoon almond extract

Beat together all ingredients.

Peach Buttercream Frosting

½	cup butter	1	(1-pound) package powdered sugar
½	cup diced peaches	1-2	tablespoons milk (optional)

Combine butter, peaches and sugar. Depending on juiciness of peaches, you may need to add milk to thin, or add extra sugar to thicken.

Banana Nut Pound Cake with Caramel Glaze

1	cup butter or margarine, softened	½	teaspoon baking powder
1	cup shortening	½	teaspoon baking soda
2	cups light brown sugar, firmly packed	½	teaspoon salt
1	cup granulated sugar	½	cup milk
5	eggs	1	large ripe banana, mashed
3	cups all-purpose flour, plus extra for dusting	2	teaspoons vanilla
		1	cup chopped pecans

Caramel Glaze

4	tablespoons butter, softened	¼	cup granulated sugar
¼	cup light brown sugar, firmly packed	¼	cup whipping cream
		1	teaspoon vanilla

Preheat oven to 325 degrees. Cream butter and shortening with an electric mixer. Add sugars and beat 5 minutes. Add eggs, one at a time, beating well after each addition. In a separate bowl, mix flour, baking powder, baking soda and salt. Beginning and ending with dry ingredients, beat in dry ingredients and milk alternately in small amounts. Mix in banana and vanilla. Lightly dust pecans with extra flour and stir into batter by hand. Pour batter into a greased and floured tube cake pan. Bake 1½ hours or until a toothpick inserted in the center comes out clean. Glaze cake while still warm.

To make glaze, combine butter, sugars and cream in a saucepan. Bring to a boil and cook, stirring constantly, until well blended and thickened. Remove from heat and stir in vanilla. Allow to cool. While cake is still warm, brush with glaze using a pastry brush.

Savannah born, Southern genre writer, Flannery O'Connor said, "The South is not Christ-centered, it is Christ-haunted." Rebellious though we may be, Spirit permeates the South, and is reflected in a rainbow of religious preferences. Flannery O'Connor, from Mystery and Manners.

To help cakes rise evenly, cut strips from towels to fit the depth and size of the pan. Wet strips with water and ring out. Wrap strips around the outside of the pan and attach with a T-pin or safety pin. Bake according to directions.

Apple Cake

4	(6-ounce) packages dried apples, cored	4	eggs
2	cups water	2	cups all-purpose or cake flour, plus extra for dusting
1¾	cups sugar, divided		
1	teaspoon allspice	2	cups chopped pecans
1	cup butter, softened	2	cups golden raisins

Combine apples, water and ¼ cup sugar in a large saucepan. Cook over high heat until bubbles form. Reduce heat to low and stir in allspice. Cover and cook until apples are tender. Remove from heat and puree with a hand mixer.

Preheat oven to 325 degrees. In a large mixing bowl, whip butter and eggs with an electric mixer until light. Add remaining 1½ cups sugar and flour. Mix well. In a separate bowl, dust pecans with extra flour. Add raisins and 2 cups of pureed apple mixture to nuts and toss until mixed. Stir nut mixture into batter by hand and mix well. Pour batter into a greased and floured tube pan, or 1 large and 1 small loaf pan or 3 small loaf pans. Bake in tube pan for 1½ hours, or for 1 hour, 25 minutes in large loaf pan and 1 hour, 5 minutes in small loaf pan. Use a toothpick inserted in the center to check for doneness.

If using metal loaf pans, place a pan of water in the oven to prevent overbrowning.

For a novel gift idea, bake apple cakes in children's shoe boxes with lids on. Cut a brown paper bag to fit inside a shoebox and grease the paper for easy removal. Batter will fill 3 children's shoeboxes. Place a pan of water in the oven to prevent boxes from turning brown. Baking in shoeboxes allows the cake to be wrapped attractively for gift giving.

Temptation Turtle Cheesecake

2	cups crushed chocolate cookies or vanilla wafers (about 8 ounces)	1½	tablespoons all-purpose flour
4	tablespoons butter, melted	¼	teaspoon salt
2½	(8-ounce) packages cream cheese, softened	1½	teaspoons vanilla
		3	eggs
1	cup sugar	2	tablespoons whipping cream
		¾	cup chopped pecans, toasted

Caramel Topping

½	(14-ounce) package caramels	¼	cup whipping cream

Chocolate Topping

4	(1-ounce) squares semisweet chocolate	2	tablespoons whipping cream
1	teaspoon butter		

Preheat oven to 450 degrees. Combine cookie crumbs and butter and press into the bottom of a 9-inch springform pan. Beat cream cheese with an electric mixer until creamy. Beat in sugar, flour, salt and vanilla. Add eggs, one at a time, beating well after each addition. Blend in cream. Pour over crust in pan. Bake 10 minutes. Reduce oven to 200 degrees. Bake 35 to 40 minutes longer or until set. Loosen cake from rim of pan. Cool completely before removing rim.

Meanwhile, prepare toppings. For caramel topping, combine caramels and cream in a small saucepan. Stir over low heat until smooth. For chocolate topping, combine chocolate, butter and cream in a small saucepan. Stir over low heat until smooth. Drizzle toppings over cooled cake. Refrigerate. Sprinkle with pecans just before serving.

Makes 1 (9-inch) cheesecake

Place a tray filled with water on the bottom rack of oven before preheating. Leave in oven during baking time to prevent cracking in cheesecake.

The first Greek Orthodox Church was founded about 1900. In 1918, a Greek school was established to help maintain a connection with the old country. In 1941, the present Greek Orthodox Church was organized, at a new location, with a Hellenic Center established in 1951. Savannah looks forward to the Greek festival each year in the fall.

Chocolate Nut Pie

1	cup semisweet chocolate chips (6 ounces)	3	eggs, slightly beaten
1	(9-inch) pie crust, unbaked	½	cup light brown sugar, firmly packed
2	cups assorted unsalted nuts, such as cashews, pecans, macadamia or peanuts	½	cup light corn syrup
		2	tablespoons butter, melted
		1	teaspoon vanilla

Preheat oven to 375 degrees. Sprinkle chocolate chips over pie crust. Top with nuts. In a mixing bowl, lightly whisk together eggs, brown sugar, corn syrup, butter and vanilla. Pour mixture slowly into pie crust, rearranging nuts as needed. Bake 40 to 50 minutes or until golden. Cool at least 30 minutes before slicing.

Serves 8

For a bourbon nut pie add 1 to 2 jiggers of bourbon and 1 cup chopped walnuts or pecans to pie.

French Silk Chocolate Pie

Crust

1	cup flour	½	cup butter, softened
¼	cup powdered sugar		

Filling

¾	cup butter, softened	1	teaspoon vanilla
1	cup plus 1 tablespoon sugar	3	eggs
2	(1-ounce) squares baking chocolate		Whipped cream (optional) for topping

Preheat oven to 400 degrees. Combine all crust ingredients and press into a well greased 10-inch pie pan. Bake 10 to 12 minutes.

For filling, cream butter and sugar. Melt chocolate and cool. Blend cooled chocolate and vanilla into creamed mixture. Add eggs and beat 10 minutes or until thickened. Spoon into crust and refrigerate until set. Top with whipped cream when ready to serve.

Serves 8

Marbled White Chocolate Raspberry Cheesecake

Soft rocky road cookies, crumbled

5 (8-ounce) packages cream cheese, softened

½ teaspoon vanilla

1½ cups sugar

3 tablespoons flour

½ teaspoon salt

4 eggs

2 egg yolks

¼ cup whipping cream

3 tablespoons seedless raspberry jam

3 (3-ounce) packages quality white chocolate, finely chopped

Preheat oven to 450 degrees. Press cookie crumbs into a 9-inch springform pan to make a crust. Mix together cream cheese, vanilla, sugar, flour, salt, eggs, egg yolks and cream in order listed. Remove ¾ cup of batter and mix with jam until smooth. To remaining batter, mix in chocolate. Pour chocolate batter over crust in pan. Drizzle with jam batter. Gentle swirl batters together. Bake 12 minutes. Reduce oven temperature to 350 degrees and bake 55 minutes longer or until firm. Chill.

Chess Pie

2	cups sugar	1	tablespoon white vinegar
1	tablespoon all-purpose flour	½	teaspoon vanilla
2	tablespoons yellow cornmeal	4	eggs
		¼	cup buttermilk
½	cup butter, melted	¼	teaspoon salt
		1	pie crust, unbaked

Preheat oven to 350 degrees. Combine all ingredients except pie crust in order listed. Pour mixture into pie crust. Bake 50 minutes. Cool completely on a wire rack.

Serves 8

Chess Pie Variations:

Coconut Chess Pie:

Add 1 cup toasted, flaked coconut to filling before pouring into pie crust.

Chocolate-Pecan Chess Pie:

Add 3½ tablespoons cocoa and ½ cup chopped, toasted pecans to filling before pouring into pie crust.

Lemon Chess Pie:

Add ⅓ cup lemon juice and 2 teaspoons lemon zest to filling before pouring into pie crust.

Simple in preparation and timeless in appeal, this is the ultimate pantry pie. Chess pie may have originally been called "chest pie" because it held up well in a pie chest, a common piece of furniture in the early South. Another story of origin is that when the husband asked "What kind of pie is this?" the cook replied, "I don't know. It's ches' pie." Try these variations to this timeless confection.

Golden Pecan Pie

½ cup granulated sugar

½ cup dark brown sugar, firmly packed

1 cup light corn syrup

¼ teaspoon salt

3 eggs, well beaten

5 tablespoons butter, melted

2 teaspoons vanilla

1 cup chopped pecans

1 (9-inch) pie crust, unbaked

Preheat oven to 325 degrees. Combine all ingredients except pie crust. Pour mixture into pie crust. Bake 1 hour.

Serves 8

Crème de Menthe Pie

12	chocolate cookies, crushed	2	tablespoons plus
2	tablespoons butter, melted		2 teaspoons crème de
20	marshmallows		menthe
¼	cup milk		Pinch of salt
		1	cup whipping cream, whipped

Sprinkle three-fourths of cookie crumbs in a pie pan. Pour butter over crumbs. Melt marshmallows in milk in a saucepan over medium heat; cool. Fold cooled marshmallow mixture, crème de menthe and salt into whipped cream. Spoon over cookie crumbs in pan. Sprinkle with remaining crumbs. Freeze at least 2 hours.

Serves 6 to 8

Apples and Pears Sautéed in Brandy Butter

4	tablespoons butter	3	apples, peeled and sliced
½	cup brown sugar, firmly packed	3	pears, peeled and sliced
		½	cup brandy

Melt butter with sugar in a large heavy skillet. Add apples and pears and cook until fruit is softened. Add brandy and simmer 1 minute longer. Serve warm.

Serves 6

Can be eaten alone or served over ice cream.

Super Fudge Sauce

½	cup butter or margarine	2	tablespoons rum
1	cup sugar	⅓	cup cocoa
⅛	teaspoon salt	1	cup whipping cream
1	teaspoon instant coffee	2	teaspoons vanilla

Melt butter in a saucepan. Blend in sugar, salt, coffee, rum and cocoa. Add cream and bring to a boil. Reduce heat and simmer 5 minutes. Remove from heat and stir in vanilla. Serve warm.

Excellent over ice cream or pound cake.

Basic Crème Brûlée

2	cups whipping cream	½	cup light brown sugar,
5	egg yolks		firmly packed
½	cup granulated sugar		Fresh raspberries and
1	tablespoon vanilla		fresh mint sprigs for
			garnish

Preheat oven to 275 degrees. Combine cream, egg yolks, granulated sugar and vanilla in a bowl. Whisk until sugar is dissolved and mixture is smooth. Pour into five 5x1-inch round baking dishes. Place dishes in a large roasting pan or jelly-roll pan. Add ½ inch of water to pan for a water bath. Bake 45 to 50 minutes or until almost set; the center will still be liquid and a knife inserted will not come out clean. Cool in the water bath on a wire rack. Remove from pan, cover and refrigerate 8 hours or overnight. When ready to serve, sprinkle about 1½ tablespoons brown sugar evenly over each custard and place custards in a jelly-roll pan. Broil 5 inches from heat or until sugar melts. Let stand 5 minutes for sugar to harden. Garnish as desired.

Serves 5

This elegant dessert is both delicious and easy to prepare. When broiling the brown sugar, place the custards as close to the heating element as possible or use a small kitchen propane torch to caramelize the sugar. Crème Brûlée is even more extraordinary when the custard is cold and the topping is warm. Here's the secret: pack the custards in ice before you broil them.

Chocolate Crème Brûlée

Combine 4 (1 ounce) squares semisweet chocolate and ½ cup whipping cream from basic recipe in a small heavy saucepan; cook over low heat, stirring constantly until chocolate melts. Add remaining 1½ cups whipping cream; reduce vanilla to 1 teaspoon. Proceed as directed in basic recipe, baking for 55 minutes. To make a Chocolate-Raspberry version, place 8 to 10 fresh raspberries in each baking dish, add chocolate custard, and increase baking time to 1 hour and 5 minutes.

Country Vanilla Ice Cream with Quick Caramel Pecan Topping

2	cups milk	2	cups half-and-half
1¾	cups sugar	1	tablespoon vanilla
½	teaspoon salt	4	cups whipping cream

Topping

1	cup water	¾	cup coarsely chopped
1½	cups sugar		pecans

Scald milk until bubbles form around edge of pan. Remove from heat. Add sugar and salt and stir until dissolved. Mix in half-and-half, vanilla and cream. Cover and refrigerate 30 minutes. Transfer to an ice cream maker and freeze according to machine's directions.

For topping, gently heat water and sugar in a small heavy saucepan until sugar dissolves. Brush down sides of pan with cold water to remove crystals. Increase heat to medium-high and bring to a boil. Boil until mixture turns pale golden brown. Stir in pecans until well coated. Continue cooking until mixture is a rich, tawny caramel. Pour immediately into a greased baking sheet and cool until hardened. Use a rolling pin to break cooled caramel into pieces. Serve sprinkled over ice cream.

Makes 4 quarts ice cream, 1 quart topping

Peach Ice Cream

6 pounds peaches, peeled and chopped (about 10 cups)

4 cups whipping cream

2 teaspoons vanilla

1 tablespoon ground ginger

Place half the peaches in a large mixing bowl. Puree remaining peaches in a blender or food processor. Add pureed to chopped peaches. Stir in cream, vanilla and ginger until well mixed. Place in an ice cream maker and freeze according to machine's directions. Let flavors blend at least 30 minutes in freezer before serving.

Serves 6 to 8

Although there is an ongoing debate about which state produces the best peaches, we Georgians know the answer. There is no question that peach ice cream is the favorite Southern ice cream. It's always good over apple pie, but try it over bread pudding, peach cobbler - anything!

Teacup Whiskey Trifle

2	dozen ladyfingers, split, or thinly sliced angel food or pound cake
½	"teacup" (about ⅓ cup) whiskey or rum, or to taste

1	cup jam or preserves, such as raspberry, blackberry, apple or peach, or 1½ to 2 cups chopped fresh fruit sweetened with sugar
1-1½	cups whipped cream for topping
½	cup slivered blanched almonds, lightly toasted

Custard

¾-1	pound sugar
2	tablespoons cornstarch
	Dash of salt
2	cups half-and-half

4	egg yolks, well beaten
2-3	tablespoons butter
1½-2	teaspoons vanilla
1½-2	cups whipped cream

Arrange ladyfingers over the bottom and sides of a deep, wide trifle bowl or a punch bowl. Sprinkle with whiskey, saving some if ladyfingers will be layered in the bowl. Spread jam over top of ladyfingers. Repeat layers 2 or 3 times, if desired.

Prepare custard in a double boiler. Mix sugar, cornstarch and salt. Gradually stir in half-and-half. Cover and cook over hot water for 6 to 8 minutes. Uncover and cook 8 to 10 minutes longer. Add egg yolks and butter. Cook briefly, then cool, stirring often. Stir vanilla into cooled custard. Fold in whipped cream. Pour custard over layers in bowl. Top with whipped cream and almonds.

Serves 10 to 12

On occasion, top off your favorite dinner with drizzled, dipped fruit. Let fresh pineapple spears, Mandarin orange sections and cantaloupe cubes dry so the chocolate for dipping will adhere. Melt 1 cup of semisweet chocolate chips with 1 tablespoon shortening in a double boiler. Let stand until 110 degrees or until lukewarm. Dip each piece of fruit into the chocolate using wooden picks and place on a rack sprayed with nonstick cooking spray. Chill until set. Melt 1 cup of white chocolate chips with 1 tablespoon shortening in a double boiler. Cool as before. Drizzle over the chocolate coating. Chill until set and store in the refrigerator until serving time. Garnish with sprigs of fresh mint.

Best of the Bunch Baked Banana Pudding

3	cups whole milk	1	teaspoon vanilla, or
¾-1	cup sugar, divided		½ teaspoon vanilla and
¼	cup flour		½ teaspoon banana
⅛	teaspoon salt		flavoring
3	eggs, separated	¼	teaspoon cream of tartar
		1	(12-ounce) box vanilla wafers
		4	bananas, sliced

To make a custard, heat milk in the top of a double boiler until skim forms on top. Stir in ½-¾ cup sugar (to taste). Add flour and salt and blend well. Cook over boiling water, stirring frequently, until mixture thickens. Reduce heat to medium-low. Cover and cook 10 to 15 minutes, stirring often. Beat egg yolks in a large bowl. Pour milk custard slowly into egg yolks while stirring constantly. Stir in vanilla. Cool to lukewarm.

Meanwhile, preheat oven to 325 degrees. To make meringue, combine remaining ¼ cup sugar, cream of tartar and egg whites in a bowl. Beat until stiff peaks form. Line a greased medium baking pan with a single layer of vanilla wafers. Stand more wafers along the sides of the pan. Arrange a flat layer of banana slices over wafers. Pour half the custard on top. Repeat layers. Spread egg white meringue over top layer. Bake 15 to 20 minutes.

Serves 6 to 8

The first Jewish Congregation in Georgia came only five months after Oglethorpe landed in 1733. It is the oldest recorded congregation in America practicing Reform Judaism. The congregation, Mickva Israel (Hope of Israel), treasures its ancient scriptures, the "Sephar Torah."

Catholics were not officially allowed to settle in the Colony until after the Revolutionary War due to fears that they might ally with the Spanish. The first Catholic Church in Savannah, the Cathedral of St. John the Baptist, was organized in 1796.

Bread Pudding with Bourbon Sauce

Pudding

1	(1-pound) loaf firm white sandwich bread	1	tablespoon cinnamon
2	eggs	1	tablespoon vanilla
1	cup granulated sugar	2	cups whole milk
½	cup brown sugar, firmly packed, divided	½	cup raisins

Sauce

2	eggs	½	cup unsalted butter, melted and slightly cooled
¼	cup sugar		
2	tablespoons bourbon		

Preheat oven to 350 degrees. To make pudding, tear bread into small pieces and place into the bowl of an electric mixer fitted with a dough hook. In a separate bowl, whisk together eggs, granulated sugar, ¼ cup brown sugar, cinnamon, vanilla and milk. Stir in raisins. Pour mixture over bread pieces. Let soak 5 minutes. Blend on low speed until bread is completely moistened. Transfer pudding to a greased 2-quart baking dish. Force remaining ¼ cup brown sugar through a medium sieve onto pudding. Place dish inside a larger baking dish filled with 1 inch of hot water. Bake in center of oven for 1½ hours or until set. Allow to settle before serving.

Make sauce while pudding bakes. Beat eggs and sugar in a metal bowl with a hand-held electric mixer until combined. Set bowl over a saucepan of simmering water and beat 6 minutes or until light and thickened. Remove bowl from heat and beat in bourbon. Beat in butter in a slow steam until well combined. Serve pudding warm or at room temperature with sauce.

Serves 8

The earliest Scots, mostly lowlanders, were in Savannah by 1734, where they formed an unofficial St. Andrew's Society. This group was not popular with the Trustees, against whom they spread seditious gossip. Most everyone was glad to see these "Malcontents" move to South Carolina in 1740. In contrast, the 200 Highlanders were most welcome and they supported Oglethorpe to the fullest. They soon made their home south of Savannah, in what is now Darien. These Highlanders were skilled warriors and helped defeat the Spanish at the Battle of Bloody Marsh, in 1742. In 1762, the Saint Andrew's Society of Savannah was recreated with highest standards, which remain to this day.

Chocolate Bread Pudding with Raspberry Cabernet Sauce

The Moravians came in 1735, on the ship with the Wesleys. They set up the first church in North America organized by the Christian Communion, founded in Bohemia. The Moravians, hoping to educate the Indians, were evangelical and refused to bear arms, even for defensive purposes. In 1740, they left to join another group of Moravians in Bethlehem, Pennsylvania, as it was not working out for them in the colony of Georgia.

¾	cup chopped pecans	6	eggs
½	(1-pound) loaf cinnamon raisin bread	½	cup sugar
		¼	cup coffee liqueur
6	ounces bittersweet chocolate, chopped	1	teaspoon vanilla
		½	teaspoon freshly, finely ground black pepper
2	cups light cream or half-and-half, divided		Powdered sugar for garnish

Raspberry Cabernet Sauce

1	(12-ounce) container frozen raspberries, thawed	1	(750 ml) bottle Cabernet Sauvignon wine
1	cup sugar	2	grinds black pepper

Preheat oven to 350 degrees. Toast pecans in oven for 10 minutes. Cut enough bread into ½-inch cubes to equal 6 cups. Place bread cubes in a 9x5-inch loaf pan that has been sprayed with cooking spray. Combine chocolate and 1 cup cream in a double boiler. Heat slowly over simmering water until melted. Stir to mix well. Combine remaining 1 cup cream, eggs, sugar, liqueur, vanilla and pepper in a blender. Blend on high speed for 1 minute. Reduce to low speed and slowly add melted chocolate mixture, blending well. Pour mixture over bread cubes. Sprinkle with toasted pecans. Cover with foil and refrigerate at least 4 hours or overnight if texture of bread is very dense. Bread cubes should be completely saturated.

When ready to bake, preheat oven to 325 degrees. Place pan in a water bath. Bake 75 to 90 minutes or until bread feels slightly firm to the touch. Remove foil and cool slightly. Serve on dessert plates in a pool of Raspberry Cabernet Sauce. Sift powdered sugar on top for garnish.

To make sauce, combine all ingredients in a 12-inch skillet. Boil over high heat until reduced to 2 cups. Transfer to an electric blender. Cool slightly. Place lid on blender and cover with a kitchen towel. Blend on high speed until pureed. Pour through a fine sieve to remove seeds. Refrigerate until ready to serve.

Serves 12

Lemon Charlotte

2	(3-ounce) packages unfilled ladyfingers, split	5	eggs, beaten
1	(¼-ounce) envelope unflavored gelatin	½	cup sugar
¼	cup fresh lemon juice		Pinch of salt
		2	teaspoons lemon zest
		1	cup whipping cream

Sauce

3	tablespoons apricot preserves	1	tablespoon fresh lemon juice
3	tablespoons orange marmalade	2	tablespoons butter
	Juice of 1 orange	¼	cup slivered almonds

Line the bottom and sides of a 7- or 8-inch springform pan or a bowl with ladyfingers. Softened gelatin in lemon juice in a bowl. Place bowl over hot water to dissolve gelatin. Combine eggs, sugar and salt in the top of a double boiler over simmering water. Beat with an electric mixer until thick and light colored. Add gelatin mixture and lemon zest, beating a few more seconds. Whip cream while mixture cools. Fold cream into cooled mixture. Pour over ladyfingers in pan. Refrigerate overnight. To serve, spoon sauce over individual servings.

To make sauce, heat preserves, marmalade, orange juice and lemon juice in a saucepan over low heat until melted. In a separate pan, melt butter. Add almonds and sauté until lightly browned. Add almonds to sauce. Blend well and remove from heat. Serve sauce at room temperature.

Serves 8 to 12

John Wesley became smitten with a young woman named Sophey Hopkey, but was worried that his ministry would suffer if he became too involved. Thus, Wesley cooled his attentions and Sophey accepted another proposal of marriage. Wesley refused to perform the marriage and the couple went to South Carolina to be wed. Upon their return, Wesley also refused to give Sophey communion. Her husband sued, but Wesley claimed this to be a church matter. A court date was set, but Wesley posted his intentions to return to England, which he did almost immediately.

Oreo Mousse

½	(half-gallon) container vanilla ice cream, softened	1	(8-ounce) container frozen whipped topping, thawed
		12	Oreo cookies, crushed

Sauce

½	cup cocoa	3	tablespoons butter
1	cup sugar		Pinch of salt
1	cup light corn syrup	1	teaspoon vanilla
½	cup half-and-half		

Mix ice cream and whipped topping together. Fold in cookie crumbs. Pour mixture into a flat 8x8-inch container. Freeze 8 hours. Cut into squares and serve with warm sauce on top.

To make sauce, combine all ingredients except vanilla in a saucepan. Bring to a boil and cook 3 minutes. Remove from heat and stir in vanilla. Serve warm over ice cream.

Serves 4 to 8

Use as an elegant dessert or have on hand in the freezer for the kids to enjoy. You will want to double this recipe since it is eaten so quickly. Make each batch separately to avoid overheating your mixer. If doubled, use a 9x13-inch pan.

In 1755, the first Presbyterian Church was organized. It was the first church for the followers of the Doctrines of the Church of Scotland. Destroyed by fire in 1796, it was rebuilt as the Independent Presbyterian Church in 1819. Fire took it again in 1889, but it was rebuilt in the same manner in 1891.

Strawberry Biscuits with Sugared Cream

12	frozen Southern biscuits	¼	cup sugar
1	pint fresh strawberries, sliced	½	cup cold Sugared Cream

Sugared Cream

½	cup sugar		Juice and zest of ½ lemon
2	cups whipping cream		

Bake biscuits according to package directions; set aside. Sprinkle strawberry slices with sugar; set aside. Prepare cream sauce.

To make cream sauce, stir sugar into cream until dissolved. Add lemon juice and zest and stir until thickened. To serve, slice biscuits in half and spread a teaspoon of cream sauce over the bottom half of each biscuit. Top with an overlapping layer of strawberry slices and a dollop of cream sauce. Cover with top biscuit half and a strawberry fan. Serve immediately.

Serves 12, makes 2½ cups sauce

Apricot Almond Dream

½	cup sliced almonds, toasted	1	teaspoon almond extract
3	tablespoons margarine or butter, melted	1	(1-quart) block vanilla ice cream
1	cup crushed vanilla wafers	1	(12-ounce) jar apricot preserves

Combine almonds, margarine, wafer crumbs and almond extract. Set aside ¼ cup of mixture. Sprinkle half of remaining mixture in 9x9-inch dish. Layer with half of ice cream and half of preserves. Repeat layers. Sprinkle reserved ¼ cup of crumb mixture on top and freeze.

Serves 8

This is one of our favorite Damon Fowler creations. We agree that, "It's a beautiful sauce to serve with a fruit compote, pound cake or a fruit tart. Best of all, it's as simple to make as it is good. Whipped cream with no whipping!"

Crème fraîche, a cultured mixture of buttermilk and whipping cream, is thicker than heavy cream but not quite as thick as sour cream and has a tangy, nutty taste. It may be purchased in the gourmet cheese section of some supermarkets or selected specialty stores.

Peach or Raspberry Pecan Shortcake

2	cups all-purpose flour		1	cup whipping cream
2	tablespoons sugar		1½	cups whipping cream, whipped and flavored with 2 to 3 tablespoons bourbon
½	teaspoon salt			
1	tablespoon baking powder			
4	tablespoons butter, chilled		1	pint raspberries or 2 to 3 cups sliced peaches, or a combination
½	cup very finely ground pecans			

Preheat oven to 450 degrees. Combine flour, sugar, salt and baking powder in a mixing bowl. Cut in butter until crumbs are the size of small peas. Mix in pecans. Gently stir in liquid cream until just blended. Pat dough into about a ¾-inch round. Use a floured 3-inch cutter to make 6 shortcakes. Place shortcakes on a lightly greased baking sheet. Bake 13 to 15 minutes or until puffed and lightly browned. Cool slightly on a wire rack. Split slightly cooled shortcakes in half. Spoon a generous amount of whipped cream onto bottom half of each shortcake. Top with berries or peach slices. Cover with top half of each shortcake. Serve immediately.

Serves 6

Fresh Peach Sauce

4-5	fresh ripe peaches	Sugar to taste
½	lemon	Whole nutmeg

Peel and chop peaches over a bowl to catch juice. Drop chopped peaches into juice. Squeeze a small amount of lemon juice - just enough to keep peaches from browning - over peaches. Mash peaches to a smooth pulp. Taste pulp and stir in sugar as needed. Grate a little nutmeg over sauce and let stand 30 minutes.

Makes about 2 cups

The first Salzburger Lutherans landed in Savannah in 1734, fleeing religious persecution in Austria. They set up their own religious colony at Ebenezer (Stone of Help) near Savannah. They built the first church building of any denomination in 1740. When the wooden structure rotted, they began the Jerusalem Lutheran Church in 1767. It was completed in 1769/1770 and is the oldest standing church in Georgia.

Georgia Pecan Apple Crisp

4	cups thinly sliced tart apples	½	cup rolled oats
¾	cup brown sugar, firmly packed	¾	teaspoon cinnamon
		¾	teaspoon nutmeg
½	cup all-purpose flour, sifted	½	cup butter
		½	cup pecans

Preheat oven to 350 degrees. Spread apples over the bottom of a 9x9-inch baking pan. Blend sugar, flour, oats, cinnamon, nutmeg, butter and pecans until crumbly. Sprinkle mixture over apples. Bake 30 to 45 minutes or until apples are tender and top is golden brown.

Serves 8 to 10

Simple Peach Cobbler

2	cups peeled and sliced peaches or fresh blueberries	¾	cup flour
		2	teaspoons baking powder
1½	cups sugar, divided	¼	teaspoon salt
½	cup margarine	¾	cup milk

Preheat oven to 350 degrees. Combine peaches and ½ cup sugar; set aside. Melt margarine in oven in an 8x8-inch baking dish, tilting dish to coat bottom. In a mixing bowl, stir together remaining 1 cup sugar, flour, baking powder, salt and milk. Pour batter into baking dish without stirring. Arrange peach slices on batter. Bake 40 minutes or until crust is light brown and puffy.

Serves 8

Charles Wesley was chosen as Oglethorpe's personal secretary. Then, while they were in Ft. Frederica, Wesley accused Oglethorpe of adultery with two married women (due to idle gossip, probably). For a time, Charles Wesley swapped parishes with John Wesley to avoid more trouble. It is noteworthy that Charles Wesley wrote the words for about 6,000 hymns during his lifetime.

Cinnamon Pear Crumble

The First African Baptist Church was established by a slave, George Leile. Leile preached along the river beginning in 1775, and gained his freedom in 1777. The British evacuated him to Jamaica. Before leaving, Leile baptized Andrew Bryan, a slave. This church was organized in 1788, and is the Oldest Black Congregation in America.

4	tart, crisp pears, peeled and chopped	½	cup butter, melted, divided
¼	cup fresh lemon juice	4-6	teaspoons granulated sugar
½	cup light brown sugar, firmly packed	2	cups plain soft white bread crumbs
1	teaspoon cinnamon	1	cup finely chopped pecans
½	teaspoon allspice (optional)		

Topping

4	tablespoons butter, melted (optional)	¼	cup brown sugar, firmly packed
½	cup finely chopped pecans	1	jigger rum (optional)

Combine pears, lemon juice, brown sugar, cinnamon and allspice in a large bowl with a lid. Toss until pears are evenly coated. Refrigerate at least a few hours to allow pears to slightly soften.

When ready to bake, preheat oven to 375 degrees. Brush about 1 tablespoon of melted butter in a round casserole dish. Sprinkle granulated sugar over bottom and sides of dish. In a bowl, pour remaining butter over bread crumbs. Toss to evenly coat. Stir in pecans. In dish, make 3 layers each of pear mixture and bread crumb mixture, ending with crumbs.

Combine all topping ingredients and pour evenly over top layer of crumbs. Bake 45 to 60 minutes or until pears are cooked and topping is golden brown.

Serves 6 to 8

For a Pear Brown Betty, omit topping.

Cookies, Bars, and Candies

The *First* Girl Scouts

Juliette Gordon Low was the founder of the *first* Girl Scouts in America. Begun on March 12, 1912, the Girl Scouts has grown to be a worldwide organization, which has positively influenced about 50 million women. Each year 15,000 Girl Scouts come for educational programs at "the birthplace," and another 50,000 visitors pass through this most special house museum. In 1965, the Juliette Gordon Low Birthplace became Savannah's *first* National Historic Landmark. It is furnished in the style of the 1880's and 1890's, as it was when Juliette "Daisy" Gordon Low was living there. "Daisy" was born on Halloween night in 1860, to the wealthy Gordon family. She married in 1886, and was widowed in 1904. In England, she met Lord Baden-Powell who gave her the inspiration for Girl Scouts. She was a tireless worker on behalf of "Daisy's Scouts," often supporting the venture with her own money. "Daisy" was a "maverick" whose life's work made a worldwide contribution.

Spirited Savannah

A poignant story is told about "Daisy's" parents, General William and Mrs. Nellie Kinzie Gordon. "Willie" and "Nellie" led a storybook life together for 54 years, from 1858 until the General's death in 1912. This had not been assured, since the General was Confederate and Nellie was a New Englander, with family fighting for the Union. In 1917, as Nellie lay dying, she urged her family to not mourn for she would soon be with her "Willie" again. Her daughter-in-law, Margaret Gordon, having bid Nellie a final goodbye, was sitting in an adjoining room, which had once belonged to the General. Suddenly, Margaret was startled to see the General in full Confederate regalia, coming out of Nellie's room. He walked through his own room, past Margaret Gordon, and descended the stairs. On his face was an expression of "grave gladness." At that moment, Margaret's husband came to say that Nellie had died. Nellie had been wearing an expression later described as that of a "radiant bride, going to meet her bridegroom." Downstairs, they found the old family retainer in tears as he told of seeing the General in the same way. It seems that the General had come to escort his Lady, himself.

"Reclaiming the Cookie-Baking Mom"

Somewhere along the line, the phrase "cookie-baking mom" lost its true meaning. We believe it got lost in the shuffle created by those who insisted that the cookie-baking mom had to be only that – instead of – being the labor force, outside of the home – and vice versa. Maybe we missed something where we are, because this idea mystifies us completely. We can see no reason why one precludes the other. Not one among us could generally recall anyone in their family who couldn't work all day, at whatever they did, and on into the night on a regular basis. After that, they were still able to produce homemade treats, such as cookies and candies when they were needed, and do it well. Certainly there was the occasional lily-livered cousin who made a career out of enjoying poor health. Oddly enough, she usually managed to turn out some of the most delicious delicacies. These goodies were even worth hearing about what a trial they had been to make. General Sherman said that the Savannah women were the toughest he had ever known. We consider this to be a given. We just don't get this either/or instead of separation, nor are we particularly interested in trying to! We've been doing both, or "having it all," since Oglethorpe set foot on the bluff overlooking the Savannah River.

So, here and now, we would like to reclaim the phrase "cookie-baking mom." Here it does not necessarily mean the type of mother who irons the socks. More accurately, it means the mother who lets the laundry sit untended, while she and her family work memorable magic with sugar and butter, and wonderful flavorings. And, furthermore...if she wants to iron the socks later...she can do so.

Praline Cookies

Cookies

1⅔	cups flour	1½	cups brown sugar, firmly packed
1½	teaspoons baking powder	1	egg
½	teaspoon salt	1	teaspoon vanilla
½	cup butter or margarine, softened	1	cup pecan pieces

Icing

1½	cups whipping cream	1	cup powdered sugar
1	cup brown sugar, firmly packed		

Preheat oven to 350 degrees. Combine flour, baking powder and salt in a bowl; set aside. In a separate bowl, beat butter with an electric mixer until creamy. Add brown sugar and beat until blended. Add egg and vanilla and mix well. Add dry ingredients gradually, beating well after each addition. Drop by rounded tablespoonfuls onto an ungreased baking sheet. Bake 10 minutes. Remove from oven and press 4 to 5 pecan pieces into each cookie. Cool on wire racks for 5 to 10 minutes.

To make icing, combine cream and brown sugar in a saucepan. Bring to a boil, stirring constantly. Boil for 2 minutes, stirring constantly. Remove from heat. Add powdered sugar and beat until smooth. Drizzle over cookies.

Make 2 dozen cookies

Lace Cookies

1 egg, beaten

1 cup sugar

2½ tablespoons all-purpose flour

1 teaspoon salt

¼ teaspoon baking powder

1 cup quick-cooking oats, slightly crushed

½ cup butter, melted

1 teaspoon vanilla

Preheat oven to 350 degrees. Combine all ingredients and mix well. Drop batter by half teaspoonfuls, 2 inches apart or more, onto foil-lined baking sheets. Bake 12 to 14 minutes or until golden brown. Cool completely before removing from foil.

Makes 5 dozen

Praline Graham Cracker Bites

Graham crackers

1 cup butter

1 cup brown sugar, firmly packed

1 cup chopped pecans

Preheat oven to 300 degrees. Line a jelly-roll pan with a single layer of graham crackers. Melt butter in a small saucepan over medium heat. Mix in sugar and pecans. Stir until sugar is dissolved. Pour mixture over crackers and spread evenly. Bake 20 minutes. Cool for a few minutes and transfer to wax paper. Cool completely, then break into pieces.

Sweet Benne Cookies

1	cup benne (sesame) seeds	¼	teaspoon baking powder
¾	cup butter, melted	¼	teaspoon salt
1½	cups light brown sugar, firmly packed	1	teaspoon vanilla
1¼	cups all-purpose flour	1	egg

Preheat oven to 300 degrees. Toast benne seeds on a baking sheet, stirring occasionally, for 10 to 15 minutes or until golden. Remove from oven and increase temperature to 325 degrees. Let seeds cool. In a large mixing bowl, combine all ingredients and mix thoroughly with a wooden spoon. Drop batter by half teaspoonfuls, about 1½ inches apart, onto a well-greased foil-lined baking sheet. Bake 15 to 20 minutes or until evenly browned. If pale in the center and puffed, the cookies are not done baking. Watch constantly to avoid burning. Cool on baking sheet a few minutes, then carefully peel from foil and cool completely on a wire rack. Regrease foil between batches. Store in an airtight container.

Makes about 85 cookies

After cooking the first batch of cookies, you must allow the foil to cool completely, then regrease it before dropping another batch. If you don't, the cookies will "run."

Butter Pecan Dreams

1	cup butter or margarine, softened	2	cups all-purpose flour, sifted
2	tablespoons granulated sugar	2	cups finely chopped pecans
2	teaspoons vanilla	2	cups powdered sugar

Preheat oven to 325 degrees. Cream butter and granulated sugar. Add vanilla. Stir in flour and pecans. Mix well. Form into small balls or crescents. Bake 25 to 35 minutes. While still warm, roll cookies in powdered sugar. Roll again when cool.

Makes 24 to 30 cookies

Ultimate Peanut Butter Chocolate Chip Cookies

1½	cups all-purpose flour	½	cup crunchy peanut butter
1	teaspoon salt	2	teaspoons vanilla
½	teaspoon baking soda	1	tablespoon light corn
½	teaspoon baking powder		syrup
½	cup butter, softened	2	eggs
1	cup granulated sugar	1	cup old-fashioned oats
½	cup light brown sugar, firmly packed	1	cup crispy rice cereal
		2½	cups mini chocolate chips

Preheat oven to 350 degrees. Sift together flour, salt, baking soda and baking powder into a medium bowl. In a large bowl, beat butter and sugars until creamy. Add peanut butter. Beat well. Add vanilla, corn syrup and eggs. Beat until blended. Stir in oats, rice cereal, chocolate chips and flour mixture. Drop by teaspoonfuls onto ungreased baking sheets. Bake 10 minutes or until lightly browned. Cool 1 to 2 minutes before removing from pan to a wire rack.

Makes 4 dozen cookies

These cookies are loaded with chocolate chips. Feel free to reduce amount of chips according to your family's taste.

This is a versatile cookie recipe. Try using chocolate crispy rice cereal and leave out the chocolate chips or add chopped nuts.

Chocolate Chip Cookies are sometimes called Toll House Cookies because there was a real Toll House, built in 1709. Coach passengers ate while the horses were changed and a toll was paid for the use of the highway. It was at this tollhouse that the first cookies with chocolate chips were made.

Pecan Meringues

1 egg white, stiffly beaten

¾ cup brown sugar, firmly packed

2 cups finely chopped nuts

¼ teaspoon vanilla

Preheat oven to 300 degrees. Combine all ingredients. Drop by teaspoonfuls onto a lightly greased baking sheet. Bake 15 to 18 minutes or until golden brown. Cool 10 minutes before removing from pan.

Margarita Mousse Cookies

1	teaspoon unflavored gelatin	2	teaspoons lime zest
2	tablespoons tequila	¼	cup fresh lime juice
2	tablespoons Triple Sec or Grand Marnier	1½	cups whipping cream
		¾	cup sugar

Pecan Crisp Shells

2	tablespoons brown sugar, firmly packed	¼	cup all-purpose flour
2	tablespoons butter, melted	¼	cup chopped pecans
2	tablespoons light corn syrup	¾	teaspoon vanilla

Sprinkle gelatin over tequila and liqueur in a small saucepan. Let stand 1 minute. Cook and stir over low heat until gelatin dissolves. Stir in lime zest and juice. Cool. In a mixing bowl, beat cream until foamy. Gradually add sugar and gelatin mixture and beat until soft peaks form. Cover and chill. Spoon or pipe into shells. Garnish with lime zest and serve with fresh fruit.

To make shells, preheat oven to 350 degrees. Combine brown sugar, butter and corn syrup in a saucepan. Cook over high heat, stirring constantly, until mixture boils. Remove from heat. Stir in flour, pecans and vanilla until well blended. Drop batter by level teaspoonfuls, 3 inches apart, onto well-greased baking sheets. Do not bake more than 3 cookies at a time. Bake 8 minutes or until golden brown. Cool on pan on a wire rack for 1 minute. Grease the handle of a long wooden spoon and lay spoon across 2 mugs. Working quickly, place cookies over handle of spoon, allowing ends to drape and resemble taco shells. Cool. Store in an airtight container up to 3 days ahead.

Serves 12

Key Lime Whippersnaps

1 (18¼-ounce) package lemon cake mix

2 cups frozen whipped topping, thawed

1 egg

1 teaspoon Key lime juice

¼ cup sifted powdered sugar

Preheat oven to 350 degrees. Combine cake mix, whipped topping, egg and lime juice in a large bowl. Stir until well mixed. Drop by teaspoonfuls into powdered sugar and roll to coat. Place 1½ inches apart on greased baking sheets. Bake 10 to 15 minutes or until light golden brown. Remove from baking sheets to cool.

Makes 4 dozen

Fruitcake Cookies

1	cup sherry	4	ounces crystallized citron
1	pound almonds, chopped	3	eggs
4	ounces pecans, chopped	1½	cups dark brown sugar, firmly packed
1	(8-ounce) package dates, chopped and rolled in sugar	⅔	cup butter, melted
8	ounces golden or black raisins	1	teaspoon baking soda dissolved in 1 tablespoon buttermilk
4	slices crystallized pineapple, chopped	1	teaspoon vanilla
8	ounces crystallized cherries, chopped	3	cups all-purpose flour
		1	teaspoon ground cloves
1	(4-ounce) can flaked coconut	2	teaspoons cinnamon
		¼	teaspoon nutmeg

Combine sherry, almonds, pecans, dates, raisins, pineapple, cherries, coconut and citron in a container. Cover and soak overnight.

When ready to bake, preheat oven to 350 degrees. Mix together eggs, brown sugar, butter, dissolved baking soda and vanilla in a bowl. Set aside. In a larger bowl, sift together flour, cloves, cinnamon and nutmeg. Add liquid mixture to dry ingredients. Mix well. Add soaked fruit and nuts with all of the sherry. Mix well. Drop by teaspoonfuls onto a greased baking sheet. Bake 10 to 12 minutes or until firm and light brown. Store in a tightly covered container. Place an apple, cut in half and set on foil, inside the container, making sure the apple does not touch the cookies.

Cowboy Cookies

1 cup butter, softened

1 cup brown sugar, firmly packed

1 cup granulated sugar

2 eggs

1 teaspoon vanilla

2 cups flour

1 teaspoon baking soda

½ teaspoon salt

½ teaspoon baking powder

2 cups rolled oats

1 (12-ounce) package semi-sweet chocolate chips

½ cup nuts

Preheat oven to 350 degrees. Cream butter, sugars, eggs and vanilla until fluffy. Blend in flour, baking soda, salt, baking powder and oats. Stir in chocolate chips and nuts. Drop by tablespoonfuls onto baking sheets. Bake 12 to 15 minutes.

Makes about 4 dozen

Key Lime Bars

Crust

1¼	cups all-purpose flour	¾	cup butter, softened
1	cup graham cracker crumbs	½	cup powdered sugar

Filling

2	cups granulated sugar	Zest of 1 lime
¼	cup all-purpose flour	Powdered sugar for
4	eggs	dusting
½	cup lime juice, preferably from Key limes	

Preheat oven to 350 degrees. Combine all crust ingredients in a bowl. Mix to form a soft dough and press into an ungreased 9x13-inch baking pan. Bake 20 to 25 minutes or until lightly browned.

Meanwhile, prepare filling. Beat together granulated sugar, flour, eggs, lime juice and zest until well mixed. Pour over hot crust and bake 20 minutes longer or until set. Cool on a wire rack; center will be soft, like custard. Dust with powdered sugar and cut into bars.

Makes 24 to 30 bars

Brown Sugar Pecan Squares

1 (1-pound) package light or dark brown sugar

½ cup butter

3 eggs

2 cups self-rising flour

1 teaspoon vanilla

2 cups chopped pecans (optional)

Preheat oven to 325 degrees. Heat sugar and butter in a large saucepan over medium heat until butter melts. Cool 2 minutes. Add eggs, one at a time, mixing well after each addition. Stir in flour, 1 cup at a time. Add vanilla and pecans. Transfer to a greased 9x13-inch baking pan. Bake 30 minutes. Cool before cutting into 2- to 3-inch squares.

A great Southern alternative to brownies for picnics or cookouts.

Saints' Bars

Choose the variation you want first, then follow recipe.

First Layer

1	(18¼-ounce) package cake mix	½	cup butter or margarine, melted
2	eggs		

Second Layer

1-1½ cups chopped nuts   1-1½ cups candy chips

Third Layer

1	(8-ounce) package cream cheese, softened	1	(1-pound) package powdered sugar
3	eggs, beaten	½-1	cup chopped nuts

Preheat oven to 350 degrees. Combine first layer ingredients and spread in a 10x15-inch baking pan. Mix second layer ingredients and sprinkle over first layer. Blend third layer ingredients thoroughly and spread over top. Bake 50 to 60 minutes. Bars will be sticky and moist inside with a light outer crust.

Spice: Use spice cake mix, butterscotch candy chips and pecans.

Chocolate: Use dark fudge cake mix, chocolate chips, toffee bits and pecans or walnuts.

Lemon or Orange: Use lemon or orange cake mix, crushed lemon candy and almonds.

At five years old, Juliette "Daisy" Gordon could bring laughter even to Sherman, as he occupied the city. When "Daisy" saw that Union General Howard was missing an arm, she said, "I shouldn't wonder if my Papa did it, He has shot lots of Yankees!"

An 8 x 8 x 2-inch pan will yield 16 (2-inch) square bars. A 9 x 13 x 2-inch pan will yield 3 dozen bars, depending on the size desired.

Classy Tassies

Crust

½	cup unsalted butter, softened	1	cup all-purpose flour, sifted
1	(3-ounce) package cream cheese, softened		Dash of salt

Filling

1	egg	3	tablespoons butter, softened
¼	cup brown sugar, firmly packed	½-1	teaspoon vanilla
¼	cup granulated sugar	1	heaping cup very finely chopped pecans

Preheat oven to 350 degrees. Mix together all crust ingredients thoroughly and refrigerate. When chilled, form dough into 20 to 24 equal-sized balls. Press each ball into the bottom and up the sides of an ungreased mini muffin cup.

To make filling, beat egg well in a mixing bowl. Beat in sugars, butter and vanilla. Set aside. Sprinkle pecans evenly over crust in muffin cups. Spoon filling over pecans, filling each cup no more than three-fourths full. Bake 20 minutes or until filling sets. Cool briefly, then carefully remove from muffin cups and cool completely on a wire rack.

Makes about 2 dozen

Throughout the years, Pecan Tassies have been popular at teas, church socials, and weddings. Long considered a "stylish" confection throughout the south, they are usually served on a silver cookie tray. Natalie Dupree tells one story of a young woman entertaining the mother of the man she hoped to marry. Her table was set with fine linens, flowered china and bud vases filled with honeysuckle and wisteria. Hoping to impress her mother-in-law-to-be with all her Southern social graces as she began to serve dessert, the woman announced, "I wasn't going to eat any dessert, but you've tempted me down memory lane." As they enjoyed their tassies, the ice melted in their glasses and in their conversation as well, as they spoke of the man they both loved. From Southern Memories.

Pumpkin Bars with Cream Cheese Frosting

2	cups flour	4	eggs, beaten
2	teaspoons baking powder	2	cups pumpkin
2	teaspoons cinnamon	1½	cups sugar
1	teaspoon baking soda	1	cup vegetable oil
1	teaspoon salt		Chopped pecans (optional)

Cream Cheese Frosting

1	(3-ounce) package cream cheese	1	teaspoon vanilla
½	cup butter or margarine, softened	2	cups sifted powdered sugar

Preheat oven to 350 degrees. Stir together flour, baking powder, cinnamon, baking soda and salt; set aside. Combine eggs, pumpkin, sugar and oil in a mixing bowl. Add dry ingredients and mix well. Spread batter into an ungreased 10x15-inch baking pan. Bake 25 to 30 minutes. Cool. Frost and sprinkle with pecans. Cut into bars.

To make frosting, beat together cream cheese, butter and vanilla until light and fluffy. Gradually blend in sugar and beat until smooth. Spread over cooled cake.

Serves 12

Savannah had the first motorized fire department in America, beginning in 1911. Savannah is also home to two cherished fire bells. There is "Big Duke," acquired in 1873, then moved to the Chatham County Firefighters Memorial in 1968. There it memorializes courageous firefighters as part of the "Last Alarm." There is also the City Exchange Fire Bell, imported from Amsterdam in 1802, and thought to be one of the first bells in Georgia.

Vienna Raspberry-Chocolate Bars

1	cup butter, softened		1	cup semisweet chocolate chips
1½	cups sugar, divided		4	egg whites, room temperature
2	egg yolks		¼	teaspoon salt
2½	cups all-purpose flour		2	cups finely chopped pecans or walnuts
1	(10-ounce) jar raspberry jam			

Preheat oven to 350 degrees. Cream butter. Beat in ½ cup sugar. Mix in egg yolks, one at a time. Stir in flour. Press mixture into a lightly greased 10x15-inch jelly roll pan. Bake 15 to 20 minutes. Spread jam over baked crust. Sprinkle with chocolate chips. Beat egg whites until foamy. Add salt and remaining 1 cup sugar and beat until peaks form. Fold in nuts. Spread egg white meringue over chocolate chips, spreading to edges to seal the crust. Bake 25 minutes. Remove from oven and cut immediately into bars.

Makes 5 dozen bars

Toasted Pecan Clusters

3 tablespoons butter or margarine

3 cups pecan pieces

12 ounces baking chocolate

Preheat oven to 300 degrees. Melt butter in oven in a 10x15-inch jelly roll pan. Spread pecans evenly in pan. Bake 30 minutes, stirring every 10 minutes. Melt chocolate in a heavy saucepan over low heat. Remove from heat and cool 2 minutes. Stir in toasted pecans. Drop by rounded teaspoonfuls onto wax paper. Cool.

Makes 4 dozen candies

Snowy Chocolate Peanut Butter Bites

1	(6-ounce) package semisweet chocolate chips		½	cup butter or margarine
½	cup creamy peanut butter		8	cups Rice Chex cereal
			1	cup sifted powdered sugar

Combine chocolate chips, peanut butter and butter in a saucepan. Heat until melted. Remove from heat and stir until smooth. Pour mixture over cereal and stir until evenly coated. Spread cereal mixture on 2 wax paper-lined baking sheets. Sprinkle sugar evenly over cereal. Store in an airtight container.

Orange Blossom Bars

1½	cups sugar	2	teaspoons baking powder
¾	cup vegetable shortening	½	teaspoon salt
1	teaspoon vanilla	½	cup milk
2	eggs	1	cup chocolate chips
2½	cups flour		

Glaze

1	cup powdered sugar	¾	teaspoon orange zest
2	tablespoons orange juice		

Preheat oven to 350 degrees. Cream sugar and shortening in a mixing bowl. Add vanilla. Beat in eggs. Sift together flour, baking powder and salt. Mix dry ingredients, alternating with milk, into creamed mixture until completely blended. Stir in chocolate chips. Spread mixture in a greased 10x15-inch jelly roll pan. Bake 25 minutes. Meanwhile, combine all glaze ingredients and stir until smooth. When done baking, spread glaze over hot bars. Cool completely before cutting.

Makes about 3 dozen bars

Mint Cream Brownies

1	(20-ounce) package fudge brownie mix	¼	cup whipping cream
		¼	cup crème de menthe
½	cup margarine, softened	1	(1-pound) can chocolate icing
4	cups powdered sugar, sifted		

Preheat oven to 350 degrees. Prepare brownie mix according to package directions. Spread batter in a well-greased 9x13-inch casserole dish. Bake 25 minutes. Meanwhile, combine margarine and sugar in a mixing bowl. Gradually beat in cream and crème de menthe until mixture is light and fluffy. Spread over baked brownies and chill 1½ to 2 hours. Top with icing. Refrigerate until ready to serve, then cut into squares. Store, covered, in the refrigerator.

During the War of 1812, Juliette Gordon Low's great-grandmother, Elizabeth Gordon, is said to have sat in a rocking chair atop the bales of cotton she was shipping down the Savannah River. Elizabeth Gordon counted on the soldiers to be gentlemen and not risk shooting a lady. Fortunately, she was right.

Praline Brownies

1	(22½-ounce) package brownie mix without nuts	¾-1	cup chopped pecans
4	tablespoons butter or margarine	¾-1	cup light brown sugar, firmly packed

Preheat oven to 350 degrees. Prepare brownie mix according to package directions. Spread batter in a greased 9x13-inch baking pan. Melt butter in a small skillet. Add pecans and sugar and cook and stir until sugar dissolves. Sprinkle pecan mixture over batter. Bake 25 to 30 minutes.

Serves 12 to 15

Savannah Candy Kitchen Divinity

½	cup corn syrup	2	egg whites
2½	cups sugar	¼	teaspoon vanilla
¼	cup water	1	cup pecan halves

Combine corn syrup, sugar and water in a saucepan and stir until sugar dissolves. Cook over medium heat until a candy thermometer registers 250 degrees. Do not stir while cooking. While mixture is cooking, beat egg whites until soft peaks form. When sugar mixture reaches 250 degrees, beat in egg whites using an electric mixer. Add vanilla. Mix 10 minutes or until divinity loses its glossy appearance. Drop by spoonfuls onto wax paper. Top each with a pecan half. Allow to dry at room temperature.

Store candy in an airtight container or freeze.

Can add ½ cup chopped pecans just before spooning onto wax paper.

A story is told that originally a cook left baking powder out of a chocolate cake batter and thereby created a dense, chewy bar later called a Brownie. The first recipe for Brownies was published in 1897, in the Sears and Roebuck Catalogue (the recipe was already well known by word of mouth).

This is perfect for a holiday candy dish or a bake sale. It is best to make the candy on a sunny, dry day; use 1 tablespoon less water on humid days. Divinity freezes well and will keep for days if tightly covered. Use a heavy stand mixer for best results.

Mints

⅓	cup light corn syrup	½	teaspoon salt
4	tablespoons butter, softened	1	(1-pound) package powdered sugar, sifted
1	teaspoon peppermint extract		Food coloring of choice

Blend corn syrup, butter, extract and salt. Add sugar and mix by hand with a spoon until smooth. If coloring is desired, add 1 drop per ⅓ cup of mixture. Roll a small amount of mixture into a nickel-sized ball. Flatten with a fork onto wax paper. Let stand several hours to dry. Remove from paper and store in an airtight container.

Savannah Pralines

1½	tablespoons light corn syrup	1	cup granulated sugar
½	cup evaporated milk	⅛	teaspoon salt
3	tablespoons butter	½	cup pecan halves, toasted
½	cup brown sugar, firmly packed	½	cup pecan pieces, toasted
		1	teaspoon vanilla

Combine corn syrup, milk, butter, sugars and salt in a buttered, heavy 2-quart saucepan. Cook and stir over medium heat until blended. Continue to cook over medium heat, stirring frequently, until mixture reaches 240 degrees on a candy thermometer. Add pecans and continue to heat until temperature reaches 246 degrees. Remove from heat and cool 2 minutes. Beat in vanilla with a spoon until creamy. Quickly drop by spoonfuls onto wax paper, making 2-inch circles. Candy should drop easily from the spoon; if candy hardens too quickly, add a few drops of milk and heat and stir gently until creamy. Store cooled pralines in an airtight container, separating layers with wax paper.

Makes 24 pralines

Warm summer evenings conjure up memories of days gone by, when taffy pulls and mint pulls were pastimes for the entire family. A cold marble slab, buttered hands, and straining muscles have since been replaced with a simple rolled mint recipe. Sadly, however, the family memories have been replaced as well. Invite everyone into the kitchen to talk of days past and enjoy making these simply delicious candies together. A bowl of hand-made mints is a must for any Southern luncheon, tea, bridal shower, or wedding reception.

A story is told by hostess and friend alike of a recent bridal shower given at Tybee in the heat of summer. The hostess was remodeling her home and asked a friend to cater the event. Much to everyone's dismay, the air-conditioner was out that day. While fans and well-chilled Southern Comfort Whiskey Punch cooled the guests, the mints and caterer began to melt from the heat. Luckily for both, the freezer was able to hold them long enough for them to regain their composure. The shower and the mints were a big success.

Chocolate Almond Bark

1½	cups sliced almonds or pecans, divided	1	cup sugar
1	cup butter	10	(1.55-ounce) solid chocolate candy bars

Sprinkle half the nuts on a foil-lined baking sheet. Melt butter in a small saucepan. Add sugar and cook, stirring frequently, until mixture reaches 300 degrees using a candy thermometer. Pour mixture over nuts on baking sheet. Arrange candy bars, side by side, in a single layer on top. Broil 3 to 10 seconds or until chocolate melts. Smooth with a knife. Sprinkle remaining nuts over chocolate. Refrigerate until chilled. Just before serving, remove from refrigerator and break into pieces.

Downright Decadent Chocolate Fudge

5	cups sugar	1	(12-ounce) package semisweet chocolate chips
1	cup butter		
1	(12-ounce) can evaporated milk	2-3	cups chopped pecans
24	large marshmallows		

Combine sugar, butter and milk in a large saucepan. Bring to a boil over medium to high heat, stirring frequently off the bottom of the pan. Continue to cook 13 minutes, stirring almost constantly. Remove from heat and add marshmallows and chocolate chips. Stir until melted. Add nuts. Pour into a 10x15-inch jelly roll pan. Cool and cut into squares with a pizza cutter.

Makes 5 pounds

Bibliography

No project such as *First Come, First Served...* is possible without the finest resources, for information and for inspiration. The following selection of books is shared favorites, each one absolutely recommended for their excellence and classic style.

Hospitality and Cooking:

Calendar Cookery: St. Andrew's School. Savannah, Georgia: PIP Printing, 1990.

Classical Southern Cooking: A Celebration of the Cuisine of the Old South by Damon Fowler. New York: Crown Publishers, Inc., 1995.

Georgia Entertains: A Rich Heritage of Fine Food and Gracious Hospitality by Margaret Wayt DeBolt, with Emma Rylander Law and Carter Olive. Nashville, Tennessee: Rutledge Hill Press, 1988.

Magnolias: Uptown Down South Southern Cuisine by Donald Darickman. Charleston, South Carolina: Wyrick and Company, 1995.

My Mother's Southern Kitchen: Recipes and Reminiscences by James Villas with Martha Pearl Villas. New York: MacMillan, Inc., 1994.

Savannah Entertains by Martha Giddens Nesbit. Charleston, South Carolina: Wyrick and Company, 1996.

Savannah Seasons: Food and Stories from Elizabeth's on 37th by Elizabeth Terry, with Alexis Terry. New York: Doubleday, 1996.

Savannah Style by The Junior League of Savannah, Inc. Nashville, Tennessee: Favorite Recipes Press, 1980.

The Lady & Sons Savannah Country Cookbook by Paula H. Deen. New York: Random House, 1998.

History and Stories:

A Visitor's Guide to Savannah by Emmeline King Cooper and Polly Wylly Cooper. Charleston, South Carolina: Wyrick and Company, 1998.

Georgia Ghosts by Nancy Roberts. Winston Salem, North Carolina: John F. Blair, Publisher, 1999.

Savannah: A History of Her People Since 1733 by Preston Russell and Barbara Hines. Savannah, Georgia: Frederic C. Beil, Publisher, 1992.

Savannah: People, Places and Events by Ron Freeman. Savannah, Georgia: H. Ronald Freeman, Publisher, 1997.

Savannah Spectres and Other Strange Tales by Margaret Wayt DeBolt. Virginia Beach, Virginia: The Downing Company, 2000.

Sojourn In Savannah from the Franklin S. Traub Trust. Garden City, Georgia: The Printcraft Press, 2000.

Southern Memories by Natalie Dupree, New York: Potter Publishing, 1993

Tybee Island: Images of America by James Mack Adams. Charleston, South Carolina: Arcadia Publishing, 2000.

Contributors

A book of this type would not be possible without the help of countless volunteers. To those who contributed recipes and memories, we offer a big thank you. A cookbook is only as good as its recipes and we have some of the best. We regret that we were not able to include all that we received due to space limitations and duplications. Know that your submissions were appreciated and contributed greatly to the overall quality of the book. To those who spent numerous hours testing and evaluating recipes, writing, editing, compiling, proofing, marketing, and selling, our heartfelt thanks. Thanks as well to those whose efforts are yet to come as this book continues to be read and enjoyed. To everyone whose name we have inadvertently omitted, please accept our sincere apologies. Lastly, to our families who have waited so patiently with us for this book to become a reality, a very special thank you.

Berta Adams
Terri Adams
Rozanne Aimone
Charlie Aimone
Linda Albritton
Mark Albritton
Beth Aldrich
Steve Aldrich
Bob Allen
Melissa Allen
Diana Arenander
Karen Arpin
Suzie Bailey
Karen Ball
Melissa Ball
Betty Barnette
Wendy Bath
Leo Beckmann
Nancy Beckmann
Judy Branham
Sarah Buchanon
Jan Bugos
Randy Bugos
Donna Cantrell
Debbie Cates-Trahan
Rosemary Christensen

Kathy Chu
Patrice Cole
Misty Coleman
Kathleen Collins
Lynn Cooper
Lynn Corbin
Mary Jane Crouch
Mary Jo Crowe
Phyllis Curlee
Judy Curley
Lake Daly
Davis Produce
Suzanne Davis
Paula Deen
Karl DeMasi
Patty Demere
Chris Dickson
Frank Dickson
Debbie Dixon
Lisa Donlan
Kerstin Donohue
Bob Eason
Maureen Eason
Linda Easterlin
Nancy Easterlin
Sue Estus

Sonja Fishkind
Margaret Forman
Jane Foster
Pam Foster
Damon Fowler
Captain Bear Frazier
Betsy Freeman
Keith Freeman
Barbara Friedenberg
Nancy Gates
Kim Gattis
Tracy Gonzalez
Patricia Graham
Carol Gray
Sally Greenberg
Judi Griffin
Jodi Groover
Janet Guerry
Jill Guthrie
Sandra Haggberg
Gloria Harrison
Debbie Helmken
Howard Helmken
Jameson Heidt
Sandra Hill
Patsy Hinely

Dale Holloway

Sheree Holloway

Cindy Howard

Brenda Hubbard

Em Hubbard

Lucie Hughes

Debbie James

Beth Johnson

Bruce Johnson

Jana Johnson

Ken Johnson

Pat Johnson

Julie Kehoe

Susan Kelleher

Carlton Knight

Jeanie Knight

Pop Knight

Donna Krauss

Jeffrey Lasky

Stacy Lasky

Dianne Lee

Diane Lewis

Caroline Lindner

Mary Locklear

Beverly Long

Sandy Lovell

Dana Lutz

Kathy McCarthy

John McLean

Kathy McLean

Lisa McNeil

Mike Mahaney

Susan Mahaney

Pat Mainz

Connie Malloy

Vikki Maner

Brenda Manning

Norman Massey

Torrey Massey

Nella Maxwell

Ann Merritt

Jane Merves

Mary Ruth Miller

Pauline Munro

Martha Nesbit

Cynthia O'Brien

George O'Brien

Tracey Oetgen

Nancy Oosterhoudt

Cheryl Ostman

Laura Overstreet

Gay Parks

Karen Perrie

Norma Perry

Melanie Phillips

Laurence Plapinger

Susan Plapinger

Lynn Porter

Lisa Prescott

Maria Rabeler

Julie Radelmiller

Debbie Rauers

Lata Raut

Joyce Rayburn

Leighton Reeve

Janet Robertson

Francine Robin

Annette Rock

Barbara Roth

Jeannie Rozier

Leigh Ryan

Russo's Seafood

Kathy Salter

Alan Sampson

Tamara Sampson

Rebecca Sasser

Paige Saussy

Diana Scheinbart

Clayton Scott

Joseph Scuderi

Gail Shanklin

Patty Short

Diane Smith

Dot Smith

Kim Smith

Michele Smith

Marilyn Solana

Diana Solomon

Bess Soper

Connie Stephenson

Carol Ann Stovall

Stan Strickland

Tonya Strickland

Don Stubbs

Susie Stubbs

Debbie Suglia

Martha Sullivan

Martin Sullivan

Monica Sullivan

Sue Svoboda

Elizabeth Terry

Judy Thompson

Tami Timms

Sandy Trenaman

Sally Tyson

Caroline Verner

Patrick Walsh

Claire Watts

John Watts

Peggy White

Debbie Wilkowski

Kathryn Williams

Sarah Yates

Susie Ziegler

Index

Index

Index

255

Index

O

OKRA

ONIONS

OYSTERS *(see Seafood)*

P

PANCAKES

PASTA

PEACHES

PEARS

PEAS *(see Beans and Peas)*

PECANS *(see Nuts)*

Index

Index

Index

First Come, First Served... In Savannah

St. Andrew's School
PO Box 30693 Savannah, GA 31410
912-897-4941
www.saintschool.com

Name _____

Address _____

City _____ State _____ Zip _____ Phone (____) _____

Please send _____ copy (ies) .... $19.95 each _____

Shipping and handling .... $ 5.00 each _____

Total _____

Enclosed is my check made payable to **St. Andrew's School** in the amount of $ _____

Please charge my (circle one) MC / VISA

CARD # _____ EXP Date _____

Signature _____

First Come, First Served... In Savannah

St. Andrew's School
PO Box 30693 Savannah, GA 31410
912-897-4941
www.saintschool.com

Name _____

Address _____

City _____ State _____ Zip _____ Phone (____) _____

Please send _____ copy (ies) .... $19.95 each _____

Shipping and handling .... $ 5.00 each _____

Total _____

Enclosed is my check made payable to **St. Andrew's School** in the amount of $ _____

Please charge my (circle one) MC / VISA

CARD # _____ EXP Date _____

Signature _____